Made, Laid and Betrayed in Hong Kong

Made, Laid and Betrayed in Hong Kong

The scandalous revelations of two young and disparate recruit Hong Kong bobbies

Victor Blair

Copyright © 2023 Victor Blair

The moral right of the author has been asserted.

Apart from any fair dealing for the purposes of research or private study, or criticism or review, as permitted under the Copyright, Designs and Patents Act 1988, this publication may only be reproduced, stored or transmitted, in any form or by any means, with the prior permission in writing of the publishers, or in the case of reprographic reproduction in accordance with the terms of licences issued by the Copyright Licensing Agency. Enquiries concerning reproduction outside those terms should be sent to the publishers.

Troubador Publishing Ltd
Unit E2 Airfield Business Park
Harrison Road, Market Harborough
Leicestershire LE16 7UL
Tel: 0116 279 2299
Email: books@troubador.co.uk
Web: www.troubador.co.uk/matador

ISBN 978 1 80514 146 4

British Library Cataloguing in Publication Data.
A catalogue record for this book is available from the British Library.

Printed and bound by CPI Group (UK) Ltd, Croydon, CR0 4YY
Typeset in 10pt Source Sans 3 by Troubador Publishing Ltd, Leicester, UK

Illustrations and maps by BGY
Electronic maps by Lumotimedia

Matador is an imprint of Troubador Publishing Ltd

Dedication

Dedicated to the few friends who are still as they were, and to the majority as they used to be. (And to dear, departed parents, who would no doubt be amazed, if not justifiably scandalised. That is, all except Geoff Bottomley, who would have been pleased as punch to be included so prominently in the narrative.)

Contents

Introduction	ix
Maps of Hong Kong in 1975	x
List of Characters and Abbreviations	xiii
Chapter 1 – Bob 'Steady Eddie' Yates	1
Chapter 2 – Alan Victor 'AV'/ 'The Bucket' Bottomley	26
Chapter 3 – Seminar, Hong Kong Office, London	71
Chapter 4 – Leaving on a Jet Plane	85
Chapter 5 – The Induction Introduction	93
Chapter 6 – That Was the Week That Was[1]	109
Chapter 7 – Finding Their Feet	128
Chapter 8 – Stepping Out but Hardly Up	145
Chapter 9 – Up and Running	165
Chapter 10 – Learning the Drill	182
Chapter 11 – The Nitty Gritty	200
Chapter 12 – Moving on Up!	222
Chapter 13 – Fun and Games	242
Chapter 14 – The Final Stretch	267
Chapter 15 – End Games!	291

---

[1] © Copyright BBC

Introduction

'Young man, rejoice in thy youth - but watch out for the buggers around you.'
(*Ecclesiastes,* and Victor Blair.)

'Had we only known that we'd be asked to recall people and incidents from fifty years ago, then we'd have paid more attention to what was going on around us way back then. Nevertheless, here goes.' (The San Miguel Three)
'A curious, colourful and salacious amalgam of fact with only occasional snippets of fiction, fantasy and smoking mirrors aimed at entertaining, enraging and – thank you very much, sir, you're so kind! – possibly slightly enriching its various contributors. (Well, you didn't imagine that we've done all this for nothing, do you?)'

Victor Blair
July 2023

Made, Laid and Betrayed in Hong Kong

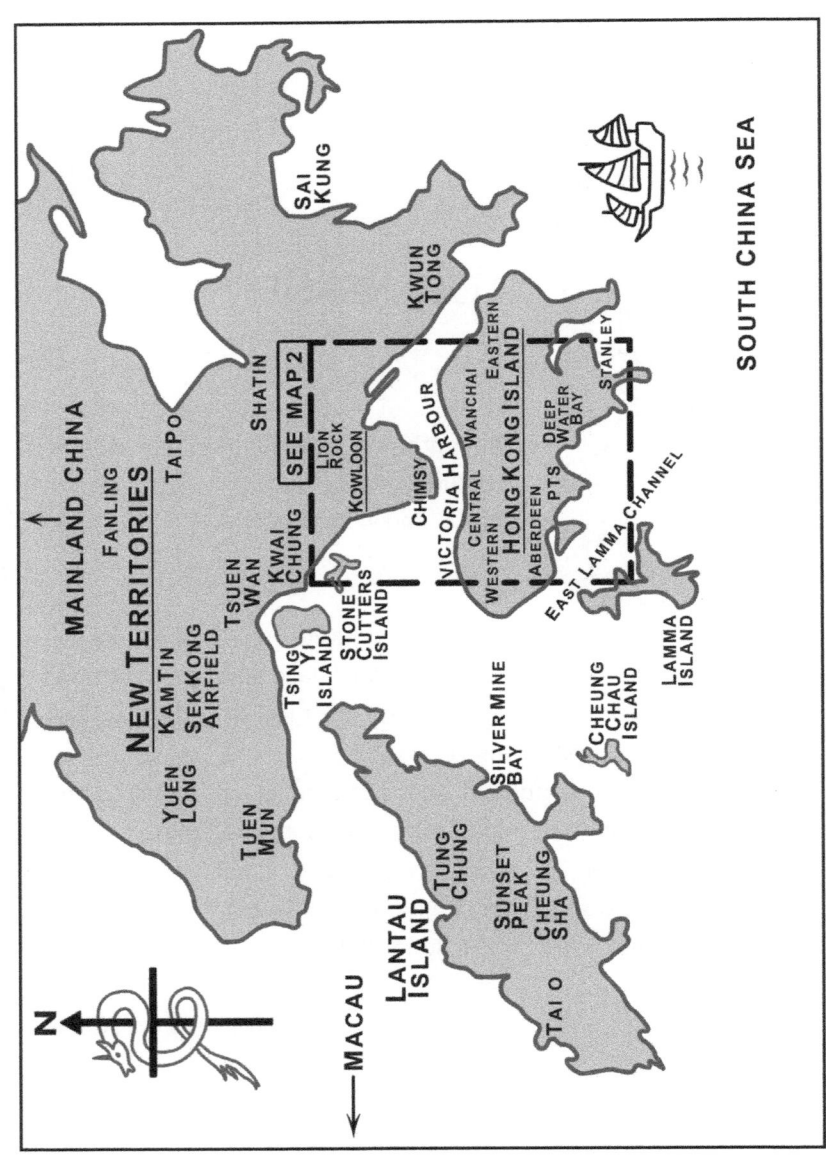

Hong Kong Colony, 1975

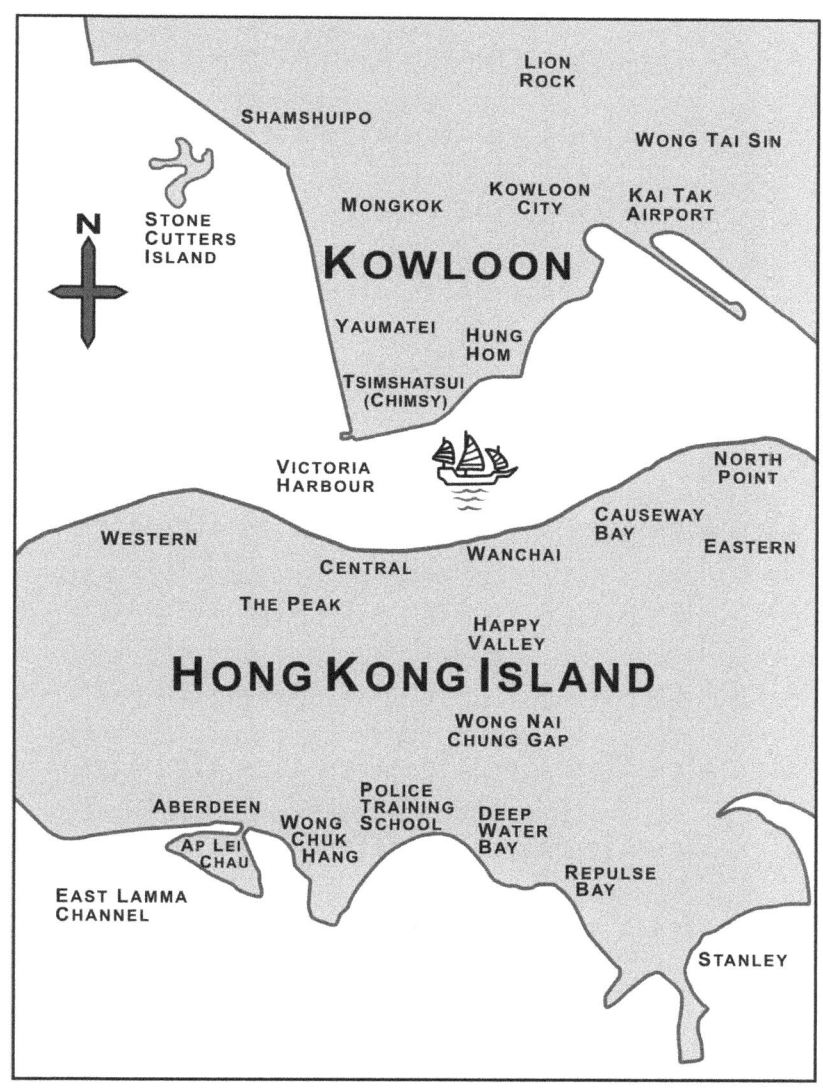

Closer view of Hong Kong Island and Kowloon, 1975

List of Characters and Abbreviations

Dear Reader – given the number of characters in this story (all based on real people and situations encountered), below is an aide-memoire to help you place them as you read through the book. **Just in case you were to forget who's who, as and when you encounter them again later in another chapter. Hence it does not apply to any persons who are only referred to once in the story.**

The page and chapters numbers shown against each refer to when they are first encountered in this narrative.

You may also find the list of abbreviations at the bottom helpful. Here goes!

Alphabetical list of characters

Alan 'The Bucket' Bottomley aka 'AV'	Page 26, Chapter 2
Arthur Glossop	Page 207, Chapter 11
Bandy Yat-ding Lam	Page 195, Chapter 10
Bill 'The Reverend' Robinson	Page 98, Chapter 5
Billy 'Whizzer' Nairn	Page 151, Chapter 8
Blake 'Motor Mouth' Piggard	Page 98, Chapter 5

Bob 'Oriental Tailors'	Page 158, Chapter 8
Bob 'Steady Eddie' Yates aka 'BY'	Page 1, Chapter 1
Brian Wilkins	Page 250, Chapter 13
Callum 'Sunny Boy' Colgate	Page 152, Chapter 8
Charlie (Red Lips Bar)	Page 192, Chapter 10
David Greening	Page 3, Chapter 1
David Kensington	Page 133, Chapter 7
David Man aka 'Ham Sap Man'	Page 146, Chapter 8
Debbie 'Dee Dee' (Popeye's Bar)	Page 191, Chapter 10
Denny 'Mad Dog' Browning	Page 160, Chapter 8
Dick Snyder	Page 93, Chapter 5
Farrier, JB	Page 191, Chapter 10
Frank Topley	Page 109, Chapter 6
Frankie Chan	Page 259, Chapter 13
Franny Fong	Page 182, Chapter 10
Frick Jacobs	Page 109, Chapter 6
Fulton Puller	Page 202, Chapter 11
Geoff Bottomley	Page 32, Chapter 2
Gina Bottomley	Page 32, Chapter 2
Ginty the poodle (honest guv, a real dog)	Page 215, Chapter 11
Gobbler Wong	Page 273, Chapter 14
Gordon Banda	Page 12, Chapter 1
Henry the dog (another real dog)	Page 87, Chapter 4
Iain D. Bullingham aka 'Faidee' or 'Faidi Aidi'	Page 134, Chapter 7
Jack 'Fingers' Claymore	Page 173, Chapter 9
Jerry Benfield	Page 239, Chapter 12
Jim Brady	Page 55, Chapter 2
Keith Franks	Page 94, Chapter 5
Kevin 'Tits' Monkman	Page 183, Chapter 10
Laura & Lena Bottomley	Page 35, Chapter 2
Laurence 'Lats' Latimer	Page 120, Chapter 6
Lillie 'Lil' Parrish	Page 32, Chapter 2
Lilly (San Fran Bar, Wanchai)	Page 162, Chapter 8

Linda Bailey	Page 68, Chapter 2
Margaret (Maggie) 'Pigswill' Pickersgill	Page 26, Chapter 2
Martin 'Dogs' Dinner	Page 96, Chapter 5
Marvin 'The Perve' Purvis	Page 54, Chapter 2
Maurice 'Plod' Smiley	Page 111, Chapter 6
May Ling & Ah Cheung	Page 157, Chapter 8
Mingus Muffet	Page 274, Chapter 14
Morgan Effin-Jones (CDMI)	Page 117, Chapter 6
Mungo McMee	Page 122, Chapter 6
Neville 'Nev' Tenspeed	Page 115, Chapter 6
Nigel Bland	Page 151, Chapter 8
Norman 'Norrie' Pinkney	Page 132, Chapter 7
Paddy Loughlin	Page 117, Chapter 6
Paul 'Clicker' Cannon	Page 153, Chapter 8
Perry Sherry	Page 72, Chapter 3
Peter Godber	Page 81, Chapter 3
Peter 'Punjab' Spicer aka 'King of the Khyber Rifles'	Page 60, Chapter 2
Phillip Johns	Page 135, Chapter 7
Phillip Yip	Page 195, Chapter 10
Richard 'Clusterfuck' Clutterbuck	Page 75, Chapter 3
Richard 'Dick' Short	Page 138, Chapter 7
Ron McFyffer	Page 96, Chapter 5
Sadler Wells	Page 111, Chapter 6
Seamus O'Stropley	Page 13, Chapter 1
Stella Lai	Page 275, Chapter 14
Steve Greening	Page 188, Chapter 10
Teresa 'Terry' Bailey	Page 68, Chapter 2
Terry Carpenter	Page 122, Chapter 6
Tiger (yet another dog)	Page 5, Chapter 1
Tina (Popeye's Bar)	Page 202, Chapter 11
Titsalina	Page 33, Chapter 2
Toby 'Jugs' Robling	Page 255, Chapter 13

Tommy 'Two Dicks' Allcock	Page 94, Chapter 5
Tony Carpio	Page 140, Chapter 7
Tony Ho	Page 182, Chapter 10
Wilhelmina Mkele	Page 12, Chapter 1
Wolfgang 'Kaiser' Sheitzer	Page 173, Chapter 9
'Yorkie' Bill Towser	Page 95, Chapter 5
Zoe Cheung	Page 311, Chapter 15

Abbreviations

ADS	Assistant Divisional Superintendent
ASDI	Assistant Sub Divisional Inspector (rank Senior Inspector)
AV	Alan Bottomley
BY	Robert (Bob) Yates
CCR	Creedence Clearwater Revival
CID	Criminal Investigation Department
Chimsy	Tsimshatsui area in Kowloon
DMI	Drill and Musketry Instructor
DS	Divisional Superintendent
HK	Hong Kong
HKI	Hong Kong Island
ICAC	Independent Commission Against Corruption
MOTS	Member of a Triad Society
NFA	No Further Action
NST	Nobs, Snobs and Toffs
NT	New Territories (mainland part of the Colony attached to China)
OC	Officer Commanding
PC	Police Constable
PHQ	Police Headquarters
PTS	Police Training School
PTU	Police Tactical Unit

Red Lips	Red Lips Bar, Tsimshatsui
RHKP	Royal Hong Kong Police
San Fran	San Francisco Bar, Wanchai
San Mig	San Miguel beer
SDI	Sub Divisional Inspector (rank Chief Inspector)
SDS	Special Duties Squad (Divisional Anti-Vice squad)
SIP	Senior Inspector of Police
SM3	San Miguel Three (Alan Bottomley, Bob Yates and Nev Tenspeed)
Wally Mats	Waltzing Matilda Bar, Tsimshatsui
Wanch	Wanchai area on Hong Kong Island
WCH5	Wong Chuk Hang Five (Alan Bottomley, Bob Yates, Nev Tenspeed, Lats Latimer and Tommy 'Two Dicks' Allcock)
WIP	Woman Inspector of Police
WPC	Woman Police Constable

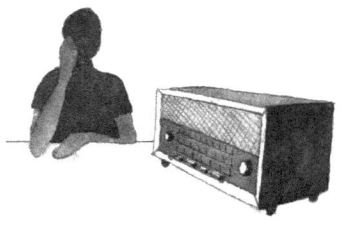

Chapter One

Bob 'Steady Eddie' Yates

One of the more endearing things about living and working in London is that you can obtain the Sunday newspapers on a Saturday evening, but if that hadn't been the case, then Bob Yates, on that dull, icy, evening on 18th January 1975, might have missed the chance of a lifetime.

For as he glumly trudged to work as the sole nightwatchman at Goldstein and Sons' warehouse in Clapham, and on the absolute spur of the moment, merely because he'd forgotten his *Flight International* and *National Geographic* magazines in his hurry to beat the clock, he'd bought a *Sunday Telegraph* from the somehow always cheery newspaper seller opposite the grim, grimy building that would be in Bob's charge from 10pm until noon the next day.

The four storey Victorian edifice was stacked with caged, locked and sealed beers, wines and spirits, and all the uniformed Bob had to do was to conduct hourly patrols, sign visiting books at key locations, and check the grilled and barred doors and windows for any signs of tampering.

Obviously, he needed to stay awake between patrols and keep his eyes and ears alert for any suspicious movement or noises from the outside and, God forbid, within the building itself.

To help pass the time, and the nights did sometimes drag, and apart from wheeling himself along the wide corridors in an old wheelchair, he invariably had his favourite magazines to hand, but this night, as he'd been forced to make his own sandwiches back in Balham as his dear parents were visiting his father's family in Dumbarton, he would have to make do with the *Sunday Telegraph*, as the first-edition tabloids hadn't arrived at the news stand. Still, a bit of heavy reading would do him good. He stashed it in his office drawer and would take it out some hours later.

This job was just a temporary position, one of several night watchman roles he'd been engaged in, and he found the general peace and quiet conducive to take stock of where his life, at twenty, had led him to date, and to help him decide, whenever, what to do with at least some of the rest of it, beyond mere nebulous plans to somehow pursue a career in civil aviation, or return to Zambia.

Yes, *return* to Zambia, as he'd been brought up in that country from the age of five, where his Scottish father Colin was a senior mine extraction engineer, who in 1959 had obtained a married posting in Luanshya, a mining town 200 miles from the Zambian (or at the time, Northern Rhodesian) capital of Lusaka, smack bang within the extensive, and burgeoning, Copper Belt area in the centre of the country.

His German wife Magda was more than happy to escape the still depressed, weary and war-recovery blues of late 1950s Britain, and enthusiastically followed her husband to pastures new with their three young sons, Bob, Kevin and Michael, in tow.

And how keenly and easily they settled into living and working in Africa and into the colonial way of the expatriate community, while embracing local African culture and customs.

Colin Yates's arrival had been much anticipated by the Zamsad

Mining Corporation at the local Roan Antelope Copper Mine (named after a roan antelope that had revealed copper deposits as its head struck a rock after being tracked and shot by an early twentieth-century prospector/explorer). This was part of a drive to increase productivity amongst the local native workers and he was almost immediately set to work.

Working with the local Zambians, and some full-time and contract expats, and assorted African labourers from mainly the eight countries bordering landlocked Zambia, the deep-mine operation, running on a twenty four hours, seven days-a-week rotation basis, took up the majority of his time.

Meanwhile, Magda busied herself with settling her family into the company-provided bungalow with a big garden, set in a shallow valley overlooking the nearby Luanshya River. She began vetting local school facilities and checking out the hospital, markets and town amenities so glowingly mentioned in the introductory notes provided to her before arrival by the mine's personnel department.

Once they'd arrived, they even hosted a coffee afternoon in her honour so she could become acquainted with some of the community's leading lights and their ladies, while they, in turn, of course, had the chance to give her the once-over.

Bob, the eldest son, willingly began his studies at Rivercross Primary School and, being an open, kind hearted and energetic lad with an engagingly winning smile and pleasant disposition, soon made friends with most fellow expat children and locals alike, glorying in the open bush countryside and anthills, and the many secret paths leading to and from the Luanshya River. All told, a tremendous natural adventure playground for any expat child.

Only one arrogant little brat objected to someone new stealing some of his apparent thunder, a very forward and 'up himself' young nipper called David Greening who thankfully was packed off to boarding school in Cape Town and was never even brought to mind by Steady Eddie until many years later when he was working in the Far East. More on this later.

The actual 'bush', forbidden to some children by their parents, as if that was going to really stop them, started almost immediately beyond the grid-pattern, residential streets where the expats lived (named appropriately in alphabetical order after local flora by the mining company, which totally dominated the local economy).

That apart and as the town had developed, in true colonial fashion, the Brits had introduced such niceties as a golf course and a mine recreation club for the expats. Yes, little England in the middle of Africa.

A combination of altitude above sea level (4,000 feet), distinct wet and dry seasons and not particularly fertile soils meant that the surrounding bush itself mainly comprised of dispersed trees amidst lower scrub and occasional tall-grassed areas. Not much of the land was farmed – occasionally there were patches of maize and groundnuts, often grown at a subsistence level. Apart from a plethora of snakes, insects and some birdlife, virtually all large wild animals had either been shot, eaten or driven from the surrounding bush, the whole locale a completely different environment from what Bob could remember from his infant days in London and Scotland.

On the urging and introduction from other wives, Mrs Yates hired two domestic servants to help around the house and garden, who soon became an integral part of the family. These wonderful people were Emson 'Thanksa' Million, the general house servant, and his nephew, Tembo Mabwe, aged eighteen who was the factotum handyman and gardener. Emson and his ever-smiling wife Freda lived in a small, simple house (called a *'khia'* in the local dialect) at the back of the big garden whilst Tembo lived in a nearby African township.

Talking of domestic servants, a brief diversion regarding social etiquette at the time in a typical southern African domestic setting.

It was quite normal for expats to employ both a house and garden servant (called somewhat derogatorily 'house boy' and 'garden boy' respectively). The former was regarded as the more senior of the two. Now they say 'imitation is the sincerest form of flattery' and sure enough, on one occasion in Luanshya, an unmarried expat told the story of him arriving unexpectedly at home only to find the house boy sitting in his 'master's' bed, wearing his pyjamas, being served tea and toast on a tray by the garden boy!

Emson and Temba kept a close eye on the security of the house and the safety of the Yates siblings. Indeed, in time, people were more in danger from the wild-ranging exploits of the Yates boys and their mates than from actual criminals or trespassers.

Away from school, it was a wonderful time of freedom, exploration and excitement, and naturally, the African bush brought some dangers with it but Temba was like a cross between a pit-bull terrier and a Rhodesian ridgeback in protecting the boys at the slightest hint of danger.

Just as well, as the mongrel dog the Yateses adopted, named 'Tiger', would bark a lot, but at the first sign of even possible danger, would run for the safety of the bungalow's verandah.

The sun drew Bob out, and he soon developed into a tall, lithe, athletic type, and while not truly excelling at any one particular sport, or academically, was well in the top twenty percent at everything that he tried at primary school.

Socially, the Zamsad Mining Corporation looked after its employees quite generously, especially the senior and expat staff, establishing the 'Homestead Bar and Social Club' within an otherwise private cul-de-sac in its outer compound.

The Social, or to some angry wives, 'That bloody Social,' if and when some spouses, shall we say, overindulged, was generally men-only at lunchtimes and evenings Monday to Friday, but Saturdays and especially Sundays were family days, with swings, roundabouts, see-saws and a paddling pool for the kids and a piddling pond for the infants, all supervised by a nurse and some volunteering wives, leaving adults relatively free to imbibe the much-vaunted Lion and Castle beers, both imported from South Africa and offered at subsidised prices.

For the less hardy, or perhaps the more restrained, soft drinks were also on offer, along with sweets and light snacks, although Saturday was fish and chips day, which was usually pretty well attended.

However, Sunday was *braai* or barbecue day and the Homestead was absolutely heaving with what appeared to be miles of coiled 'all meat a real treat' South African *boerewors* sausage, ready for charcoal grilling on open-fire ranges, with mounds of potato, mixed salads, corn on the cob and finger snacks aplenty, again at subsidised prices.

Tables, chairs and canopies were set over the Social's generously grassed front and back lawns, with indoor seating at tables around the large, though rustic U-shaped bar.

Otto Kemper, a retired Austrian miner, ran the Social, and his early-life skills as a former butcher really came to the fore in preparing the meat, while his wife Gretchen 'womanned' the bar and till, chiding and chivvying the three late-teen Zambian schoolgirls who waited on tables and, my oh my, they really earned their money, which was fleshed out by generous tips from the well-refreshed and mostly sated miners and their families.

As at most Social *braais*, the grilling duties generally fell as a right and privilege to a company head honcho, usually to Pete Reichert who was one of the Transport Managers and it's no exaggeration to say that if he hadn't bullshitted, crawled and stabbed people so much in the back to get to where he was, and to remain there, his much-admired skills as a grill chef, keeping up to forty assorted pieces of meat on the go at the same time, all to individual tastes, would surely have enabled him to obtain a top position at the Savoy Grill in London, or at an equally prestigious eatery.

Indeed, many at Zamsad would have gladly provided him with a glowing reference *and* have paid his one-way airfare. However, he wasn't totally disliked, as his party piece, apart from his culinary skills, was, after a few beers, taking out his one glass eye and throwing it into the paddling pool and then jumping in with other suitably 'refreshed' customers and hopefully finding it with a joyous shout to the bemused children of, 'I'm keeping my eye on you lot!!'

Just in case he couldn't manage to find it, he at least had the presence of mind to keep a spare in the club's safe, although it was of a different colour to his one remaining or 'good' eye.

Bob, as he had got older, somewhat half gathered through overheard and snippets of whispered conversations, delicious banter and half-truths repeated at school that the mining community, and thus a good, or bad third of the town itself, seemed to be a veritable Petri-dish of disgruntled, jealous troublemakers, who turned particularly bitter and twisted late on Sunday afternoons, when copious amounts of Lion and Castle beer awoke the inner demons of some of the more tired and emotional miners on what was supposed to be a pleasant afternoon off.

Yet while his mother and father attended most Sunday brunches, Mrs Yates delighting in speaking German with Gretchen (when the manageress could spare a few moments between running the bar and cashing up), Mr Yates always projected an air of quiet dignity, leaving the party or individual parties before the almost inevitable alcohol-fuelled venom started to gush forth, the most vociferous and aggrieved people seeming to be expat workers nearing the ends of their contracts, shit-scared that they'd not be granted new ones or extensions to their present ones.

And the major figure of their hate seemed to be the Deputy Personnel Manager, Joe Stonehouse, who was a very close friend of Pete Reichert's, rumour having it that Reichert had some 'black' on Stonehouse, and this could influence appointments, with just a word needed from Joe to the Personnel Manager - 'God' himself - Mr Matanga Bwanga.

Mr Bwanga had been educated at University of Fort Hare, South Africa, overcoming the terrible 1950s discrimination through apartheid, to be awarded a first-class honours degree in mining engineering and technology, and was highly prized by the Zambian mining company as a sign of the country's investment in its own people. Yes, by now the country had gained its independence, with Kenneth Kaunda as its head of state.

However, it was apparent that a number of white expats had been retrenched since his appointment, though replaced, it must be said, by highly qualified locals, some recommended, according to the ever-churning rumour mill, by Reichert, for a fee through Joe Stonehouse, resulting in allegations against both of them as 'White Kaffirs' and of going 'bush' or 'native'.

This nepotism, if not corruption, was further borne out, some said, when Mr Bwanga's son, who attended Bob's school, and who was a tremendous rugby player, had been continually referred to as 'Munty', a racially derogative term, by his teammates, although they said it was in jest, the alleged chief 'tormentor' being the son of a South African, expat miner whose contract, with six weeks to run, had not been renewed, although he'd allegedly earlier been informed that it would be.

Sour grapes or not, it hadn't made for a convivial working environment and of course had set the proverbial gossiping cats amongst the palpably paranoid pigeons.

But talk about piss pots calling kettles black, as it was well known that many, and probably very many, of the single expat workers, black and white, senior and junior, and some married staff but with single postings and even (can you believe it?) a few with wives with them in Luanshya, all at various times used the services of the same local and transient prostitutes (nicknamed 'Night Fighters') congregating, nay lurking, in a small area of isolated huts and kitted-out containers some way outside the town limits, and called the Wazza, cheekily so-named after the famous First World War brothel area in Cairo, apparently so-beloved by the British, and then the Anzacs.

Yes, the economic, sexual and biological forces of supply and demand were at work, although most people paid lip service to the shame and degradation of it all, though it did perhaps perform a useful role in minimising the pestering and molestation of the town's 'decent, and more respectable women' and gave a reasonable income to some poor unfortunates, and a few 'spends' for those protecting and running the small operation.

It also ensured a Dr Pretorius earnt a decent living from his, the only dedicated, pox clinic in town, by curing, or at least attempting to cure, a conveyor belt of sores, lesions, bite marks and dripping dicks, the patients invariably full of regrets, drunken remorse and 'never agains'!

And while Dr Pretorius was damned expensive, he was the only qualified specialist in town, and those stricken were not only paying for his professional services, but also his silence. A trip to the company's own on site and well stocked and staffed mine hospital would have meant the whole camp, and thus town, would soon have learnt about who most recently needed to be referred to a piccolo player to show them how to block the holes in their dick.

And, more seriously, perhaps be subject to disciplinary proceedings for breaching what Health and Safety Rules they had back then, especially if their faces didn't fit, or management were just waiting for an excuse to 'let them go'.

Bob of course knew very little about all this, still being the innocent mangenue most lads are at his age, and certainly knew nothing about the various extra marital affairs being conducted around and out of town, the whoring and whatnot being most definitely frowned upon by Mr and Mrs Yates, and never a casual conversational matter within their home or in the hearing of their three sons.

Now Colin Yates, not involving himself in company politics or labour problems beyond those affecting himself, or those working for him, and to pre-empt people thinking him a threat to them in the promotion stakes, had made it plainly clear that he was very content with his position, with no thoughts of ever putting in for promotion, or wanting to inherit 'dead man's shoes'.

He'd seen enough of life, what with having travelled the world as a sea-faring engineer, and then having served in the Second World War, to know when he was well-off, the welfare of his wife and three children being his overriding concern.

Further, although by no means wealthy, he considered himself 'comfortable' and, in many ways, blessed. Magda freely concurred and if people thought them staid, lacking in ambition and 'too full of the milk of human kindness to catch the nearest way', then that was up to them, just leave them out of it. They certainly weren't the sort of people to be beholden to anyone, let alone explain themselves when no explanation was actually necessary.

The family developed a wide circle of friends, not only from within the mining community, but also from the local Moth Club (an old soldiers' club), the golf club, and the Caledonian Club, as well as the nearby Makoma Dam Club with its man-made lake and smart clubhouse, although there was inevitably some overlap, often entertaining both locals and expats, the guests delighting in Magda's cooking and the unforced hospitality and friendship.

The boys generally mucked in, freely joining the chit-chat, happy and quite at ease in mixed-race company, which to them of course, had become the norm.

Now while Colin did enjoy social activity, it more often than not included family, and he never drank more than two or three beers on those occasions, except perhaps on New Year's Eve when he'd possibly indulge in a wee dram or two to toast absent friends and relatives back in Dumbarton, and to celebrate or acknowledge his proud Scottish roots.

When he did 'take a few on board' though, it was inevitably at Theo's corner bar in the town centre, which drew a more varied range of expats, many without direct connections to the mining community, such as teachers, policemen and shopkeepers, for example. He found their varied and perhaps more expansive view of the world in general pleasantly refreshing and Theo always made sure his beers were kept ice cold, which wasn't always the case at the Homestead in view of the great demand for beer on Sundays.

Whilst young Bob may have over the years tried or sniffed a nip of whisky from Dad's glass, or an occasional sip of beer, perchance slipped to him by careless adults, or older, miscreant school chums, in truth he didn't much like the taste of alcohol. Not even Lion or Castle lager, and while in so many ways a 'real Steady Eddie' in developing into the mirror image of his father, there was no indication back then that in the right or wrong place, with the right or wrong company, he had it in him to become the magnificent pisshead he very nearly completely turned into for a while, a few short years later.

About this time, he'd moved on to secondary education at Luanshya High School, again in a mixed-race, mixed-gender environment, where the teachers in the main commanded much due respect and taught the traditional subjects and syllabus according to the South African model. Again, he quickly made friends, with his new classmates and with some fellow pupils having accompanied him from the primary school to the so-called Big School.

He immediately tried his hand at more serious and higher-level sports such as cricket, rugby, football and general tomfoolery, punching way above his weight, and thus was readily accepted by those in classes above his year, finding yet more people with whom to run wild, outside of school hours.

He was particular friends with two female classmates, Wilhelmina Mkele and Malindi Sakala, and two lads who became his sparring partners, as it were, Mulumba Kaunda and Gordon Banda, all but Gordon having fathers working at the mine.

While totally embracing their new life, by now fully part of the local scene, the Yateses still regularly kept up with news from Blighty via BBC Radio's World Service, the boys thrilling to England's World Cup football triumph in 1966 and, three years later, the Apollo moon landing of 1969.

Bob in particular was over that moon when London's West Ham United's youth team played a local eleven at Luanshya's stadium, his fondness for West Ham stemming from the time they won the European Cup Winner's Cup in 1965, again followed on the radio, reinforced by Bobby Moore, Martin Peters and Geoff Hurst just a year later playing such pivotal roles in the England World Cup winning team.

Indeed, when later living in the UK, Yates Junior tried to attend their home games, another of the many things that made living in London fascinatingly bearable.

Yes, more of that later.

But it wasn't all mine-mine-mine, school-school-school, and weekends down the Social, as while Zambia itself was land-locked, there was no reason why its inhabitants should be, and when Colin could be persuaded to take well-deserved long leaves, the family variously holidayed in Beira, Mozambique, Rhodesia and South West Africa (Namibia) and, most memorably, at the magnificent Victoria Falls, which they reached after a two day journey on a wonderfully old train, pulled by a Garratt steam locomotive, from Ndola railway station.

And then there were occasional Sunday trips to Kitwe's racecourse, some ninety minutes by road from Luanshya, with a suitably colonial, festive atmosphere amongst the crowd in pageantry, manners and attire, and although it wasn't quite Ladies

Day at Ascot, and some of the races themselves might not have borne close Jockey Club scrutiny, a tip-top day out was invariably had by all, made even more special by Magda's bumper picnic spreads, near a favourite flatted anthill, where the boys could run free, yet be discreetly watched over by Mum and Dad. Tiger was left by himself at home to fend for himself and supposedly protect the property.

While Bob was doing very well at school, now well up in the top ten per cent at academic and sporting endeavour, particularly well thought of by Jahangir Patel, the chemistry teacher, there was *one* fly in the ointment, a very large and particularly nasty one in the form of the headmaster, of all people.

A cross between Mr Creakle in *'David Copperfield'* and Mr Gradgrind in *'Hard Times'*, this florid-faced, pot-bellied, balding, middle-aged and plainly psychopathic throwback to the Dickensian era was an Irishman, appropriately named Seamus O'Stropley. His avowed purpose in life seemed to be to shame everyone, especially those in whom he perceived any weakness, hint of defiance or indication of true academic or sporting prowess, unless their parents were either known to him, or were likely to take him to task if they ever discovered he was verbally or physically bullying their child or children.

He not only carried a well-used and springy hickory cane, but also strode around with a mature, snarling Doberman dog on a leash, often lengthening its lead to frighten the children or, even better, any child he caught alone, and thus without any witnesses to his sadism.

Sad to say, he was also the school's rugby coach, and would gratuitously beat most boys, even those who were now young men in the 1st XV, who unnecessarily, solely adjudged by him, had the temerity to punt the ball away, his ethos being to 'Run with the bloody thing!'

Of course, he couldn't in any shape or form stand 'Munty', as he would weave and kick all over the place to look for an opening (he went on to become a top player in South Africa), but 'The Mad Mick' O'Stropley daren't do or say anything physical or racist against 'Munty' as his father was, of course, the Mine's Personnel Manager.

No, he wasn't quite that stupid.

However, speculation was later rife as to exactly who it was that gave O'Stropley a damned good hiding one night as he staggered alone to the golf club's outside toilets, dogs not being allowed on those hallowed premises, not even *his* ill-trained, badly used and evil-tempered beast.

But did it stop the headmaster abusing his position to bully and vent his spleen on his pupils? No, not for long, and only until his cuts, bruises and broken arm had healed, but, as sure as night follows day, he was 'back at it' in a couple of months, although 'Munty' had left school by then, much to O'Stropley's relief, as it had been so hard to control himself.

To his credit, though, he never let-on who it was who'd bashed him, which in a way was a great pity as many people in town, and at the school, and indeed past pupils, would gladly have contributed to a 'Thank you!' fund in appreciation of a totally justified job being so well done.

It would have been a greater blow to his ego than the beating itself to have realised that, while he had a small clique of hardened obsequious sycophants amongst the longer-serving teachers, mostly out of fear that he could, on a whim, cook their collective golden geese, he was universally despised by the remainder, who only put up with his shenanigans because of his position, and who were perfectly aware that he was a blatant coward and bully, hiding behind his own insecurities by taking it out on underlings and those not in positions to challenge him.

Such is the modus operandi of such creatures, and while 'Steady Eddie' didn't know it at the time, he would sooner rather than later find out there are O'Stropleys spread far and wide, and that one doesn't have to look hard to find them, either.

And so, life continued down in Zambia, with Bob's brothers Kevin and Michael following his path at Junior and then to Luanshya High School, running wild and free, often shirtless, around open countryside in the mainly temperate tropics, the only brakes on their wheels being school, and the more violent storms during the rainy season.

However, that world was to come crashing down around them, when, in 1969, their parents sat them down and informed them that their father was taking early retirement within six weeks, with arrangements in hand with relatives in Dumbarton for them to return to England and live in a large, rented house in Balham, in London's Wandsworth district.

Where?

Bloody hell!!

This was to enable the boys in turn to sit O and A levels within the much-esteemed British Educational System, and for the parents, in time, to catch up with Magda's scattered family, and for both of them to enjoy the fruits of their labours while still young enough to actively pursue whatever leisure activities or travel plans that they may later decide upon.

The decision had not been made lightly, but the boys' education was paramount, with Luanshya High taking Bob as far as he could go at fifteen. An alternative was boarding school in Rhodesia or South Africa but there was no way the parents wanted to split up the family. Surely the boys could see that?

As yes, though admittedly only after silent tears shed on downy pillows, they indeed did, and so it was to be 'offski' after all. After eleven marvellous years during the most formative days of their lives.

Bloody hell!

Strong remonstrations were made by the company for Colin and Magda to reconsider, but the die had been cast and they remained implacable, with Mr Yates taking a month to hand over to his Zambian protégé Curtis Ngosa, who fitted in very adroitly. Then it was a seemingly endless round of farewells, hosted by friends and organisations from all across town.

Bob and his brothers Kevin and Michael bade their goodbyes at school a week before departure, and were provided with glowing testimonials, Bob additionally furnished with full details of his curriculum and proficiency so he could hopefully slip seamlessly into an O level course involving multiple subjects in London.

O'Stropley even shook Bob's hand and seemed genuinely moved, never having had occasion to unduly berate or bully any of the brothers. Perhaps he was ruing missed opportunities, but let's be charitable, shall we?

But of all the people likely to miss the Yateses, surely their absence would be most keenly felt by 'Thanksa,' Freda and Temba, whose relationships with them had developed far beyond employer and employee over the full eleven years. Magda gave them generous severance pay, and all the possessions, furniture and household items she wasn't packing off to London *and* found fresh positions for them all within the family of the new protestant vicar, Harvey Wolseley, an arrangement that as an alternative was perfect for all parties, with Mrs Yates having vetted the new arrivals very carefully to ensure they'd be treated with the dignity, consideration and respect due to them.

Unfortunately, not all people were so considerate or as enlightened as the Yateses, with many tales of mistreatment, cruelty and exploitation of domestic servants, even by people who held themselves up to be veritable pillars of society, and leading lights down the Social.

People! Ye Gods! One of the alleged worse in his treatment of domestic staff was the divorced and woman-hating Mr O'Stropley, with tales emerging from his housemaid, Polly Choma, of bullying, cruelty and sexual demands. Such allegations were later supported by his house boy, Newlove Kapwepwe, who also lived in terror of his temper and sadism, although they never formally reported it, as where else could they find paid employment, accommodation and meals thrown in, and occasionally at them? Yes, economic terrorism and exploitation at its worst.

Poor Steady Eddie, for untold to this day had been his developing affection for Wilhelmina, whom he had known from his very first week in Luanshya, having even progressed to holding hands and the odd kiss.

Yes, yes, promises of writing, swopped addresses, photos and 'I'll miss you's,' all deeply meant and meaningful, even Bob's vow to return, if he possibly could, once his schooling had been completed. Young love. And so it goes. And so it went. The L word. 'Love.'

But despite that awful loss, and leaving his schoolmates and way of life, Bob was actually looking forward to the flight to Europe, starting out of Ndola Airport some twenty miles from Luanshya, having developed a passion for all aviation matters, incorporating civil, commercial and military aircraft, flight paths, airports, and the history of flight, eagerly devouring such aviation literature as he could get his hands on.

Indeed, he had also hooked onto the as-yet-unconfirmed notion of perhaps becoming a commercial pilot, somewhere and sometime along the line, should he obtain the necessary A level passes to be considered for flight training.

This fascination had been fuelled by the family taking a holiday trip back to the UK in May 1966, Bob absolutely thrilled with the Schreiner Airways DC7 propellor aeroplane belching out fiery exhaust plumes on their journey to Gatwick via Lagos, being assured by the cabin attendants that this was completely normal.

And while the Yateses never stayed for the July, 1966 England World Cup triumph, they did remain long enough to purchase their World Cup Willie souvenirs, which they held when listening to the games on the radio back in Luanshya.

Bob still retained his aviation fascination well into his sixties, incidentally, even at one stage planning to buy part of a VC10 fuselage to place in his back garden as a conversation piece, which no doubt would really have pleased his wife, and the neighbours.

And thus it was that the Yates family bade a sad farewell to Zambia and we shall pick up the story of their new life in London, and eventually see how Bob 'Steady Eddie' Yates, on that cold night of 18th January 1975, in a Clapham warehouse, opened up his *Sunday Telegraph* and came across an advertisement for an opportunity of a lifetime, just a very few hours before Alan 'The Bucket' Bottomley, down in the wilds of Gloucestershire, did exactly the same thing!

And so to Balham, in South London, where friends of the Yateses had arranged a large flat with several rooms at the top of a detached Victorian house in a comparatively quiet, leafy road, this before the de-gentrification of London in general, with only a few of the later ubiquitous tower blocks having been erected within Balham itself.

Initial impressions? Bloody cold, with everything and everyone so grey and impersonal, and although nothing could be done to change the vagaries of the British weather, they'd soon overcome some of the notorious standoffishness of the English inhabitants there once they had gotten to know the area and some locals.

And how true was the adage, 'You never know England, until you've left England!'

Bob, within a few weeks, had been enrolled at Henry Thornton Comprehensive School about a mile away from his new home and very fortuitously was immediately admitted to the Sixth Form, even without O levels, such were the testimonials he'd brought with him, and he was allowed to study for and take those examinations the following year.

Being in the Sixth Form meant he was in the school's elite from the very start, thus away from the junior and middle school pecking-order struggles, bragging rights, schoolyard fights and whatever area-specific type of 'Off Ground Galloping Knob Rot' they had down there in South London.

If he could banter with the Bantu, then he could certainly bullshit with the Balham and Wandsworth boys, easily mixing with the various ethnic groups within the new school, his classmates soon enough recognising him as the 'Steady Eddie' type, a non-confrontational, honest and straightforward chap.

Some *were* a little nonplussed though by the 'Kenneth Kaunda-type' handkerchief he carried in his satchel during the first hot spell they had, and even more so when he took it out and used it.

But they were more underwhelmed by a tee shirt he sported on one Saturday morning football session which bore the legend, 'Never mind the Elephants! Save the Whites!' a souvenir given to him in South West Africa (Namibia), which, once it had been worn to Henry Thornton that one time, never again saw the light of day except to clean his football boots with.

Yes, Steady Eddie was a quick learner, and never dared to wear his West Ham United shirt to school, becoming aware of the fierce rivalry between supporters from different London teams such as Chelsea, West Ham, Spurs and Arsenal.

Bob though was initially amazed at the somewhat undisciplined approach to study shown by many pupils, which was anathema to the desire to learn displayed at Luanshya High, but to be fair, those who remained at school by choice to study for A levels were equally as keenly competitive and most conscientious.

Unfortunately, the facilities for sports were not the best, and thus while Bob excelled at the high jump, competitive team sports were just not available, the shared footie pitches being some miles away.

This success would be invaluable to him as he'd be in the high jump many times over during the coming years, and in something a lot messier too, not always solely, or of his own making.

For the first year, Bob was perhaps still adjusting himself to the teachers and the novelty of living in London, and how day-to-day life unfolds, and what museums and other joys London has, often for little or no charge.

His love affair with West Ham United continued but he only attended a few games as the early 1970s saw the rise of the football hooligan, with the Hammers plagued by a violent bunch of so-called supporters who nicknamed themselves the Inter City Firm, and single supporters, of both home *or* away teams, caught walking alone, even if just there for the footie, could be in danger just by being in the wrong place at the wrong time.

And *that* was all in the name of fun! No thank you very much. Much safer watching West Ham on *Match of the Day* on BBC TV.

But just you try telling Mrs Yates about problems in adjusting, she having to choose washing days or even washing hours to fit in with breaks in the bad weather, while attempting to keep a houseful of five people clean and tidy.

Oh Emson, come back; all is forgiven. But she was a lot happier when the crates of furniture, carpets and other household items, turned up from Zambia, and she could then tastefully personalise their newly rented accommodation to make it more homely.

Bob failed a couple of O levels but, with a change of teacher, passed the re-sits, his first maths teachers having taught him all about poker but unfortunately that was not on the official syllabus.

But lo and behold, he passed three A levels; Physics, Geography and British Constitution, a nice mish mash of Arts and Science but where oh where was the Maths A level to add to those to perhaps qualify him for training as a commercial pilot or obtain a flying officer cadetship with the RAF?

Making most of the time off to think how to proceed and what to do, Bob joined his family in taking trips around the UK, and up to his father's folks in Dumbarton, and then the Highlands and Lowlands, enjoying the long summer break from school, with Kevin and Michael to return to Henry Thornton the following term, Bob mulling over a Maths re-sit or whether to get a part-time job, and look around first, choosing the latter option.

And there, my pedigree chums, we have him, after having had a few other nightwatchmen jobs, at Goldstein's warehouse in Clapham at about 3am on Sunday 19th January 1975, munching on his doorstep-sized cheese-and-pickle sandwiches, sipping lukewarm coffee from his Thermos, and turning over the pages of the *Sunday Telegraph*, from the sports reports to the less interesting features on the inner pages, when a boxed advert shot off the pages, its bold headline hitting him like a thunderbolt:

'Going anywhere in the next three years? If not, why not join the Royal Hong Kong Police?' (Hereinafter and throughout referred to as the RHKP.)

Followed by an equally striking sub-heading, **'2am in Kowloon is a fine time for self-discovery.'**

And as Steady Eddie read on, he was enthralled by the lure of an exciting career as an Inspector in the RHKP on a three year contract basis, promising adventure, comradeship, responsibility, experiences and opportunities only afforded to a very select few. The salary offered was way beyond what he was then earning or could possibly reasonably hope to earn in the foreseeable future, and – *look at that!* – a thirty percent gratuity at the end of the three years, along with four and a half months' paid leave.

That could pay for commercial pilot training and, after all, what was three years when one is only twenty?

But wasn't there some sort of corruption scandal involving the RHKP? And wasn't Hong Kong due to be handed back to China sometime in the future? And hadn't there been communist-inspired riots there in the mid-sixties?

And what about that plastic 'Made in Hong Kong' souvenir football that he'd bought at Victoria Falls and which had holes in the seams which meant that it could never be inflated? Bob had been as mad as hell over that.

But colonialism itself was under fire from many quarters, with the majority of Britain's admittedly few remaining 'Dependent Territories', as they were later more politically termed, seeming to be actively and vociferously seeking independence, so how much longer would China be content to allow Hong Kong to remain a Crown possession?

But he had the required three A levels, with experience of living and working overseas, so what did he have to lose in writing away for the information pack and application forms?

And, crikey, the Hong Kong Office was only in Grafton Street in London, so on the Monday why not pop along and see what gives, straight from the horse's mouth, as it were?

And then, as his parents were due back the coming Wednesday, he could talk it over with them with more information to hand, and Mr. Yates could advise Bob on whether to pursue it, or possibly help him find a position back in Zambia within the mining industry.

Yes, there was an extra spring in his wheelchair as he pushed himself around the corridors for the rest of his shift.

And so it came to pass, that at 9am on Monday 20th January 1975, as the as-yet-unknown (well, to Steady Eddie anyway) 'Bucket' Bottomley was spewing in a wastepaper basket at the offices of Nat West Bank in Stroud, Bob was making his way to the Hong Kong Office in Grafton Street and, while they wouldn't interview him immediately, or ask him to fill in an application form, they took his details and gave him an information booklet and away he went, as happy as a sand boy.

The booklet contained an extremely comprehensive introduction to Hong Kong and outlined the role of the Colony's police and what was expected of its new recruits, and as he was guarding the hallowed portals of the main Masonic lodge in London's West End later that evening, he took in as much detail as he could, and was becoming more and more convinced that he should apply.

(It's a pity he couldn't have picked up a few Masonic buzzwords, secret handshakes or finger pulls, as they could have opened a lot of doors to him later on, but, hey, we were all young once, across the seas and down the centuries ago, and what then did young Robert know of such things?)

His parents were full of enthusiasm for him to venture to the Far East, with his father pointing out the then current transportation problems and a drop in copper prices in Zambia. This, combined with political unrest in Rhodesia, Mozambique and Angola, with South Africa involving itself in those struggles, suggested that mining in that part of the world may not be an industry in which to presently seek a career.

Steady Eddie, with that in mind, phoned to Luanshya and spoke to Wilhelmina, now married to Gordon Banda, (so it goes), and found the town wasn't so welcoming as before, and had become extremely commercial; but the downturn in the copper business, while surely only temporary, had caused redundancies and consequently there weren't so many expat contracts on offer.

The high school? Much the same, except that Mr O'Stropley had been fired for going on a drunken binge after his Doberman, Zoltan, had been accidentally run over and killed when slipping the leash O'Stropley had used to tie him to the golf club's fence while the headmaster went to the bar.

The binge would have been forgiven, in itself, had he not been found in a bush near the Wazza, bound hand and foot, gagged, naked, with his springy and well-used hickory cane poking out of his backside. Despite his claims that he'd been set up, the school authorities sacked him on the spot - well, they let him get dressed first - and off he went, cane between his legs, back to Cork.

So, it wasn't all doom and gloom then. However, it's a small world and O'Stropley would resurface a few years later in Hong Kong as, of all things, a management consultant, although most definitely not for long!

Unable to resist his nature and some of the more exotic, even erotic pleasures of the Far East, as discussed later, he was arrested for caning a Filipina girl he'd met in a bar (yes, he'd taken 'Old Hickory' with him) not thinking she'd mind, as she'd willingly accompanied him back to his apartment. She called the police, who matched the marks on her buttocks to the well-used and much-travelled cane, and thus it was 'Good night Vienna!' for the Mad Mick.

He was given six months in prison in which to contemplate his sadism, although he could perhaps have been slightly proud of how 'Young Yates' had turned out, being the Police Duty Officer the night O'Stropley had been dragged to the police station cells, and who had processed the old pervert's detention.

But the UK wasn't all sweetness and light either; there'd been an IRA attack in Balham in 1974 (part of a larger campaign), memories of power cuts and the three day working week were recent, a change of government ushered-in a huge conflict with the unions, the National Front had come into being and was a portent of racial tensions that would erupt in the not-too-distant future, there was *always* the unpredictable weather, the Beatles weren't going to reform, Glam Rock was coming to an end, but, unfortunately, *Coronation Street* looked and still looks as if it never would or will.

So why *not* go to Hong Kong, then? Particularly as Mum and Dad still had Kevin and Michael under their care, so it wasn't as if Bob was running out on the family, now was it?

And so it came to pass that once Bob decided that a career in the Far East *was* for him, things in the early part of 1975 took on a speed and life of their own.

By early April 1975, he had applied for, been interviewed for, sent for a medical because of, and duly accepted for the position of Probationary Inspector in the RHKP, scheduled to travel to Hong Kong as soon as 18th April.

Before that, though, he was directed to attend a seminar at the Hong Kong Office to complete administrative formalities and be given a full briefing and presentations about Hong Kong in general, and the police in particular. At the same time, he would have a chance to briefly meet the twenty two other British chaps who'd be joining the RHKP with him, having no idea whatsoever that a few of them there would become, through many shared experiences, interests and scrapes, friends for life.

So, without further ado, let the games truly commence as I now duly direct you to Chapter 3, 'The Seminar', that is, once you've survived saying hello to a certain Alan 'The Bucket' Bottomley in Chapter 2.

Enjoy!

Chapter Two

Alan Victor 'AV'/ 'The Bucket' Bottomley

One of the more annoying things about living and working in Stroud, Gloucestershire, in the 1970s was that unless you'd pre-ordered, and had been included on a newsagent's delivery round, there was usually no bloody chance whatsoever of obtaining a Sunday newspaper on a Sunday, the trading laws being what they were back then.

So, on the 19th January 1975, if Alan ('AV') 'The Bucket' Bottomley hadn't had yet another turbulent argument with his girlfriend Maggie, then stormed out of his dingy bedsitter close to the town centre, thus bumping into Stan Tremlin just finishing his large paper round, and, on a whim, buying from him the *Sunday Telegraph* the holidaying Mrs Swinford had forgotten to cancel, he might very well have missed the chance of a lifetime.

His nerves somewhat calmed after chatting to Stan, especially as there was only an hour left until the pubs reopened for the

Sunday lunchtime session, he returned defiantly to what he termed 'The Cave' in the hope that Maggie had also quietened down, and that the eight or twelve 'little drinks with the big kicks' she'd guzzled the previous evening were temporarily sufficient to her need and addiction for the remainder of the weekend, and that she'd very shortly bugger off and leave him in peace.

The argument had once more been over the L Word. L for Love, the same as Bob and Wilhemina in Luanshya? No, not quite. It was L for Loan. A very specific loan, as in M for Mortgage, followed by another dreaded M, as in M for Marriage. Yes, three years in and now she was coming out with all that crap, mouthing off every time she was drunk, this time being particularly forward as she'd won first prize in the Cross Hands raffle very late on Saturday night, a very large, boxed presentation of choice fruit and veg, kindly donated by Alf Ollerenshaw, the town's biggest high street greengrocer.

Yes, a huge bastard, all twenty three stone of him if he was an ounce.

But the success had seemed to go to her head, especially as she wasn't used to any, and AV reckoned they were lucky to escape unhurt, as they seldom used that pub, only bursting in at ten minutes to closing time last evening as his screaming bowels had been close to exploding, and it was extremely fortuitous that the one cubicle in the 'gents' had been vacant as he rushed through the crowded public bar and noisily splatted out his waste matter.

Their intended and much preferred hostelry for a final drink or two was the Horse and Groom, a hundred yards further down the hill, but there was no way that AV could have made it before he messed himself.

And so, once he'd rearranged his clothing, washed his hands, and rinsed the sweat off his brow, manners dictated they buy their nightcaps where he'd crapped, although he seldom wore one as a rule, and a quid for the remaining five raffle tickets *did* seem too good to miss.

But my oh my, weren't the pub's regular customers mightily miffed, so much so that he'd urged, nay begged, the exuberant and glaze-eyed Maggie to re-donate the prize, but she was having none of it. Obviously, she'd taken to heart her mother's tales of banana shortages during the war, and the spuds, broccoli and savoy cabbage would 'do' her large family very nicely in supplementing and complementing the traditional Sunday roast beef.

Anyway, he opened the first floor 'Cave's' only door to find that Maggie had gone to the tenants' shared toilet, a fact he deduced from arse-sized sheets of paper torn out of his *'New Statesman'* and *'Spectator'* magazines, his prized toilet roll wisely hidden under the walnut wardrobe that dominated the small room.

She had only to ask, he mused to himself, but supposed that she'd been taken very short.

His own thought processes were jaded rather than stimulated, but he became disgustingly aware of assorted fruit and veg scattered and strewn willy-nilly round the floor, and now-black, semi-peeled squashed bananas on his single bed's cover and, damn it, laying on the pillow and inside the bed itself.

Of course! He remembered!

They couldn't go to the Chinky carrying that box of fruit, so had munched on some of it as a late-night repast, instead of the usual fare of chicken fried rice and pork Chow Mein. And royally so, judging by the mess they'd made.

But his queasy stomach told him that a mixed salad breakfast was totally out of the question, although the Greyhound Pub, just fifty yards along the road, usually had a few stale cheese-and-onion rolls left over from the evening, so that would serve as Sunday's dinner, unless Maggie's family were so delighted with their now admittedly ripped-to-pieces fruit and veggies that they sent their daughter down with a fully plated roast dinner later that afternoon.

There were pros and cons to this; the pro was that they always provided a spiffing feed. The con was that he'd have to put up with her at least until the pub's evening session started, and he was in no mood for her, 'You gonna give I one, or what?' today. Nor for any more arguments over potentially shared futures.

Actually, a full traditional roast would be nice as the woman in the adjacent flat was well cheesed off last week when she'd caught AV, well pissed, dipping the half-chewed bottom segment of a cottage loaf into her simmering gravy, as it lay atop the shared kitchen stove.

And as if that hadn't been bad enough, he'd received several jolts of electricity through the cooker being defective, the Bisto gravy conducting the electric current through the bread and into his hand, as if it was some sort of aversion therapy for recidivist gravy thieves.

Then he trod on what turned out to be a peach stone, then crushed a grape – if the landlord's cat hadn't left another turd on the threadbare carpet – between his now unshod and unsocked toes.

He heard Maggie's waddling thump coming down the stairs, so hid the *Sunday Telegraph* with the Andrex, just in case she hadn't finished her business yet but was merely coming back to resupply with paper. He'd read the broadsheet later.

In she came, tight-lipped, red-faced from the strain of the past few minutes, hardly uttering a word beyond telling him to clean his room up himself, and that she didn't feel like ironing his work shirts and he could go to the bank scruffy for all she cared.

But no mention of the L or M words, so that particular issue had been temporarily shelved, but definitely not for long, knowing her.

Then stuffing what fruit and veg was still retrievable and edible into two Fine Fare carrier bags, she huffily announced she was off but would be down in the week.

Yes, AV thought, every bloody night in the week, unless he was badly off the mark. She struggled through the door, only turning back to grunt, 'I wouldn't go into the bog for a few minutes if I were you!' and then she was gone.

Freedom! At last! The claustrophobia had been driving him damned near mad.

Yes, but just *how* he missed playing football over the weekend since Whitbread Brewery and Bond Worth carpet factory now insisted that their players all be current employees, both within the Stroud League and the Gloucester Sunday League, and he'd found himself in mid-season without a team to play for.

He'd tried refereeing, but after obtaining his qualification he found it wasn't as easy or enjoyable as he'd thought, and anyway he found himself in more arguments and altercations than when playing the game, being suspended after fighting with the captain of a local youth team.

The fact that the girl was big for fifteen and had hit Alan first had not been taken into consideration at the disciplinary hearing, most unfairly in his humble opinion.

Still, who needs any of them?

Thus, it was that he found his weekends an extremely taxing and unfulfilling two days of pubs, chip shop dances, afternoon cinema (but not so often since the Odeon had turned multi-screen), telly, popping bubble wrap, staring into space and squiring Maggie around the place, although not necessarily in that order of unimportance.

The bank where he worked was very much nine to five, although he would have gladly gone in at the weekend, even without pay, but what need of a Grade 2 clerk when the place was obviously closed?

He pondered all of this in the shared bathroom as he casually doused his face, shaved his stubbly chin and furred tongue, brushed his teeth, and used someone's wet flannel hanging on the towel rack to wipe his dick with, laughingly hoping it belonged to the woman who'd been so protective of her gravy, oh so recently.

Besides, it might help to cure her spots. The bitch!

A change into his cleanest, soiled shirt (hell, he really must get to the Soap and Suds launderette soon!), on with his jumper and jacket, then time to toddle off for a reviver or two in the Greyhound.

But just as he was about to leave, he happened to glance in the wardrobe's full-length interior mirror as the unkind midwinter sunlight, streaming through the semi-drawn curtains, showed him in all of his starkly unkempt glory, and he was startled at what he saw: a frowning, overweight, generously-buttocked, five feet, seven inches small, Beatle-fringed, Noddy Holder-bewhiskered, pointy-nosed, butterfly-lipped, twenty two year old male of the species, attired in denim jacket, multi-coloured tank top, striped suit trousers, pink round-collared shirt, loose yellow kipper tie and open flip flops (yes, in midwinter).

He would ordinarily have been wearing his prized and much-admired blue platform shoes, but he'd fallen off their three inch heels at the hop above the chip shop the previous night, while stomping to a Gary Glitter song, thus turning his left ankle. And humping that box of fruit and veg all over town hadn't done him much good either.

Christ, he *was* looking good. Feeling like crap, mind you, but image *was* everything and you've either got style or you haven't!

But with dear Margaret increasingly getting on his tits, his realisation that bedsit land wasn't an instant portal to bohemia and the permissive society, acceptance that his erstwhile, nebulous goal of saving for university wouldn't now be reached, and that a diet of fry-ups, fish and chips, curry, kebabs and Chinese takeaways was doing him very little good, and obviously quite the reverse, he had to admit that he'd made a truly terrible mistake in not moving with his late parents and siblings down to Hampshire the previous year, which now felt like ten years to him.

(No, his parents weren't dead, merely late of Stroud. Calm down! There's no reason why this can't be fun you know.)

He was obviously suffering from withdrawal symptoms and needed an immediate top-up of Forest Brown Ale as his brain yet again raced and examined exactly how he'd come so early in life to where he seemed to be in a complete rut. More importantly, his brain was further wrestling with the quandary and dilemma of just how on earth its host could find a way out of the quagmire he had gotten himself into.

So, dear readers, to start from the beginning...

Alan Victor ('AV' - get it?) Bottomley was sired by Geoff Bum, as he was unkindly locally known, out of Gina Parrish in 1952, part of the post - Second World War baby boom. Geoff hadn't quite thought about it that way, though, having shoved Gina up the duff in his family's cider apple fields one very cold, late February night, the very evening before he once again left to re-join the 10th Hussars back in Germany, part of his National Service.

Both were your typical Gloucestershire country-stock, although Gina's mother Lillie originally hailed from 'somewhere up north', which none of the family liked to talk about except privately, and in hushed tones.

Now Stroud prides itself as being at the centre of five valleys, and in many ways is still an incestuous, narrow-minded little place where people tend to be wary of others outside of their own valley and, indeed, hamlet or village. Grudges are borne for generations and 'Twitchy Window Land' spying and the love of gossip and rumour-mongering have developed along those hillsides, and at the tops and bottoms of the valleys into an evil-purposed, busy-bodying, prying, nosey-parker disposition amongst very many of Stroud's inhabitants, both the well-established and the 'newcomers' who've only been there a couple of generations.

Procrastination has however long been freely acknowledged as the principal trait of Stroudies, but as most of them don't know what the word means, one can call most of them procrastinators and they'll smile and probably thank you. But there again, I'm not quite sure about that. (See! I told you!)

But Geoff and Gina differed from most of the locals, in that both had very highly developed senses of humour which really helped them through most of the troubled times ahead.

Lil's husband Jim had retired as a foundryman and they lived in a rented cottage in Thrupp, along the Golden Valley, with the main London Road at its bottom. Geoff's father had died many years before Alan was born, which was probably just as well, as, according to both Geoff, his mother Eliza and local legend, he was apparently something of a psychopathic tartar, and God only knows what he would have made of AV as he later turned out.

Eliza lived alone, apart from when Geoff was on leave, in a farmhouse way up on the wooded hillside of the Nailsworth Valley, still tending the several fields of cider apples.

Nailsworth Valley. Golden Valley. *There* was conflict from the very start, and it was exacerbated as Lil and Gina Parrish on one side, and Eliza Bottomley on the other, hated one another with a vengeance and worshipped the very ground the other party or parties should be buried under. This hate was historical for some long-forgotten reason but was rekindled and magnified untold times when news of Gina's pregnancy hit the village jungle drums.

Didn't the shit hit the fan! And for the very first but most definitely not for the last time, the as-yet-unborn Alan Victor Bottomley was the indirect cause of absolute panic, mayhem and total pandemonium.

Geoff meanwhile was in ignorant bliss of the problem he'd helped cause, well out of it, living the life of Riley and enjoying the comparative freedom within the Allied Army of Occupation on the Rhine, and the favours of the local hostelry's main non-alcoholic attraction in the shape of a well-stacked German barmaid nicknamed Titsalina.

Now Gina hadn't conceived in the modern era where bastards are quite the norm, but at a time when their mothers would be palpably shunned and openly pointed at, subject to derision and scorn. Consequently, Gina and Lil were distraught until their telegram to Geoff's commanding officer, a Colonel Edgington, resulted in Corporal Bottomley being granted compassionate leave to return to Blighty and face the music. But that was almost impossible to do with such a bloody cacophony of sound going on around him, and hard to make out who was the principal conductor, Eliza or Lil?

In the end Geoff did the decent thing, much against his mother's wishes and indeed orders, and married Gina at Stroud Registry Office, with neither his mother nor his two elder brothers attending.

After Gina tried living in Army married quarters down in Bagshot, Surrey, while Geoff returned to active service in Bad Hessen, she soon wrote crying to her mother about hordes of drunken and loud-mouthed Scottish and Northern squaddies with their horrible wives and brats living on the base, none of whom she could understand, let alone get on with.

Both Lil and Gina then so mercilessly and ceaselessly pestered poor Geoff, through his base and senior officers, that he eventually capitulated and put in his papers, and with a very heavy heart bade farewell to his beloved British Army, his fellow 'Shiners' or Tank Drivers and, worst of all, to Titsalina.

His deep regret over this haunted the poor bastard for the rest of his life, and it just goes to show what trouble one's dick can get one into, allied to a bellyful of beer and a pocket full of serviceman's pay heftily bolstered by an 'Active Service Allowance'.

Again, none of this was Alan's fault, although in later life Geoff did seem to sometimes blame his son for the direction his life had taken.

But let's face it, AV *hadn't* told the sperm that helped form him to swim a bit faster than the other three, had he? Again, it's so unfair!

The small family then lodged with Jim and Lil in their tiny Thrupp cottage until Gina fell pregnant again following a lot of pushing from her husband. The Council then very kindly moved them to the much larger village of Whiteshill, the other side of Stroud, into a three-bedroomed house on a sprawling estate. Some welcome escape from the in-laws for Geoff, with him easily finding regular employment within the local transport and long-distance haulage industry.

Laura was duly calved, followed a year later by Lena, rat-tat-tat, with life in Whiteshill seemingly set fair until Jim threw a spaniel in the works by tripping over one on his way back from the Wagon and Horses in Thrupp, thus fracturing his skull and croaking a few days later. Rumour has it that the pub took up a collection, not for a floral tribute for Jim, but to buy the dog a collar and a case of the finest dog food.

Gina awaited until the last of the obligatory curled, sweaty ham sandwiches and brown ale had been polished off at the post-funeral, platitude-laden piss-up, always having some sense of decorum, before dropping a bombshell on Geoff.

No, not pregnant again, but worse. She wanted to move back to the Golden Valley to be closer to her now widowed mother; either that, or the old lady could move in with them. But wouldn't it be better if they took out a mortgage, and bought their own house?

Admittedly, Geoff had been doing quite well, but carped at such a financial commitment, until Lil and Gina went to work on him yet again and finally, but after more of a struggle this time, he gave in, mainly in the hope of final spousal forgiveness for trying to secretly re-enlist in the Army so he could fight in Korea, with Gina absolutely furious as the first she knew about it was when she opened his rejection letter, 'by mistake'. The Army would not send married men to fight in such a limited conflict, apparently.

'Why did he want to go and fight, anyway?' she grilled him. 'Was it to escape her and the kids?' 'To do his bit!' Geoff confusedly blurted out.

Yes, how noble, but the truth was much more prosaic, being: to travel to so-called exotic lands, to embrace a completely different culture, to meet people from a different ethnic background in their own environment and, the crux of the matter, to shag as many of their young women as he could on R and R while he was still full of vim and vigour (assuming the communists hadn't shot his bollocks off by then) as some slight recompense and revenge for the loss of Titsalina.

Now despite agreeing to the demands of Lil and Gina, he was still inwardly peeved as any confessed, or even suspected, contact with his own mother Eliza still resulted in Gina completely 'going off on one', particularly after she and Eliza had bumped into one another in the main post office in Stroud on Pension and Family Allowance Day, Alan and Laura in pushchairs.

A horrendous slanging match and cat fight ensued, much to the delight of the Family Allowance brigade, but to the terror of the many pensioners who'd formerly been limply queuing in line.

Alan at almost seven was doing quite well at Whiteshill Primary School in a class of twenty five, six-to-eight year old juniors, the thirty or so nine-eleven year olds being seniors. Indeed, he'd once been called in front of those older pupils and asked to solve a simple long division problem annotated on the blackboard by Miss Phelps, which he managed in a trice, in all his innocence and stupidity. Then he heard Miss Phelps grimly accost the cowed seniors with an 'Alan is only six! If he can solve it, why can't you?'

She thanked AV and led him to the classroom door as he felt thirty pairs of hostile eyes boring into his back and head, then suddenly realising he'd have been much better off pretending he couldn't do the maths. Hell, even bursting into tears or peeing himself would have been better than to forthwith be thought a smart-arse, a show-off and, the worst, a teacher's pet.

He'd be reminded of that incident many times in the future, sometimes actually before he'd allow himself to make a similar faux pas.

But within a matter of a few months, the Bottomleys had moved to the small village of Butterrow, yes in the Golden Valley, but on the opposite side to Lil, who'd been moved into a brand-new council flat, still in Thrupp and just down from her old place, which was being turned into luxury bungalows.

Butterrow was a finger village spread along two lanes branching off either side of Butterrow Hill, leading at its top to the National Trust-owned Minchinhampton Common, which stretched for many miles, linking up with the London Road at the top of Chalford Hill. There were no council estates there then, but terraced housing and Cotswold Stone cottages, with a comfortable, safe environment and friendly, reliable neighbours who felt little need to lock their doors when going to the two village shops or the small sub post office.

It took a matter of thirty minutes on foot to reach Thrupp from Butterrow, and vice versa, either along the narrow lanes, or the canal footpath next to the River Frome or, less safe, along the main London Road, delighting both Gina and Lil of course.

They moved into the heavily mortgaged 'Laurels' in the middle of a block of three Greystone houses, Alan and Laura being enthralled by the two-level back garden, and the three apple-laden trees and the rickety corrugated tin shed on its lower level, the house being a treat to explore while the furniture van disgorged familial possessions, and Gina busied herself with getting pots of tea on the go.

The split-level garden, though, held less attraction a few years later when the ten year old Alan started up his father's rotavator on the top patch, then once it was in gear, found he was not strong enough to control it, and the powerful machine, with blades churning wildly, careered over the retaining wall, straight through Geoff's flimsy shed, then onwards to demolish ten rows of runner beans and Gina's prize-winning sunflowers.

Although the runner beans were no longer caned, AV most certainly *was* when Geoff came home and then heard about and inspected the damage. Double bubble, too, as Gina had already given him a belting.

It was so unfair, particularly as Alan hadn't let go of the

damned thing until the rotavator eventually stalled, and thus had been dragged along as an unwilling participant to the swathes of destruction it was causing, and all just four feet in front of him.

Butterrow School was only ten minutes' walk along the lane, with a total of twenty five pupils, again split into juniors and seniors, and as the village was much smaller than Whiteshill, all of the children knew each other's families and were in and out of each other's homes, seeing what treats other mothers (now 'aunties') might give them.

Unfortunately, though, being on a hillside and with so few children between the ages of five to eleven, there was no chance of any organised or competitive sport whatsoever, apart from a sort of rounders, and throwing bean bags around. However, sometimes in summer, the children were either let loose in the woods adjoining the rear of the school, or were escorted by Miss Howell, the Head, and Miss Beard, the juniors' teacher, on nature walks over the common, those two ladies being kindly old souls.

Neither were strict disciplinarians although they could become hot under the collar if the times tables couldn't be recited correctly.

AV was taught flower-pressing, butter-churning, copperplate pen-and-ink scripting and that to sleep in a field of corn with a combine harvester working at its top end was dangerous – yes, life skills to be later cherished more in memory than in usefulness.

But the collective 'highlight', and which took the place of football and cricket, was country dancing, and until his dotage, AV could, if he had any inclination, or a suitable partner, or if he was drunk enough, still perform the steps to the Post Horn Gallop (which *isn't* a panicked mass escape from a brothel to avoid payment).

Just in case anyone is remotely interested, the rhythm goes one-two-three-hop, one-two-three-hop, one-two-three-hop, one-two-three.

No, Miss Howell and Miss Beard were seldom flustered although were infuriated when one, shall we say 'challenged' nine year old, once stole the school dinner money, and when Tony Milburn, aged eight, fashioned a huge papier maché penis in junior craftwork class, following a drawing that his malicious and malevolent teenaged brother had provided for him.

No one had any idea what happened to that particular work of art after Tony was punished, but rumour has it that Miss Beard stayed unusually late that afternoon and, again unusually, was the last to leave.

One highlight from those early days was both classes cramming into the school caretaker's home, attached to the school itself, and watching the 1963 wedding ceremony between Princess Alexandra and a Mr Angus Ogilvy (whomever he was) on Mrs Davies' black-and-white telly. There is some irony in this, as in 1969, Princess Alexandra was appointed as Honorary Commandant General of the newly titled Royal Hong Kong Police. The irony will become apparent a little later.

The Bottomleys, though, soon acquired a television and it immediately became the centre of the children's universe, particularly that of AV who avidly devoured everything he could in the way of popular entertainment, and somehow started to develop a solitary, sullen, remote air about him, and a sense of difference. Christ knows why as there was nothing special about him; he was just turning into a morose little bastard.

He was no longer happy in joining the other village urchins in cherry-knocking, scrogging apples and pears, setting fire to the common, annoying the telephone operator by pressing the emergency button in the phone box, firing his air rifle from the bushes at any old codger in their gardens who'd told him off for something like peeing in the bus shelter, riding up the hill on the rear bumper of the bus, filching sweets out of Critchley's Shop, putting chewing gum in girls' hair, gathering in the woods to stare at grown-ups' Health and Efficiencies or pinching beer and cider bottles from outside the pub and selling the empties back to the landlord.

But boy oh boy, he *did* enjoy the TV, though apparently not as much as one family in the posh new bungalow in Russell's Field who named their twin boys Zed Victor One and Zed Victor Two. But that was nothing compared to the couple across the way who christened their first-born son Tiller-Girl Macefield, the poor wee bairn.

He'd developed a passion for pop music too, especially for the Beatles, the Searchers and Gerry and the Pacemakers, hunkering down each night under the blankets with his small transistor radio to listen to Radio Luxembourg until his favourite tunes of the moment hit the airwaves. In fact, he only 'bothered' with his eleven-plus examination in 1964 as Gina had promised him a super-duper new Fidelity radio if he passed, and with an offer like that he shot through with flying colours.

He was the only Butterrow primary school pupil leaving that year, who opted to go to the Stroud Boys Technical School instead of the swotty Marling Grammar School situated right next to it.

But talk about a culture shock and a frighteningly rude awakening!

His grandmother Lil and great-aunt Elsie helped with the expense of kitting him out with his summer and winter uniforms, but when he nervously fronted up on the first day, bib and tucker, cap and tie, he realised he'd be up against it from the very start as he was the only fresher, or new first former, to arrive in short bloody trousers. Thank you, Mum! Further, it transpired that he was the only new arrival who had no friends or fellow new arrivals from the same school, as Butterrow was the smallest school in the whole of Stroud's educational catchment area. And not only that, but he was belted around the ear by the art teacher on the first day for writing his particulars vertically upon a sheet of paper instead of horizontally.

But with his timetable sorted, having been shown around the school and introduced to his form teacher and the subjects he'd be forced to study, and his ear ringing from the clout, 'Little Johnny No

Mates' trundled the three miles home, along the canal path and up the hill, consoling himself with an ice cream bought with what was supposed to be his bus fare money.

He didn't tell his mother about the battering, knowing full well she'd be down there the following day and cause one hell of a scene, and he was up against it as it was without making things worse, thank you very much. But while he said school was all right, he was actually wondering just what the hell they (whoever 'they' were) had let him in for, and he'd gladly return his new Fidelity radio if he could stop going and return to Miss Beard and Miss Howell's tender control.

Then, as the perfect end to a perfect day, on finding he'd been late home as he'd walked back, having blown the intended bus fare on a ninety-niner, Gina threw a tantrum and from the following day until he left secondary school in June 1971, he had condemned himself to walking the three miles there and three miles back, come rain, hail, sleet, snow and earthquakes, as 'We're not made of money you know!'

Yet another lesson learnt: Lying is sometimes better.

So off he daily shuffled, running the classroom gauntlet of Minchinhampton, Ebley and Stonehouse boys from large primary schools, to sarcastic remarks about his short trousers.

Maths first. What's *that* all about? I finished with that at Butterrow. Then English and History, which surprisingly did interest him. But French and Geography? AV reckoned that, as he never had any intention of ever visiting France, or travelling to any country outside of the British Isles, why was he required to learn anything about those subjects? He was soon made aware of the reason; 'Because *we* tell you to, laddie!' And then he was 'given' 500 lines on 'mountain ranges' for his perceived insolence.

And even though he had chosen to attend a technically orientated school, poor AV unfortunately had ten thumbs when it came to woodwork, metalwork and technical drawing, which Geoff had feared would be the case as his two daughters both showed more mechanical aptitude and manual dexterity than his little boy.

To summarise, after a month of snidey taunts and there being very few subjects that interested him, he was well cheesed-off and something had to break.

And it almost did, being Mike Bunting's nose, from a Geoff-taught head butt outside class one morning, following derision over the Bottomley name, 'Bottomley by name; bottomley by nature!' with Bunting's Minchinhampton buddy, a skinny, supercilious little tit named Phil Brindle, receiving a kick to the nuts for good measure.

And if the bell hadn't sounded for the start of class, two or three others from 'Minch' might well have been brained by the empty coke scuttle and shovel AV had seized from the stack of winter fuel handily piled next to room 1A, such was his uncontrolled fury.

No longer defensive and self-effacing to the point of being thought weak-minded and an easy mark for bullies and idiots, he had given a portent of a side of him that could on occasion gush forth and almost overwhelm him, even though only aged eleven and hardly drinking at all.

It was another lesson learnt in that it's acceptable to be defensive to the point of pugnacity as long as the pugnacity is warranted and is best carried out in a manner as befits the circumstances.

Although Baby Bunting went crying to teacher, his former buddies wouldn't back him up to say it was an unprovoked attack and thus it was put down as a mere schoolyard fracas, and there were loads of them, too many to keep track of in truth.

Mrs Bunting though saw fit to come knocking at Gina's door with her little boy in tow, still crying (or maybe he'd started again, just for the visit), to find they'd actually been at the girls' high school together so the matter went no further, and why should it have, in any case?

Bunting's street or school cred was then lower than snake shit, whilst AV's psychotic flare-up immediately sent him soaring up the first year's pecking order, and he henceforth was marked as a nutter not to be provoked, and as a second-or third-round draft pick for games of football after school, captain of the British Bulldog rough and tumble and of the peculiarly named game of schoolyard tag named 'Off Ground Galloping Knob Rot'.

No one ever teased him again about his short trousers, which in any case were replaced by long ones in late October, a birthday present from Granny Parrish.

It's fair to say that he struggled with most academic subjects to the normal O Level age of sixteen, although he continued to do well in English Language and Literature, having an insight and turn of phrase that apparently delighted some of the English faculty. His value to the school however was more appreciated on the sports field where he captained the Colts 1st XV and turned out for them, and for some half-decent far-flung village teams at soccer and cricket, much to the chagrin of the Bunting and Brindle brigade who seemed to have just faded into insignificance.

Gina, she of two-generational, small-village mental and general social constraints, tried to bring him up 'ever so 'umble, Mr Copperfield', to respect his obvious betters and not to offend those in authority by making them think he was, or could be, cleverer than them, or a threat to them, and that success breeds resentment and 'Best keep your light under a bushmill, son.'

While he tried to keep to Mummy's teachings, it sometimes created an awful inner conflict, finding he was enraged at the psychopathic tendencies of some of the teachers who'd use slippers, metal rulers, canes and even cricket bats to inflict corporal punishment at will, but who would fawn over rich kids and those likely to reflect credit on the school, and thus them, by gaining university places.

This attitude was made significantly worse when the swotty Marling Grammar amalgamated (took over, more like) with the Tech, when the Marling teachers and most of their never-to-beassimilated swots treated the Tech lads as inferiors as they'd never been forced to study Greek, Latin, Calculus, Music or German, severe drawbacks of course to a well-rounded education.

Hell, where was Latin, anyway?

However, even amongst the nobs, snobs and right little toffs, AV held his own at English and History and was one of only two lads to go on from the Tech to play for the new combined 1st XV rugby team.

Another problem, though, despite Geoff's pulling him up on it many times, was that he was and would always remain a scruffy bastard, with a preference for the most casual attire at the most formal of functions, even appearing casual when he was in formal attire. Just an unwanted knack.

More worryingly to him was that he'd peak at five feet seven inches small when sixteen, which was ridiculous for a goalkeeper, and for any rugby player without exceptional skills who wanted to really progress. Not only that but some of the lads he'd tapped-in in earlier now 'fancied their chances' now they were substantially bigger than him, plus some of the new Marling lot wanted to take him down a peg or two.

However, a loud voice, threatening demeanour, and a piece of metal shoved down the spine of his largest text book to use as a weapon, usually ended the challenge, or at least encouraged a settlement.

Despite this, he never considered himself as having so-called Small Man Syndrome, as he never actually thought himself small. Indeed, he messed up many school team photos by proudly plonking himself right in the back row, standing alongside the giants.

No, the problem as he saw it was the adverse reaction many had to a man of his stature because of his ability at some esoteric subjects, his often sardonic sense of humour, and hardly concealed contempt for bullshit, privilege, nepotism, toadyism, elitism and other isms too many to mention, plus his unwillingness to converse with posers or palpable fools or crawl to them merely because they were in positions of authority, or were nobs, snobs and/or toffs. And people like that don't like, and will never like, people like him, categorising people of his ilk as recalcitrant troublemakers. As if!

Luckily though he had inherited and even embellished both parents' razor-sharp senses of humour, quickly realising he could easily hide, deflect or minimise contentious or confrontational issues with a mere joke, pun, one-liner or casual aside, as long as it was only at his own expense. People who didn't know him, or whom he didn't like or of whom he was wary, never quite realised when he was being serious or not, and often found this, and him, annoying.

Sod it, you can't please everyone, even if for many years AV thought that he had to try.

By now, he'd given up on Saturday morning pictures, the library's weekend reading club, the Cubs, trainspotting, shooting vermin, the Blue Peter and Tingha and Tucker Clubs, rafting on, and swimming in, the canal, and smoking, though still liked to roam the woods, commons, River Frome and the towpaths. He also continued to try and fish, but with a spectacular lack of success, the only time he managed to catch anything being with a fork tied to the end of a hazelwood pole when he once speared an obviously very stupid, old or sick trout on the end of it.

Never a conservationist (but who was, back then?), he was however extremely angry when in about 1968 the meadow directly down from their Butterrow house was used to dump thousands of open tins of semi-hardened paint, which were then roughly covered with hardcore and topsoil, and then grassed over.

Surely, somehow, that wasn't right, but who could a young lad complain to, or even know how to find out who was responsible?

Things were changing within the village too, with many old folk dying, and a scarcely noticed but steady influx of 'townies' and 'city slickers' from outside Stroud itself, many commuting daily to and from London, the property prices by then increased dramatically up there. Well, scarcely noticed until it was too darned late and bang went the community, and in came double glazing, planning permissions, conservatories, renovations, double garages, Range Rovers, flowery skirts, real ale, and even folk club nights along at the Woolpack to please the new arrivals.

They tried to act countryfied, but not so deep down were merely a new breed of nob, snob and toff, the forerunners to the 'Glossie Possie' and the ubiquitous yuppies of just a few years later. But locals already had had enough of their own NSTs, thank you very much, those ponces lording it at the Conservative Club, and lauding it at the Minchinhampton Golf Club on top of the common above Butterrow.

While the golf club leased the land for its course from the National Trust, and the public still had unrestricted rights of way and free access, didn't those club-wielding, bag-toting, trolley-pulling, ball-polishing, Burberry-jumpered, Woolworth's-knickered bunch of wannabee Tony Jacklins shout like hell when the local tykes, romping the common, with or without their dogs, crossed their lines of vision at a shot-critical moment! Or when they stole their balls to either sell back to them later, or to keep and throw down from the balcony onto the heads of those in the stalls at Saturday morning pictures, if the abuse was particularly vociferous and if they couldn't be seen doing it.

Some particularly bold youngsters would variously throw balls 'in play' into surrounding woods or bramble bushes, tread them into cow or horseshit, or place them in the tin cup on the green then fill it with their own pee. Mind you, the village girls were at a disadvantage here, but the wet patches they made at least interfered with the putting.

Be that as it may, Alan duly scraped enough O Levels to be allowed to go on to A levels, choosing English and History, naturally, and Economics as the third of his subjects, still digging-in his heels over Geography and French. French? *Merde*! He'd had a nightmare at, and subsequent to, his French O level oral test, the details of which will be revealed much later in this narrative.

He'd mainly wanted to stay on at school and enter the Sixth Form, despite the mild amusement of some teachers and a few caustic remarks from stuck-up, snotty little prigs, to continue playing for the Rugby 1st XV, a sort of badge of honour in local sporting circles, with his fondness for History and English Literature almost being secondary. He had no job in mind requiring him to obtain good grades or even to pass, but once he commenced the courses, he felt duty bound to do the best he could, particularly when bearing in mind the cost his parents had to bear in keeping him at school.

Unfortunately, both English and History were extremely 'wordy' topics, and it appeared that the six teachers responsible for various aspects of both main subjects failed to liaise or even communicate over homework assignments. AV was thus often totally snowed under, and after school, to take advantage of peace and quiet not always afforded him at home, prepped for essays at Stroud library, completing them much later that night after, yes, the three mile traipse back to his village.

But back to prigs and ponces. In early 1971, Geoff's two elder brothers very belatedly and extremely briefly re-entered his life, but only on the death of their mother Eliza, and merely to chisel and weasel everything they could from her estate, the poor woman having broken her hip after a fall, with pneumonia setting in and her passing occurring a week later.

Geoff referred to his brothers as Tate and Lyle as he reckoned that they were a trifle 'sweet', as being queer was sometimes referred to in those less politically correct days. He also called them Tommy the Toilet Roll, as Uncle Tom was palpably and totally self-absorbed, and Uncle Patrick as Pat the Pig, as he was a great, fat, porcine-featured man, the two of them running some sort of butler and valet service in Fulham, attending to the catering, and maybe sexual peccadillos, of the great and good of the land.

But *how* they worked a flanker on Geoff, clearing out the furniture from the farmhouse while their young brother was arranging the funeral, and confirming the sale of both land and the building to property developers named Everard and Slack, who'd been put 'on notice' by the Toilet Roll some six months earlier, on expectation, or eager anticipation, of their mother's imminent death in view of her advanced age. Only the final signatures of the two brothers were needed before the transfers and formalities could be finalised, and money changed hands. Yes, they had been to see Eliza, unbeknownst to Geoff, some short time earlier and had somehow persuaded her to cut him from her will, something he only learnt about immediately following the funeral service.

With an expansive flourish, they bunged Geoff an envelope containing five hundred quid in fivers, and off they gaily and merrily, but very hurriedly, flitted, never to be heard of again by Geoff or any of his family. And good bloody riddance, too, leaving him almost dumbstruck and Gina, in her fury, feeling absolutely vindicated for the venom she had always felt towards her mother-in-law and, by association, her always estranged brothers-in-law.

Alan of course just chalked it cynically down to yet more duplicity and blatantly crass self-interest of nobs, snobs and toffs, made worse by being at the expense of their own kith and kin. Bastards! More lessons learnt.

Laura and Lena had both left school, working as seamstresses in a local garment factory, and had a steady procession of spotty young herberts courting them, some of whom, sad to say, were the offspring of newcomers to the area. All of the village kids he'd known at school were also at work, and as he was the sole A level student and only Marling swot (ha!) for a good few miles around, he felt more isolated than ever. His sisters indeed were part of the Woolpack regulars, both at weekends and during the week, nursing their lemonade and limes until someone slipped them a vodka or two if the landlord, and particularly their parents, weren't looking.

AV never entered that pub until Laura's eighteenth birthday party, and even then, he found himself quickly banned. Yes, yet another story for another day.

To help fund driving lessons, he'd taken an evening job, 6 to 9pm, Monday to Friday, as a petrol pump attendant at Golden Valley Garages, down on the main London Road, which, with not too many cars on the road, especially in winter, allowed him the time to complete some homework assignments when ostensibly performing his duties. In fact, he hardly missed going to the library at all, although he would miss the kind attentions of the very comely Estelle, one of the prettier librarians, although admittedly she only talked to him on a professional basis, despite how much his raging hormones wished otherwise.

All very easy-peasy. However, after filling a car with fuel one night and checking the oil, collecting the cash, and then saying a polite goodnight to the driver, just thirty seconds later he alarmingly spotted the vehicle's dipstick on top of a pump housing. Bloody hell! Not a sign of the car up or down London Road, and he hadn't known the driver or the car registration number, though all *that* would soon change.

Alan frantically yet foolishly hoped that maybe the customer wouldn't notice but at the end of his shift he cashed up, and locked up, leaving a note for Harold Berkley, the petrol station manager, about the incident and off he duly toddled.

But come the next evening, as he approached the garage along the flat road, he espied a big, black, highly polished Bentley parked just along from the attendant's booth, and two black-suited gentlemen, one either side of a very fretful-looking Harold, although worry was one of his more obvious traits. Along with procrastination.

And as he drew nearer (oh my God), one gent was obviously the chappie without a dipstick, with the other appearing damned familiar as well.

Apparently, Mr Brassley, as he was, totally unaware his dipstick was missing, had been driving up the M1 to a conference, but curiously and continually smelling oil, until thick, pungent smoke poured from his engine, thus forcing him to stop on the hard shoulder and summon the emergency services. He'd unfortunately missed his appointment as a VIP and guest speaker, causing him much inconvenience and embarrassment, and he was still as angry as hell.

And did I know who his black-suited companion was? None other than Sir Anthony Safeseat, Stroud's Conservative MP. That's who! And what was AV going to do about it? Well, nothing, was the answer, as he certainly wasn't going to stand against Sir Tony at the next election. No, fool! What was AV going to do about the dipstick? Well, you can have it back as I know exactly where it is. Harold was shaking but not from mirth but fear and apologised profusely, begging AV to also apologise, although begging would not have been required had the obvious NST not kicked off in such a bombastic and challenging manner.

To be fair, Sir Safeseat, smelling strongly of recently quaffed vintage brandy, poured oil (ha!) on troubled waters by saying that Brassley's company insurance would take care of the damage, which was the result of an accidental omission on AV's part, and was best put down to experience, to which Brassley agreed, obsequiously bowing to the MP's wisdom and good grace, and the matter concluded with handshakes all round. Apart from Harold, whose hand remained perfectly still while his body shook all around it.

Brassley, also smelling of brandy, with honour satisfied, took charge of his missing dipstick and proceeded to drive Safeseat back the half mile to the Conservative Club to renew their acquaintance with ten year old Napoleon brandy, if it wasn't past his bedtime, thus satisfactorily ending the latest brush with Nobs, Snobs and Toffs.

(But to this very day, AV has never voted Conservative, and now will probably never have the chance to, unless his Right to Vote is somehow restored.)

And so, to the final school term with exams looming and the Upper Sixth Form seemingly full of little prigs chundering-on about what grades they needed to get to which university, which was their fourth choice, how many passes they needed to find a suitable polytechnic, what A levels they required to enter Sandhurst or Cranwell or Dartmoor.

Even AV had been caught up in it, as, enjoying the English course immensely, he had asked his favourite English teacher the likely literature to be studied at places of further education, only to be greeted with an extremely terse, 'Depends where you go!' Oh! Mind you, Mr Chipping, as it later became apparent after he died, was wrestling with the late stages of terminal cancer, so his bad humour may have been down to that.

And the 'careers advisor', the Latin Head of Department, an Oliver "Greasy" Wickham, after the obligatory five minutes with AV with whom he'd never had any previous contact or interaction, and on finding that AV had no idea what he wanted to do or where he wanted or needed to go, concluded with a bland, 'Well I hope you find something,' and gestured to him that the session was over. Yes, our hero had realised he had very little, if any, ambition, or hopes and dreams, and had adopted the Micawberesque view that something would turn up, if only his toes, but best wait and see how the A levels went first.

In fact, they went swimmingly, with good passes in all three subjects, at grades which were the unfortunate envy of some of those arrogant, bragging, self-important little swots who'd thought high grades and top university places were theirs as a right, but who were now devastated as they'd fallen short of their own and Mater and Pater's expectations. (No suicide lines in those days, sorry!)

Then it was finger-pointing time; just how did that slob Bottomley do it?? And not quietly or politely expressed, but acerbically and accusingly. Well, they must have been really pissed off for them to have been so openly slanderous, which isn't the Stroudie way at all. Surprisingly, though, Alan hadn't reverted to violence at those direct insults, merely comforting himself in their abject misery, and in the fact that he'd never, in all probability, and with the highest hopes, see any of those whingeing little fuckers ever again.

He was later visited at home by another English teacher who attempted to make him belatedly apply for university, such application to be supported by the headmaster. But bearing in mind AV's dealings with NST's to date, not knowing where or what he wanted to study, the likely expense to his family and the fact that, in 1971 having three A levels opened a lot of doors, he thanked Mr Thomas profusely but politely declined.

Besides, Gina, who worked afternoons at the Bond Worth carpet factory in Thrupp, just a stone's throw from Lil's, had arranged for him to work there as a mill hand until that proverbial 'something' turned up, and for her son to put a bit of cash together, with him settling in as a factory labourer very quickly.

He enjoyed the camaraderie and banter of fellows of his own age, and older, many of whom he knew from the village and local football, immediately being roped in as their goalkeeper as the former custodian had recently been sent to prison for burglary. Admittedly, the team played in the lowest of the Stroud leagues and they'd always remain in the lower reaches of that league, but it was great being accepted into a welcoming, non-intellectual, non-competitive, non-threatening and non-NST environment.

Besides, the Friday and Saturday night piss-ups in the Horse and Groom were a refreshing change to the Union, the student and rugby XV pub where pretentious posers like him had sat around in RAF or Army greatcoats, smoking clay pipes and testing each other on their knowledge of Shakespeare, Chaucer and Arthur Miller.

No, AV preferred the spit and sawdust of the Groom, and being one of the lads, totally losing contact with most of his former school and teammates, even those who hadn't gone on to further education and who still lived locally.

The wages weren't bad either and he soon comfortably settled into what he didn't realise at the time could have been his lot in life for ever, had not Gina, after a year, given him a huge kick up the arse (which we all need now and again).

While Geoff had been content to let Alan determine his own destiny, up to a point, mainly because he'd been pushed and pulled in all directions by the Parrish women, Gina put her foot down and told him it was high time he did something with his A levels, unless he wanted a life of total mediocrity, and to be nothing other than a number on the clocking-in machine, his nebulous plan to save and put himself through university having gone to the wall, along with the old banger he'd bought and had written-off by crashing into one.

Like his father before him, he bowed to her nagging and, seeing an advert in the *Daily Mail*, applied to join National Westminster Bank, and within a month had been invited for an interview at their Stroud branch, much to Gina's delight.

So, suited and Brut-ed (splash it all over) but still resembling a bag of spuds nonetheless, he was ushered into the manager's waiting room one afternoon at 4pm, after the bank had finished its routine business for the day.

The secretary told him to knock and enter, but what a shock for both the manager and AV when they caught sight of each other, for the chap due to conduct the interview was none other than Mr Dipstick, himself, Claude (yes, Claude!) Brassley. Bloody hell!

After an initial and mutual double-take and a brief yet pregnant silence, 'Good afternoons' and handshakes were exchanged and Brassley conducted the interview in a most cordial, and professional manner, cooing over AV's final school report, and references from his rugby coach and Mr Thomas, the English teacher. Just going through the motions, thought AV, but it'll show Mum I'm not so employable as she made out.

The interrogation over, Brassley walked over to the door and informed him that Area Office would be in touch, and then, after a final handshake, quietly, almost conspiratorially, asked, 'Kept any dipsticks, lately?' to which Alan, who couldn't help himself, shot back, 'Driven any MPs pissed, lately?' Brassley then smiled and told him, 'By the way, you've passed the interview!'

And thus it came to pass that he was working as a Grade 1 bank clerk at the only Nat West in Stroud, and what a seismic change from the carpet factory. No bacon rolls and mugs of tea at mid-morning break, nor bullshit about footie, drink and shagging, but a delicate cup of freshly percolated coffee with brown sugar and a doughnut, at a time decided upon by Amelia, the mid-thirty-something, sensibly and two piecedly dressed, supervisor upstairs in the machine room, as it's called, which the public never gets to see.

Their morning break was actually a very staid affair, with gardening, holidays, offspring, and *Coronation Street* being the main topics of conversation during the five minutes or so it took to get the percolated coffee and pastry down their crops, the conversation as false as one of his Physics teacher's legs, good old Normandy Norm, whose favourite line was, 'I lost my leg in Normandy but I go back every year to see if anyone's handed it in yet.'

The only person truly pleased to make his acquaintance up there, despite the platitudes from all, was a Marvin 'The Perve' Purvis who, now that AV had arrived, would go on to bigger and better things as a cashier at front of house, while AV, of course not at all pleased to meet any of *them,* relieved him of odious tasks like sorting cheques, ordering statements, printing up chequebooks, sending out the post and general fetching and carrying as ordered by the haughty, indomitable Amelia.

The machine room housed six young female clerks and he soon realised that gossip and bitching was not just confined to small village folk, school masters and pupils, factory workers, NSTs and the sporty lot, but also to supposedly well-educated young career women as well, who seemed to gossip about each other most of the time, especially when one of them was foolhardy enough to leave the room and become 'It' for as long as she was absent, a sort of more sophisticated 'Off Ground Galloping Knob Rot' game. Yes, he was learning all the time.

Besides the Perve, there were five other male clerks, all at varying stages of their careers, and the lowest was a Grade 3, none of whom would take the slightest interest in AV until the machine room and Amelia had spat him out when a new clerk had been taken on.

The Chief or number-one cashier was a good chap, though, a retired RAF Squadron Leader Paymaster, who had a wicked sense of humour which he generally kept firmly under wraps, but he spotted in AV a kindred spirit and they often merrily quipped away when and if they had a spare moment together, which wasn't that often.

Apart from him, though, AV was made to feel the lowest of the low, even having to defer to the two typists and the manager's secretary, and he began to think that Brassley had extracted due revenge for the 'Dipstick Incident' by sentencing him to a mediocrity and insignificance beyond belief, even beyond the credulity of his mother, *and* at a salary (not a wage) less than half that of factory pay.

Brassley though had returned to his VIP position of Area Controller in Cheltenham, having merely been relief manager at Stroud while the real incumbent, Jim Brady, was on a golfing holiday in Scotland. Brady turned out to be a very personable, spritely, and well-turned-out chap, with a quick, glib patter and who was, according to him anyway, a veritable star in Cheltenham's cricketing and golfing circles.

Thank God though he wasn't a member of Minchinhampton Golf Club as he wouldn't have taken kindly to AV peeing in the tin cups up there, if he could remember him from that far back. Far back? Hell, AV still occasionally did it when on the common, just for old time's sake.

Wanting to make a favourable impression on Brady, and so as not to blot his copybook too early, Alan refrained from his factory-accustomed two pints at lunchtime, a habit he'd enjoyed with fellow mill hands up at Thrupp, though having the Post Office pub right next to the bank was very tempting. Additionally, he'd either not attend the Nat West monthly evening social gatherings if too far out of town, or, if in town, limit himself to two small light ales at most before he got the 'taste', although he would invariably stop for a quick quart or two on the way home, particularly when the bullshit and crawling to Brady had been worse than usual, with Brady seemingly not being able to see through those snivelling twats.

The male clerks were even worse in trying to outdo each other in pushing themselves forward.

And it was no good him trying it on, or cracking a few jokes with the bank girls, as they were clearly all lesbians as not one of them ever gave any indication of being fatsoever interested in AV until, as he was given more interesting tasks, he was responsible for the daily tallying of all amounts received from and for non-Nat West bank accounts, his accuracy (or not, as the case would be), determining if everyone, or anyone, could go home early, or had to stay and go through yards and yards of printed rolls to identify and rectify errors.

Then he met Margaret 'Pigswill' Pickersgill at the British Oak pub in Bowbridge, at the bottom of Butterrow Hill, while she was playing darts for the Groom pub. He was late from the bank, having helped to clear out the stationery cupboard, stopping for a slow pint or three before heading home, still attired in his bespoke Hepworth's pinstriped suit, prompting Maggie's cries of 'Little Lord Fauntleroy!' as he pushed through the swing doors to the public bar.

Her big bouncy tits, sparkling eyes and jolly smile more than made up for the perceived insult, and between throwing arrows, and chugging down pints of rough cider with Pony chasers, she made it clear to everyone, both verbally and by demeanour, that not only was she well pissed, but that she was also after a boyfriend and was not fussy whom it might be. AV, to tell the truth, had no experience of women as sexual entities, nor of any woman quite so brash and bold, but he had one hell of an inquisitive nature, at nineteen, to see what that sex business was all about before it was too late.

So, a bit of a shrinking violent around women, he got a quick half gallon down himself, and somehow arranged to meet 'Pigswill' (so nicknamed because it conveniently rhymed with her surname *and* described her propensity to drink anything put in front of her) up at the Groom over the weekend. And so it was that their rocky, often tempestuous relationship started, though initially both gave each other enough freedom ('space, man') before proprietary rights, possessiveness and jealousy set in, as they do in so many relationships once sex raises its ugly head to become a part of them. (Thank you, Dr Ruth.)

Gina of course soon heard about it, and tacitly approved, even though the Pickersgills were from the top of town, stretching it a bit to place their large house at one side of the very start of the Golden Valley. Additionally, Maggie worked full-time at the same carpet factory as Gina and while they were in no way friends, at least they weren't enemies, which is saying a lot for Stroudies.

However, rumour had it that Maggie had been so controlling over one of her previous beaus that he'd done a runner and had joined the French Foreign Legion, AV putting that rumour down to jealousy but, as time progressed, wouldn't have blamed him if the poor bastard had.

Whatever, it was nice to have a regular drinking partner who'd buy her round (she earned more than him) and he had concluded that sex, though not as he'd imagined from his dad's dirty magazines (kept in Geoff's shed) and from his beloved pop songs, wasn't too bad so he had been quite content to plod along with her for a while until something else turned up. He also had it in his mind to sometime try sex when they were both sober, which could possibly make a difference to how he felt about it.

Then, God bless Nick Baimbridge, two years behind AV at school, who had failed his A levels and who had joined Nat West bank instead of resitting, and who was therefore the new kid on the block, being shoved upstairs with Amelia and the lezzies, and thus it was AV's turn to be trained as a cashier.

So, the world turns.

It wasn't all plain sailing, though, as downstairs he'd always be under the Manager's and Chief Accountant's glare, although the one week Cashier and Accounts Course in London was a real blast, and thereafter he was indeed shoved on the till as cashier number four.

But some matters had to be sorted out immediately. 'Stop biting your nails; the customers expect well-groomed hands. Trim your hair and beard and smile at the customers - you look like the Cotswold version of Charles Manson' (the infamous 1969 Hollywood murderer, one of his victims being the actress Sharon Tate). 'Don't whistle so much - the lady customers may think you are "wolfing them."' 'Refer to male customers as "gentlemen" when directing them to the manager or to specialist clerks, not as "blokes", which could be construed as an insulting term.'

More NSTs then! Bastards!

Still, he was soon advanced to Grade 2 level and thus was 'on the ladder', despite himself, and even took out a staff-rate bank loan for a second-hand Triumph Herald.

Whoopee! Conformity!

And so it continued; Maggie, local hops, pubs and grinding away quite successfully at work, occasionally acting as Chief Cashier and Foreign Clerk.

He'd somehow become reasonably friendly with the manager, Jim Brady, sometimes caddying for him at the very posh Cheltenham Golf Club on competition days and when he was entertaining valued or potentially valuable customers. Great days out, away from daily bank routine and with a few pints thrown in too. No, not at the nineteenth hole with the great and the good, but with the other temporary caddies and chauffeurs in a gazebo jobbie, well behind and out of sight of the first tee.

He also drove Jim home in his Rover 3000, as entertaining customers often made his boss extremely 'tired'.

One thing AV had learnt though was not to let things slip out unguardedly, either in jest or when half pissed, as Brady was none too pleased when AV (he realised, very stupidly afterwards) proudly mentioned he'd been so drunk after one chip shop hop that he'd been taken home in a police Panda car and, on another occasion, he and a confederate (you could tell by the flag) had started up a double decker bus in the unguarded bus depot and had driven it along London Road until they'd reached the bottom of Butterrow Hill, then walked the rest of the way home.

Those two admissions had prompted good old Jim to consider transferring AV to a branch in Devon, in case Stroud customers had ever, or would ever, witness his drunken and hitherto unsuspected criminality. Mind you, Jim was driving drunk when he gave the bollocking, so probably thought better of it, though AV did take the hint.

Yes, Nobs, Snobs and Toffs!

Mind you, AV often thought he should try to belong, but couldn't, because he patently didn't, comforting himself, years later, to find out that one of his heroes, John Lennon, apparently had the same sense of isolationism but had expressed it so much better.

But if John Lennon couldn't and didn't, then just who exactly can?

After a while, Bottomley junior (anyone *not* yet sussed why his alternative nickname was 'The Bucket'?) grew to enjoy his role as a cashier, and while the money was still no great shakes, he never saw himself progressing, or wanting to progress beyond that level. He liked most customers and they seemed to like him, the only obvious and inevitable exceptions being the stuck-up little pricks from the Wycherly Public School's Sixth Form College. Yes, those fuckers with plums and silver spoons in their mouths.

One particularly arrogant little ponce, a Peter Spicer, so annoyed him that when he asked once a month on a Friday if his allowance had been received from India, AV would go to the rear, pretend to check the balance as at close of business on Thursday evening, and return with a glum reply in the negative, even if Spicer's account was bursting with the anticipated funds, and advise him to try again Monday. That would hopefully mess up his weekend of fagging, paper chases, toasted muffins, cream teas in the dorm and glasses of sherry with his house master.

But then a blockbuster and total game-changer: Geoff had secured a job back within the bosom of his much-missed British Army as a heavy-goods and armoured-vehicle driving instructor based in Borden in Hampshire, a pensionable position that would (and did) set him up nicely for eventual retirement.

'To cut a long story short, son, we're selling up and moving down there soonest. Are you coming?'

Well, there was little choice, put like that, and after a day or two of mulling it over, and finding out the bank would give him a generous rent allowance and didn't want to lose him, he decided to stay put, while his sisters would move away with their parents within six weeks. Thus, lo and behold, he soon found himself in bedsit land, only then realising how much his parents had kept the whole universe together, and how much he had taken them for granted. And how much he missed them, although that would come a little later.

Maggie had thought he'd stayed for her, and was highly

delighted, if delusional, not realising that AV didn't really like change, and certainly not wanting to start all over again down in Hampshire. Besides, the way his life had been to date, and the way he had treated things, something would be bound to turn up. It always does.

And it did, in the form of regular drug busts in the flats wherein he had his bedsit, and the mental strain of living in one small room with shared kitchen, bathroom and toilet facilities, and no garden or other amenities to make the ambience and surroundings any pleasanter.

And even the footie had been cut off as whined about earlier in the piece, along, later, with the refereeing.

There was a finite number of times, too, he could turn up at Lil's, especially at weekends when her 'lodger' (a once, when young, former boyfriend) had his family come to visit, who were teetotallers, and who moaned like hell after he left about how AV always smelled like a brewery.

And *who* the hell wants at his age to be romping and yomping all over the bloody common after having it on his back doorstep most of his life? And even nutters who do, somehow militate and mitigate it by taking a dog or two with them. He had even grown out of wanting to annoy the golfers up there, unless it was a Senior Ladies Day or something similar.

Further, and most assuredly, Maggie and he had no future together as a couple whatsoever, particularly if he wanted to, or had to stay at Nat West, the staff still laughing behind his back after she'd turned up 'to surprise him' at the Painswick Inn, where his banking colleagues had booked a table to celebrate Brady's forty fifth birthday.

In she'd burst with her darts team, straight across to the Nat West reserved table, swigging out of a Bulmer's cider bottle, three tins of Carly Special swinging from her left hand, and, blearily spying the obvious guest of honour, shouted out a disgustingly drunken and raucous, 'Wine me! Dine me! Sixty nine me!' before then collapsing unconscious over the table, right on top of the highly decorative and expensive birthday cake, legs akimbo.

And what a great pity that she had neglected or had forgotten to don underwear that evening, too!

Yes, on that Sunday, 19th January 1975, just as Alan 'AV Bucket' Bottomley had been preparing to head off to the Greyhound pub for a lunchtime session, *all* of the former narrative had flashed in a microsecond through his raddled and addled brain, once again letting him know exactly how he'd arrived at his present state.

The question he now had to resolve was: 'How the hell can I get out of it??'

Bugger it, on to meatier matters, but there were *no* stale rolls left at the Greyhound so it was a large draught Guinness and a packet of crisps with a pickled egg, the heaviness of the food and drink very satisfying, and settling his stomach quite nicely. So, with hunger temporarily forgotten, he took time to exchange pleasantries with the usual Sunday gang of West Indians playing cards by the fire in the corner, and some of the usual old codgers enjoying the warmth while playing crib.

People in ones or twos drifted in for a pint or three, as they did on a Sunday, then the lucky bastards shuffled off for their Sunday roasts, Brian Moore hosting the footie on ITV and then *The Golden Shot*, though it hadn't been the same since Monkhouse had been booted out.

Only lonely, miserable diehards like him made it out again for the evening sessions, but how he wished there was all-day opening so he wouldn't have to go back and 'stew' alone in 'The Cave.' A pox on those munitions workers and David Lloyd-George!

Fair enough, there had been a war on, but didn't they know it ended in 1918?

Still, probably it *was* best to have licencing hours or else he could develop into a pisshead.

After his fifth pint of 'Forest-topped', (a half pint of Forest Brown Ale 'topped' with a half pint of bitter), he'd somewhat sorted things out in his head and reckoned it'd be a good idea to phone up his parents to see how they'd feel about him moving down to join them, pretty sure that Jim Brady would be delighted to arrange his transfer to Alton, if indeed they had a branch in that town, wherever it was.

But just how many good ideas when one is drunk turn out to be goddang awful ideas in the cold light of day?

Using the public phone in the corridor, he was answered by Gina, who was thrilled to hear from him, and amongst her effusive, general chit-chat, before he had the chance to broach the subject, much of which he'd not remember an hour later, was her terrible, crushing pronouncement about how proud they all were of him for making a go of living alone, and standing on his own two feet, proving to be an independent soul, and being able to fend for himself, making a complete mockery of Geoff and his sisters' reckoning that within six months he'd be phoning up, and pathetically begging to be allowed to come and join them, as he hadn't bloody realised when he was well off.

So *what* could he say to *that*, except, 'I love you, Mum, and I'll call you again soon!'? Oh well, the best laid plans of mice, men and morons.

Out of the proverbial frying pan and into the fire, so why not try and quench it with a few more pints? It didn't work, though.

Fast-forward an hour or so, and into his private reverie came a phrase from his A level English Literature, 'Never ask for whom the bell tolls, it tolls for thee…' and it had, also for the other hangers-on in the Greyhound, as Pete Hayward, the landlord, had rung for 'Time!' and as his wife Valerie had his dinner all ready and waiting for him, out they jolly well had to go.

After a wobbly fifty yard limp back to 20 Lansdowne Road, and looking up the stairs to 'The Cave' on its first floor, he saw

Tony Hayes, the houseowner's creepy agent and flunky, on the toilet landing, cussing flashes as some ignorant, dirty bastard had blocked the toilet pipes so thoroughly with newspaper that even the industrial-sized plunger he was holding couldn't shift it, and if he ever found out who the culprit had been he'd - well - bloody druggies!

'*No! Bloody Maggie!*' thought AV, as he slumped onto the banana-encrusted bed, quickly dozing the fitful slumber of the world-weary wino, awaking with a start at about 5pm.

No Maggie. Good! But by heck, he wasn't half famished!

So, armed with half a dozen of the best pieces of sliced bread he'd salvaged from the walnut wardrobe, which he also sometimes used as a larder, fridge and occasional emergency lavatory, he crept to the kitchen to find - thank you Lord - that the family in the adjacent flat had finished their lunch, with pots and pans left in the sink to be Fairy Liquidised later and, further joy of joys, had also left their half-empty gravy boat on the draining board, and so it was therefore 'dippy bread and gravy time' yet again for young Bottomley, courtesy of Spotty.

Then time to tidy up the flat, with all the remaining green grocery stuff quickly bagged and thrown out of the window to join the rest of the thin white plastic carrier bags in the backyard, all awaiting collection the following day.

He pushed the Bissell carpet sweeper around a couple of times and tidied his bed, admitting that the black-stained sheets, pillows and blankets were annoying, but he'd change them next weekend, if he remembered to go to the laundrette. He then rinsed and very roughly ironed, three white shirts for the forthcoming week, pressed his best (and only) work-suit trousers, and then proudly considered his weekly drunken thrash at domesticity done and dusted. Frankly, he could never understand why Maggie made such a fuss about it or why she took so long in doing it. But now what?

Nothing worth watching on the telly and, besides, the detector vans had been busy in the area, and it would be just his luck to be nabbed on a Sunday by some sneaky bastard who'd think those without licences would relax their vigilance at the weekend. Some people are like that.

An hour until the pubs reopened. How the hell to pass the time, then?

Then it hit him. The *Sunday Telegraph*. And as he took it out from under the multi-functional walnut wardrobe, little did he realise that within its broad pages was an advertisement that would provide him with the opportunity of a lifetime, the same opportunity that Robert 'Steady Eddie' Yates had read about up in Clapham, just a few hours earlier.

Yes, he read the same advertisement in the *Sunday Telegraph* as had Bob Yates, and although his drink-befuddled brain took longer to assimilate the information, he too was aroused by the possibilities.

Going anywhere in the next three years? If not, why not join the Royal Hong Kong Police?

Well, he wasn't heading anywhere but the dung heap, the way things were, and he needed a complete change. But why not join the Army or even the Gloucestershire Police Force instead of heading all the way out to the Far East?

2am in Kowloon is a fine time for self-discovery!

That's great, but it's a bloody long way to go to get your head together and why does it only come right at two in the morning?

But the more he read, the more intrigued he became, and while he certainly had the educational qualifications, would they take a rough diamond like him? He felt that while he could work hard for any organisation that appreciated his energy and gung-ho work ethic, and that could perhaps promise him excitement, diversity and, all things being equal, a possible career, could he put up with the likely Nobs, Snobs and Toffs he'd encounter, or, perhaps more importantly, *they* him?

And what about the corruption he'd heard about out there? And wasn't Hong Kong being handed back to China a few decades hence? If so, he might as well stay in the bank but perhaps try and get a move to a city, anywhere, to get out of his morass.

And what about his height? Surely that would count against him, although no mention was made of physical requirements in the blurb.

Bollocks!

Why not write away, anyway? (And the salary offered *was* tremendous, after all.)

Which is what he did first thing the next day, popping the enquiry form in the bank's 'mail out' box immediately after he entered the premises and just before spewing in the waste paper basket under his till - it must have been all that vitamin C - just as Bob Yates was making his way to the Hong Kong Office in London.

He received the information package at the bank first post the following Friday morning, (delivered there as he couldn't trust the hounds in those flats not to open his mail) and he went to the reading room at the library during his lunch break, hardly able to believe what could be available to him.

Him!

But from various experiences of people counting chickens before they'd hatched, and empty promises of employment, best not get carried away. However, straight from work, he returned to the library, filled in the application form, shoved it in an envelope, put a few stamps on it, pushed it through the main post office's letter box, went for a few pints on the excitement of it all, and, a few hours later, had damned near forgotten about it.

Back to the old routine.

But blow me down and tickle my bum with a stinging nettle, he was called for an interview in London, at which there were ten other candidates, all of whom AV thought would totally eclipse him in terms of education, experience and officer potential, these thoughts increasing so much during the day that he almost did a runner at 4pm, as he was the last one left in the waiting room, still not yet called before the interviewing panel who'd given an introductory presentation some six hours earlier.

Then interviewed and out, collecting the coat and scarf he'd left, and trying to scamper down the stairs before any bastard started laughing, being stopped at the security gate before the main door and told to go back and pick up the directions to Harley Street for his medical. Medical? You don't mean I passed?

But they did and confirmed it by post just a few days later, with 18th April 1975 later set as date of departure for Hong Kong to commence training as a Probationary Inspector with the Royal Hong Kong Police.

But just a doggone minute, thar, boy! He hadn't told *anyone* about all this Hong Kong business, not his parents, not his current employers, not the teachers he'd given as referees, and certainly *not* Maggie, who surprisingly had been increasingly cool towards him (must have been time of month.)

He first told his two former teachers that they'd probably be approached as referees, which indeed they were, by visiting them one evening, both having houses adjoining Marling School. No problems there.

After that, he telephoned his father, who was absolutely delighted, but as it appeared that Geoff had 'tied one on' down the golf club, he cut short the conversation before the inevitable, maudlin Titsalina stories commenced.

Then late on a Wednesday afternoon, he called his colleagues to order, treated them to naughty-but-nice fresh cream cakes and Lipton's finest, then dropped the bombshell. Most were pleased for him, but Marvin 'The Perve' Purvis was, surprisingly, absolutely delighted, damned near in tears, and although he had of late come up to the Groom for a pint at weekends, uninvited, his response was a bit over the top, even suspicious.

Teresa 'Terry' Bailey, one he'd thought of as just another lesbian in the Nat West machine room, apparently had a sister, Linda (more on her later), working with the Independent Commission Against Corruption in Hong Kong, whatever that was, and gave AV her telephone number, as if he would ever call her up. Still, it was a nice thought and Terry was a far nicer girl than he'd allowed for. Too late to do anything about it though, he mused, and yet another 'if only'.

Jim Brady though was thin-lipped and came out with the thought that he'd better pay off his car loan before he went, or they'd convert it to the non-staff interest rate. As the gathering dispersed to balance the day's work, AV was told to finish cashing up, then wait in the staff room while Jim attended to some private matters, and he'd talk with him in an hour or so. Talk about 'Man of Mystery'!

And so, as the rest of the staff were sloping off, Jim button-holed Bottomley, sat him down, and informed him that he'd been in touch with Area Office, and they'd offer him a Grade 3 position, a significant and very early step-up, at the Nat West branch in nearby Cirencester if he'd stay, double his tax-free rent allowance, and give him a pay rise to Grade 4 commencement level.

For anyone with a career in banking in mind, *that* was a very good deal.

Jim then made it clear that a mortgage of £10,000 would be made available to him should he now wish to buy a house and thus commit his future to the bank.

However, if he didn't accept this offer, the result of some considerable machinations behind the scenes, and things went tits up in Hong Kong, then no way would the bank consider re-employing him.

A quandary then, for AV, as was his wont, was already worrying if he could 'cut it' in Hong Kong or be found out as the fraud he thought he could be, having perhaps what is now termed as Imposter Syndrome, or just nervy as he hadn't had a pint yet that day.

He'd give his answer by the weekend, after speaking to his parents again. But what a mixed reaction there, with his mother pleased if he'd stay, and his father cussing flashes and saying he'd disown any son of his who *didn't* take up an opportunity of a lifetime in joining the RHKP. When he was once on the Rhine, he had a girlfriend called Titsalina and… 'talk to you later, Dad.'

He went straight up to the Groom where he was due to meet Maggie, the landlord opening the rear doors early to regulars, and in the saloon, away from the prying eyes of passers-by, there she was already seated, but with the Perve, *and* holding the duplicitous bastard's hand, both looking a trifle worried, as well they might.

The Perve had already told her of the good news, but AV rained on their parade by delightedly informing them that it wasn't so cut and dried, and then demanded to know how long they had been 'seeing each other'. (He wasn't going to stoop so low as to use the childish 'two-timing him' and 'in a relationship' wasn't invented until the nineties, but he did come out with the coarser 'knocking each other off' and 'shagging one another'.)

Ever since the night she'd collapsed at Brady's forty fifth birthday party, apparently, when Marvin had shared the taxi that had taken her home, both claiming mutual love at first sight.

AV later pondered, the way she was so knickerlessly spreadeagled across the table at that function, just what was it that the Perve had seen to make him fall so head over heels with her? Conversely, what it was about him she found so irresistible after she first clapped eyes on him in the back of the cab, having just chundered all down her blouse and presumably him too?

But there's nowt so queer as folk, now is there?

'Love at first sight' will also affect a chap called Martin 'Dogs' Dinner later in this narrative. Apparently, it does exist, then, and is not just an urban myth like Bigfoot and snuff movies.

But my word, the Perve *was* in a tizzy, twitching like a chicken with its head cut off and Maggie, straight from work and still with fluffy white carpet wool on her Florrie Capp headscarf, obviously not wanting to remain in AV's company too long as he might kick off.

But in truth he was more amused than angry, and they'd done him a huge favour had they but known it.

So 'Let them sweat!' and, with a flourish, AV left with as much dignity as he could muster and downed a couple of pints in the Post Office pub in town, thinking that, whatever happened, whatever he decided, he was going to have a new start, in whatever shape and form that may take. But best not get too pissed as he needed a semi clear head to make a decision by Friday.

As so he did, the decision being (despite annoying Bank Manager Brady):

'Sod it! Hong Kong, here I come!'

'And if I only learn how to use chopsticks and find out whether it's true or not about Chinese girls sliding down banisters before I'm kicked out, so be it!'

(Well done that man! *That's* the spirit that won us the Empire! Now go out and help destroy some of what's left of it!)

Chapter Three

Seminar, Hong Kong Office, London

Yes, all well and good to be accepted, but just exactly where *was* Hong Kong and what was the RHKP all about? More germanely, where would Bottomley and Yates be training?

These questions would be answered in early April 1975, when both recruits were duly invited to an induction seminar at the Hong Kong Office in London, along with most of the other successful expatriate applicants who'd all be flying out on 18th April, one New Zealander not coming all the way to London just for that.

And what an assortment turned up, a mish-mash of ex UK and overseas policemen, bank clerks, lads on their 'gap between the ears year', civil and uncivil servants, blokes straight from both school and university, a teacher, and two ex-military men, all dressed very neatly, though hardly anyone, apart from the ex-military, had had a haircut or shaved their whiskers (dedicated followers of fashion)

---

2 Includes hand-painted image of the crest of the former Royal Hong Kong Police Force. Contains public sector information licensed under the Open Government Licence v3.0

and all sat to attention when the convenor, a HK government administrator named Perry Sherry, called the assembled throng to order, and away from the tea and coffee pots and the finely cut, rather delicate beef sandwiches, sausage rolls and cold chicken pieces.

A brief verbal welcome and introduction, and then some touristy films about Hong Kong, the history of the RHKP, and the Police Training School wherein the rapt audience would be spending the next eight months.

Very briefly, Hong Kong was a British Colony of over 250 islands, with about four million mainly Chinese inhabitants, the majority from South China, especially from the nearby Canton Province, although all Chinese regions were represented.

The most important land masses were Hong Kong Island, Kowloon and the New Territories, the first being where the very important Central business and banking hubs were located, a little along from the Police Headquarters, which in turn was a stone's throw away from the Royal Navy Base of HMS Tamar, close to Wanchai, the famous, nay infamous, bar area. More of that later. Much more.

On the south side of the Island lay the fishing town of Aberdeen, above which was the Police Training School, or PTS, very near to the large resettlement estate and residential tower blocks of Wong Chuck Hang.

The film of the Police Training School (PTS) was very 'skinny', just views of the accommodation block, parade square, assault course, shooting ranges, front and rear entrances, some expats on parade and in the mess, but Mr Sherry had jokingly said they'd know *all* about it in a week or two, and be sick of it in a month, depending on which Chief Inspectors had been appointed as their instructors for the eight month course.

Further along from PTS was the British Army base at Stanley, the home of the current incumbent regiment, the 1st Battalion,

Royal Hampshires, soon to be replaced by the 1st Battalion of the Light Infantry, on a two year married posting, and nearer were the popular beaches of Deep Water and Repulse Bays.

Towering above the Central skyline was Victoria Peak and Tower, affording magnificent all-round vistas and especially across to the mainland of Kowloon and, beyond, the New Territories, seemingly guarded by the Lion Rock.

Kowloon incidentally is romanised Cantonese for *'Gau Lung'*, meaning Nine Dragons, referring to the hills above Kowloon, but now there are only six or seven, the rest having been cropped, topped and used for land-fill in view of the construction boom and ongoing land reclamation around the harbour.

Hong Kong is romanised Cantonese for *'Heung Gong'*, meaning Fragrant Harbour, but it was hardly *that*, back in 1975, and things probably haven't changed much in that regard, if at all.

The seascape views, both near and far, with a plethora of assorted freight and passenger ships, tugs, lighters and other small craft, either dashing about or at anchor, never failed to awe, and the larger US Naval vessels, and especially the occasional aircraft carrier, were mightily impressive.

The mainland of Kowloon was separated from Hong Kong Island by the waters of Victoria Harbour, with the quickest access across the waterway to the always bustling and favourite tourist area of Tsimshatsui being afforded by the busy green-and-white Star Ferries, which also had routes to parts of East and West Kowloon. Then there were the larger white passenger and vehicular ferries belonging to the Hong Kong and Yaumatei Ferry Company, which also sailed its vessels to parts of the New Territories and to the Outlying Islands, the most popular of which were Lantau (larger than Hong Kong Island but quite undeveloped), Cheung Chau and Lamma Islands.

The main thoroughfare in Kowloon was Nathan Road, running right from the harbour waters in Tsimshatsui (hereinafter referred to as 'Chimsy') right up through the very spine of Kowloon, through the densely populated areas of Yaumatei, Mongkok and Shamshuipo, all these areas having a substantial police presence (divided into Divisions), and all of which will be featured later.

Kai Tak International Airport was located in East Kowloon and its presence there was one of the reasons why there were not so many high-rise buildings in Kowloon as there were on Hong Kong Island.

The New Territories in 1975 were very rural, with scant few signs of the large-scale housing and business development of the next two decades, although factory blocks were evident in upper East and West Kowloon and were spreading outwards.

The only town of any size in the New Territories was Yuen Long, and the approaches to it were very countrified and agrarian, with British Army Units, including a Gurkha Regiment, having bases spread around Kam Tin, a walled village, dwarfed by the acres of space taken up by the Army.

In fact, various British Army bases were scattered throughout the Colony, with Shamshuipo Barracks, (a former Japanese-run prisoner-of-war hell-hole), the Gun Club Barracks in Yaumatei/Chimsy, and Victoria Barracks, right in the heart of Hong Kong Island, opposite Police Headquarters, being three of the most prominent, along with the military facility at Stanley as already mentioned, with Stanley also being where the Japanese interred captured soldiers and police during the Second World War.

The ones they hadn't by then murdered, anyway.

Apart from the ferries, Hong Kong was connected to Kowloon by the Cross Harbour Tunnel running from Causeway Bay, Hong Kong, near the famous Noon Day Gun of the Noel Coward song 'Mad Dogs and Englishmen', to the Hung Hom Train Terminus, opposite the Hong Kong University, although buses plied routes to and from all major areas both on the Island and the mainland through the tunnel, a few routes with an all-night service.

However, the Star Ferries, even the ones running the busy route between Central and Chimsy, shut at 2am and to cross from one side to the other, if not near a convenient all-night bus stop, one needed to take an up-down, slip slop ride on one of the larger 'sampans', small motorised vessels, operated by private entrepreneurs and making a buck while fulfilling an obvious need, particularly if one had been, shall we say, 'socialising' and had been caught on the wrong side of the harbour to where one lives when the ferries terminated.

Meanwhile, back at the seminar, while the gathering tittered guiltily at this (as if we'd do that!), as did Mr Sherry, AV did wonder, but thought it politic not to ask, *'Was this the 2am in Kowloon self-discovery time they'd told us about in the recruitment advertisement?'*

And then a short briefing on the RHKP, itself, although the person giving the talk, a Superintendent Richard Clutterbuck, whose nickname was, a month or so later, found to be bandied around police circles in Hong Kong (hereinafter annotated as HK), as 'Clusterfuck', told the new recruits that he'd only take a few minutes as they'd learn all about this in the coming weeks, and the blurb they'd already been sent would suffice.

But to reiterate, the RHKP was established as long ago as 1844, as Imperialistic Britain claimed the territory in 1842 from the ruling Chinese Qing Dynasty, using gunboat diplomacy.

It was a paramilitary organisation, with armed beat and CID officers, with a Police Tactical Unit based in the New Territories with its companies drawn from Colony-wide Divisions and with at least one unit always under training, and another deployed on normal policing duties, available to handle any civil disturbances should they break out during its tour of duty.

In addition, Divisions operated their own PTU units, drawn from Sub Divisional uniformed officers, and rank and file, with regular ongoing training and exercises.

Within PTU was a Special Duty Unit, with specialised and highly trained officers performing or ready to perform so-called SWAT duties.

Other than mainstream Uniformed Branch, CID and/or Marine Police presence in virtually all relevant Divisions and Sub Divisions, there were specialist units at Police Headquarters, such as the Commercial Crime Bureau, the Organised and Serious Crime Group, incorporating Narcotic Bureau, Triad Society Bureau and the Criminal Intelligence Unit, along with support agencies like the Criminal Records Office, Identification Bureau and the Technical Support Unit.

The Marine District had over 250 vessels at its disposal, the largest civil navy in the world, with some 2,300 officers of all ranks, quite necessary when considering the area of 637 square miles of sea and islands to be policed.

In addition to the regular Police, there was also an Auxiliary Police Force, consisting of paid volunteers who were required to undergo formal training, and who supplemented and supported the RHKP not only in times of emergency, but also with beat, crowd control and guard duties as supervised by their own command structure, and as directed and required by senior officers of the Regulars, at whatever Division to which they were assigned.

There were of course large Administration, Welfare, Housing, Public Relations and Personnel Departments, staffed by Police officers and local administrators. being oh so necessary to attend to the needs, rights and legal and personal requirements of so many people.

There were specialist investigative, action and crime units at Hong Kong Island, Kowloon and New Territories Headquarters, with Emergency Units in each District to answer 999 crime calls as first responders.

The RHKP had its own Special Branch dealing mainly with internal security matters, and a large Traffic Police detachment, both dealing with preventative measures and advice, plus accident investigation and prosecution where necessary.

As well as the Police Training School, the Force also ran its own Detective Training School within Aberdeen itself for both rank and file and the officer cadre, with officers frequently sent for overseas training to renowned places such as Hendon in the United Kingdom.

Police also acted as Court Prosecutors and were responsible for order in the courts, and for granting various licences as per statute, and permits for large-scale public marches, processions and gatherings, and for crowd safety at such events.

In addition, there was a large civilian arm in support of the police working within police stations, such as clerks, executive officers, messengers, typists, interpreters, cooks, room boys and many more, with, in total, about 26,000 people within the RHKP, and it was expanding, never mind what the assembly had heard about handing the Colony back to China in 1997, which in all probability would be way after all of the new recruits had retired, or had otherwise long left HK.

He finally added that the majority of them, providing they finished the PTS course satisfactorily, would start off as uniformed Sub Unit Commanders, posted all over the Colony, in charge of about thirty two Constables and Sergeants, working eight hour shifts, with a Station Sergeant as second in command, answering to a Chief Inspector SDI, or Sub Divisional Inspector, thence an Assistant Divisional Superintendent and, ultimately, the Divisional Superintendent himself.

A Division, such as Central Division on Hong Kong Island, for example, consisted of several Sub Divisions, namely the Waterfront, Central, Upper Levels and the Peak Sub Divisions, all under the overall charge of the Divisional Superintendent, who in turn is answerable to his District Commander, with Hong Kong Island, Kowloon, the New Territories and the Marine area all designated as Police Districts.

'Now I trust that makes things clearer, gentlemen, and may I wish you all the best of luck! The buffet downstairs has been replenished, with some tins of cold beer also laid out for you, so I suggest we retire for thirty minutes and then continue.'

Well, forty five minutes later, the stragglers were hauled back from the buffet (the feeding frenzy and the quest for most to get at least a couple of tins down themselves as quickly as possible, causing the delay), as it was time to complete some forms, including the vital contract agreements.

There'd hardly been any time to take note of anyone all morning, what with having to appear fully attentive, bright-eyed and bushy-tailed, and even now it was quite hard, although there did seem to be quite a few Scotsmen in attendance.

Either that or the few Scottish attendees were talking amongst themselves more than anyone else, presumably having flown down the previous evening and may thus have met earlier in the hotel wherein they'd been housed for the night.

But one bloke seemed really familiar to AV, but he couldn't immediately place him at all. Where had it been? It nagged and nagged until the tall, young, moustachioed chap spoke to ask someone if he could borrow a pen with which to sign his employment contract, and it hit him!

Punjab Peter Spicer! From Wycherly College back in Stroud! He whose pater sent him funds from India, which for some reason never seemed to arrive on the Friday they should have.

Why hadn't he gone to university? Well, the answer was clear: he'd fluffed his A level grades. Well no shame in that, but AV guiltily hoped it wasn't because he'd been worried about having no money the weekend before his exams.

Yes it *was* Peter Spicer, and what's more, not only were they on the same intake, but when they were later split into two squads at PTS a few days after their arrival in Hong Kong, they were also on the same course, and became quite pally, AV never coming clean though about the many monthly deceptions he'd practiced on poor old Punjab Pete, who once at the training school was somehow given the alternative nickname of 'King of the Khyber Rifles'.

Steady Eddie Yates had been as quiet as AV at the seminar, being a trifle tired as he was still working as a night security guard, and the previous evening had been so worried about falling asleep, and not leaving work early enough to get to the meeting, that he'd had a particularly long wheelchair-pushing session at around 5am, but even so his eyes had sagged once or twice during the films.

Now he was very full, stuffed with chicken and beef sandwiches, having eaten a lot more than the pissheads who'd been almost scrapping over the tins of cold beer, which Bob hadn't fancied at all. The orange juice was fine, though, and there was plenty of it too.

Now that he'd signed his contract and things were very definitely *on*, he'd hand in his notice that very evening and spend the next couple of weeks taking it easy and relaxing with his family before the 'Big Off' on 18th April.

But then it was question time, a few answers being:

Yes, the Barrack Sergeant at PTS can provide you with size 12 boots.

Yes, the salary is high, but remember you'll be at the bottom end of the Hong Kong expat community in real terms.

Once you pass out from PTS, you'll mainly be housed in police messes, hopefully where you have been posted.

Yes, things are still very colonial-like out there, but they are changing fast.

Illegal immigrants from China are swelling the HK population and those who reach family members already living there are granted residency.

Yes, many others just go to ground within the community.

Yes, a few senior officers may be out of touch with on-the-ground policing bearing in mind the vast population increase since they were one-pip Recruit Inspectors, (pips were worn on shoulder epaulettes to distinguish the various Inspectorate ranks) and when a single robbery caused the most senior commanders to turn out at the scene of the crime.

No, it is not their job to be trawling the streets, as it were, having higher responsibilities.

There may very well be young Chinese women available but it's up to you to go and find them.

Prostitutes? Well, yes, but a police officer should never avail himself of their services.

Room boys at PTS will launder your civilian clothes and uniforms, polish your shoes, boots and Sam Browne belts, and change your bedding, and although you'll have to pay for these services, the amount is hardly extortionate for the work they do.

Room boys are also employed at most police messes, so you'll have to negotiate fees, for the same services.

Those who may later seek private accommodation will have to sort out domestic arrangements themselves, although your uniforms will still be attended to by room boys at the station where you work, irrespective of whether you live elsewhere or not.

If you resign, you'll have to pay back your air fare, proportionate to time served.

The Hong Kong riots in 1967 were communist-backed, fuelled by China's Cultural Revolution and local social grievances, some of which were redressed following the suppression of the civil unrest which was put down and quelled very professionally by the RHKP and other security services.

Don't believe that stupid *Kung Fu* TV series. If some bastard comes at you with violent intent, thump him. Or her. Or them.

Yes, there will be some localisation policy within the RHKP in view of the proposed handover of Hong Kong to China in 1997, but it shouldn't affect any of you.

Eight local Chinese recruits will be joining your two squads after you've completed your Cantonese language training, some direct entry and some promoted from the rank and file.

There will be a few expats joining you out in Hong Kong, these either joining locally or from Canada, Australia, New Zealand or South Africa, the number not yet finalised.

Yes, admittedly there *was* some former corruption in the police, but there are bad apples in every organisation. I'm sure it's just the same within the Metropolitan Police Force. (And *how*, with Operation Countryman commencing in 1978 with the aim of 'cleaning-up' the Met.)

No, the Independent Commission Against Corruption (ICAC) is not part of the RHKP, and is not primarily targeting the police, but every government department and business organisation wherein corruption has raised its ugly head.

The ICAC was formed in 1974 and is answerable directly to the Governor of Hong Kong.

It is not only an investigative and prosecuting body, but also instructs and advises.

No, I've *no* idea how Police Superintendent Peter Godber managed to stash away $600,000 US and the equivalent in HK currency that the ICAC know about, let alone how much they don't.

No, I only knew him slightly.

No, I never worked with or for him.

No, I was on leave at the time.

Chinese girls down banisters? Sorry, I don't understand the question.

'Oh, is that the time? Well, we must call an end to this seminar now or else the Scottish lads and the chap from Jersey won't catch their flights back.'

And with that, the meeting broke up, with a few nods, grunts and handshakes here and there, and Perry Sherry issuing instruction of when and where to meet at Heathrow on 18th April and making sure everyone had handed in their signed and witnessed contracts.

Then, more importantly, refunding travel expenses, in individual envelopes, the claims for which the Recruit Inspectors had given him the first thing that morning.

Bob Yates had chained his bike to the office railings and away he pedalled, all at one with the world, while AV, having seen the size, confidence and indeed arrogance of some of the folks who'd be going out there with him, was again having a bout of insecurity.

Still, the two tins of beer he'd filched from the lunchtime spread would do him nicely until he reached Paddington, and the train's buffet car would be open soon after departure, so he'd probably be fine by the time they hit Didcot, and certainly as right as rain by Swindon.

All in all, it had been an extremely useful and informative day.

They'd discover in time though that much had been glossed over, with two absolutely staggering ironies concerning what they'd been shown and told, and who had conducted the seminar.

The first was when Richard 'Clusterfuck' Clutterbuck, never mind him spouting out that police officers should not use prostitutes, was found naked, just over a year later, during a raid by officers from Uniform Branch Yaumatei, (on the Special Duty Squad), in a massage parlour, which more often than not was a pseudonym for 'brothel', with three equally unclad Chinese girls, and he wasn't there to teach them English by the look of it.

A bit of 'French' maybe, but definitely not English.

Had he not been so abusive and tried so aggressively to pull rank over the Inspector conducting the routine check of the premises, and actually threatening him, then no doubt the compartment door would have been closed, and Clutterbuck would have been politely left to get on with his pleasures or perversions.

However, while he was not arrested, he was reported to the Inspector's SDI (Sub Divisional Inspector) who had no choice but to pass it up the line in view of the intimidation aspect, and Clutterbuck was verbally cautioned by a very senior officer, and was forced to publicly apologise to Inspector Robert Yates, as he was then, yes the very same Steady Eddie who'd been at the seminar he'd conducted in April 1975.

The second was when the then Inspector AV Bottomley arrested an Auxiliary Police Constable down a side lane in Yaumatei, eleven months later, for illegal off-course betting on horse races, immediately recognising him as being on one of the training films shown at the seminar, which had portrayed the 'Auxie' as an example of how an officer should behave towards members of the public.

No, he wasn't charged, but cautioned there and then on the advice of AV's Sergeant, which at the time seemed fair.

And there was supreme irony in *that*, of which AV would become very aware later, when that Sergeant himself was arrested and charged with corruption offences relating to off-course betting and protecting illegal gambling houses in Yaumatei itself.

Very much more on drugs, and illegal street gambling and casinos in later pages, the Hong Kong Chinese in general having an almost fanatical gambling addiction. The only legal gambling was on and at horse races at the Happy Valley racecourse, or off-course through their many Jockey Club betting offices.

Then there was limited gambling allowed on mah-jong, a tile game, at licensed mah-jong associations, and also at private, social mah-jong gatherings for small stakes.

Lastly there was a weekly lottery again run through the Jockey Club, called Lucky Six or Luk Hap Choy.

Portuguese Macau, however, some one hour away by high-speed ferry, operated legal gambling casinos and brothels, allegedly Triad-controlled (the 14K chapter), where 'anything goes' and which thousands of Hong Kong residents (and many Hong Kong police officers on hotel and ferry freebies) visited weekly.

Oh, what a tangled web we weave, especially when social mah-jong gatherings amongst some cliques of police officers were allegedly used as opportunities to either launder money, or to share out 'the divvy' by letting certain persons 'win'.

What a lot to learn! What a lot to trip you up!

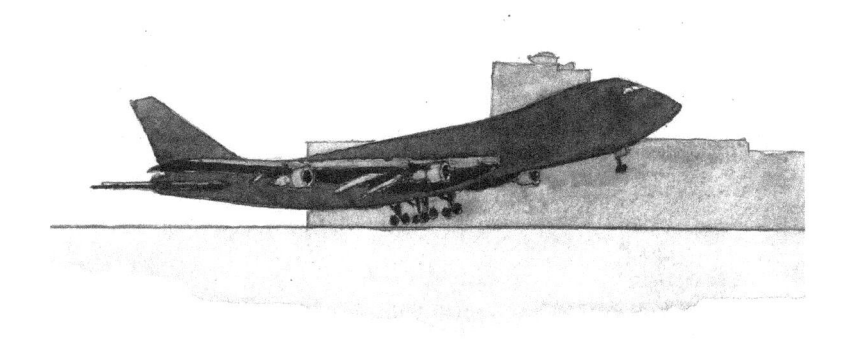

Chapter Four

Leaving on a Jet Plane

So the 18th April 1975, Departure Day, was fast approaching, and both Steady Eddie Yates and AV Bucket Bottomley found time quickly running out, with loads of administrative and personal matters to attend to.

Both had to put enough money together to last the six weeks until their first full salary from the Hong Kong Government, and then there were passports and inoculations needed, confirming resignations from jobs, paying off debts and visiting and saying goodbye to relatives, near and far, particularly the older ones as one just didn't know if they'd still be around at the end of three years.

Luckily, a former footballing colleague bought AV's Triumph Herald and he had a few quid left over after paying off the bank, but one question not asked at the seminar was whether the grub at the Police Training School was free or not. Fair enough, the drink most probably wasn't, but the food was another matter. It turned out that *no*, it wasn't, which meant they had to economise more than they had thought.

Bob, not quite yet cursed with the burden of being a drinker, had been most prudent with his savings and had quite a nest egg to tide him over, though very wisely he never let on about it, such was his caution and common sense.

Things at the bank hadn't been too clever, as Jim Brady had taken offence at AV still deciding to break away, despite their kind offer, and Marvin Purvis was keeping well out of the way of AV's forehead, coke scuttle and even presence during working hours, and had stopped meeting or associating with Maggie at the Horse and Groom in case of potentially embarrassing or hazardous moments.

AV was grateful, as while he couldn't have given a toss, really, there *was* a certain hurt pride in 'losing out' to a pratt like the Perve and, let's face it, a shag *was* a shag after all, and he *so* would have liked to have tried 'making love' (he believed that was the term) when sober.

He'd have to wait a year or more for that to happen, incidentally.

But things have a funny way of working out, and all Maggie's efforts and exhortations to become engaged, sort out a mortgage and marry, while wasted on AV, worked a treat on the young, bespectacled, tubby, spotty, swotty, dotty and formerly virginal twenty three year old Marvin, their happy future union announced the very Friday afternoon AV had left the Nat West bank for good, promising never to darken their doors again unless they wanted a quick wood stain job on the bank's front doors, and at just a little more than cost, merely as a favour to Jim Brady.

He later learnt that Maggie had been in such a desperate hurry to tie the knot with, well, anyone really, because the bloke whom many had thought had gone off to join the Foreign Legion was the chappie who had been sent to Exeter Prison for burglary, yes the fine young criminal who used to work at the carpet factory and the very ex-goalkeeper AV had taken over from in the factory footie team.

While Dobber (yes, that was his nickname) probably would have been furious to find that his ex-girlfriend had taken up with another man during his incarceration (and very damned soon after it commenced, the truth be told) he couldn't argue if he came out and find she'd married and had settled down. Convict 236584's own fault, if he cared enough to reason it out.

Thank the Lord that AV was well out of it. In fact, did he actually need to go out to the Far East at all, now that *that* formerly tricky situation had resolved itself quite nicely?

Yes, he still had his doubts, although Geoff was still pushing him, seemingly already living AV's future for him, somewhat too vicariously, actually, while Colin Yates was glorying in his son's chosen path, which he probably would have done whatever young Robert had decided.

With everything tidied up in Stroud (apart from the Golden Valley section of the London Road which is *still* in a mess in present day 2023), Geoff collected AV and drove him to Alton in Hampshire, for a few days with his parents before the 18th.

AV, unlike Steady Eddie, had never flown before and was a trifle apprehensive, only previously having travelled abroad by coach on a school trip to Italy, and a footballing coach trip (as a player, not a hooligan) to Germany, plus a rugby tour by ferry to Guernsey, which was considered foreign to most people from Stroud.

But on the Sunday before departure, the *Sunday Mirror* carried an article in its magazine about how a Jumbo Jet is scheduled, provisioned, crewed, flown and maintained, and the Bottomleys en masse sat down in their nice new house at 10 Maple Close in Alton and digested every scrap of detail contained therein, and even AV was buoyed and reassured by the apparent expertise and professionalism of the British Airways organisation at every level.

Thence to the Last Supper on Thursday 17th April 1975, Laura, Lena, Geoff, Gina, AV and Henry the Dog sat around chewing on fish and chips, pickled onions and crusty bread ('but no pickles for the dog as he'll stink the place out with his farts') in a sombre, sober mood of quiet reflection as, who knew, but that could have been the last time they'd all be together as a family.

Still, Geoff shattered all that by producing a couple of bottles of Woodpecker cider and spirits were temporarily lifted. Similar final family meals were taking place in homes of many, if not most of those flying away to God knows what in Hong Kong the following afternoon, and the Yates home was no exception, Magda laying on a feast of stuffed cabbage, cream and potato salad, with strudel and custard, Bob's favourite, although in truth he had one hell of an appetite, and a constitution and metabolism that meant he'd hardly gain a pound, no matter the passing of the years or how much or what he'd whoof down himself.

'And so to sleep, perchance to dream.' But you must be joking! Up at sparrow's fart, (not Henry's), clothes packed into the brand-new strengthened-cardboard suitcase they'd bought at British Home Stores, then most of the morning faffing around, Gina forcing in some extra underwear, probably realising AV was close to crapping himself, Gina now a civil servant on the same Borden base where Geoff worked with the Army's School of Electrical and Mechanical Engineering, and both booking a day off to take him to Heathrow in the family's VW Beetle.

And so it was a lovely stop in a pleasant pub in Windsor, right opposite the castle itself, on a beautiful spring day, enhanced by a couple of pints and a light sandwich lunch, then having to reluctantly leave and head off to the airport, AV feeling a cloud of depression and maybe guilt hanging over him, and a self-questioning 'What *am* I doing?' throbbing inside his head.

The car radio was tinnily playing hits of the day, with Steve Harley's wonderful 'Make Me Smile (Come Up And See Me)', tempered by the very apt and almost poignant Glitter Band's 'Goodbye My Love', and then the current number one, the reissued 'Honey' by Bobby Goldsboro, a real sickly tear-jerker if there ever was one, and one of the worst songs AV had ever, or would ever, hear, so off with the radio and the journey continued in silence.

Geoff parked up in the appropriate London Heathrow terminal

car park, and then the three of them walked across to the departure lounge, where the recruits had been instructed to assemble, and there were Perry Sherry and Superintendent Clusterfuck, both with clipboards and, one by one, young lads were shuffling across and collecting their tickets, and then being individually ushered to the check-in desk, so obviously not being seated all together as a group on the aeroplane.

After the boarding passes were received, there was a lot of milling around, the Hong Kong Office staff obviously trying to be very business-like, but equally aware that there was a shed load of both positive and negative emotions flying around, as mums, dads, grans, and cousin Festus, and Carole next door who drove someone up because their dad's lumbago was giving him gip, and Uncle Tom Gobbly and all, wanted a final piece of their little boy for probably the next three years and, sadly to say, in some terribly piquant and bittersweet, even tragic, circumstances, forever.

Unbeknownst to the Gloucestershire mob, amongst the crowd was Bob Yates and his parents, but Alan did recognise a few other people from the seminar, although no one really stood out apart from a tall, bright-ginger-haired fellow who apparently had no one there to bid him farewell, although it was later learnt he had flown up alone from Jersey, but he seemed happy enough about it, wandering around and nodding to a few with a cheeky, infectious grin.

It was learnt, years later, and from pints of bitter experience, that a few toots of Jersey's own Mary Anne Special beer can do that to a person.

One other bloke did attract attention, though, a stocky young chap who was a worse bag of spuds than AV, cuddling an old lady, presumably his grandmother, and although he was pleased to see he wouldn't be the only scruff, Bottomley's parents had wryly noted that everyone else travelling to join the RHKP was substantially taller than AV.

Gina even commented, 'You'll have to work harder than them, son!' with Geoff adding a snarly, 'If they give you any trouble, son, kick them in the cods!'

Easier said than done, Dad.

If his parents hadn't been there, then he would definitely have turned tail and immediately called it a day, right there and then, and bugger learning how to use chopsticks (at which his mother had laughed) and finding out about Chinese girls sliding down banisters (at which his father had letched, and then very stupidly told his wife).

And so with hugs, tears and kisses over, but with a final look back, and a wave, they slowly went through the departure lounge gate into Immigration Control and beyond, AV following like a lost sheep although he surely wasn't the only one, clutching his boarding pass and wondering if he'd ever see his luggage or his family again.

But those Scotsmen were still at it, with their loud, guttural 'Big Man' and 'Wee Man' and 'Och Ayes', with at least five or six of them in the party of twenty-odd, not bothering to even glance at or locate the remainder of the group, again probably hooking up the previous evening and forming a bond, or maybe even a White Heather Club already, aided by the fact that two of them seemed significantly older than the others and, from their patter, probably designed to impress, they already had some police experience, not that it would serve them any better once the real training commenced.

 AV viewed them with a detached curiosity, never having consciously seen a real Scot in the flesh before, as it were, let alone conversed with one, but he was soon to find out that some of them weren't bad fellows at all. Once, that is, one could get used-to, and decipher their rather guttural accents, although some of the party, in isolation, proved to have softer and more lilting, mellifluous tones, as they weren't all Rob Roys, but had thought that amongst the sassenachs they had to collectively act as if they were. (It was obviously an historical and cultural affectation.)

(No, he hadn't seen a Scot in the flesh before, but he'd often fantasised about seeing Moira Anderson and Lulu naked, right enough.)

Hell, it was only months after meeting Steady Eddie, and 'Ginger' (as we'll call him for the present) that he realised both of *their* fathers were Scottish.

And *there* was Punjab Pete himself, AV keeping his distance in case he was recognised, but realised that at some time he'd probably have to speak to him during the next eight months. But not just now.

Yes, he was in a right bloody mood with himself.

Then shuffling onto the aeroplane, cramming into a seat, and before he realised it, they were airborne, watered, fed and settled, ears hurting from those sharp headphones, but quite content to read the in-flight magazine and enjoy the music and film, holding back memories and regrets as best he could.

He'd bought the excellent '*The Moon's a Balloon*' by David Niven and was much amused by David's anecdotal and apocryphal tales, so much so he actually found himself bursting into laughter a few times, despite himself.

British Airways to Rome, where he thought about jumping off the Jumbo and leaving, but what about his luggage? And so onward to Bombay where they alighted the plane as there was an engine fault, remaining in the airport terminal for two hours.

Whatever thoughts AV might have had about skipping off and somehow making his way back to Stroud via Bombay straight away flew out of his head, as the whole countryside around the airport was a mass of heat-scorched, and burnt, brown dirt and grass with a heat haze shimmering away as far as the eye could see, reminding him of the Blaster Bates skit, 'A Shower of Shit over Cheshire.'

Bob Y was amused to see the British Airways ground engineer arriving on a pedal cycle, carrying the spare part with which the fault was duly fixed. This reminded him so much of how things had been back in Ndola and other rather 'bush' airports he'd experienced during his African heydays, while AV was thinking they hadn't mentioned this in the *Sunday Mirror* supplement.

Then back on board, and the seemingly ceaseless journey to Hong Kong continued, the avoidance of air space over Vietnam adding to the flying time apparently.

Steady Eddie was in his element when the pilot acceded to his request, through an air hostess, as they were then termed, to visit the cockpit and was treated to a look round the controls and to a brief chat with the flight crew who were both courteous and most welcoming.

'One of these days!' he mused, as he returned to seat 35A, 'One of these days!'

The Bucket meanwhile was most annoyed not to have realised that alcoholic beverages from the serving trolley were complimentary, as a British Airways apology for the delay, and, had he known it, he could have been both more 'relaxed' and certainly more 'refreshed' when they reached Hong Kong, but, in retrospect, considering what was awaiting the party, it was probably quite fortuitous that he *hadn't*.

Then finally… finally… it was time to fasten seat belts as they were due to land from the sea approach, apparently, and through the window and the early evening darkness they could initially see bright lights, ships at anchor, some tower blocks, then more fully illuminated but larger buildings, then hills, and then - a bit of an anti-climax - touchdown, and 'Welcome to Kai Tak International Airport!'

No, my pedigree chums… there was no turning back now!

And what a welcome awaited them all!

Chapter Five

The Induction Introduction

And so, at about 7pm on Saturday 19th April 1975, it was time to shuffle off the aircraft and then through the tunnel from the Jumbo into the airport's arrival lounge, where four plain-clothed British chaps from the RHKP were holding up hand-written placards 'asking' the new intake to gather around them, one fellow being in his thirties and the other three possibly in their mid to late twenties.

The older officer seemed to be the 'Big Cheese', because he was the one with the clipboard, was more serious than the others appeared to be, and was giving the welcoming speech and instructions.

He turned out to be Chief Inspector Dick Snyder (and what a name 'Chief Inspector' is to give someone, nearly as bad as Zed Victor One as mentioned earlier in this tale!) and yes, there *were* a surprising number of Dicks in the expatriate officer corps.

Mr Snyder would be in charge of the party for most of the forthcoming week during their familiarisation, but in the interim, he told them to follow him to the immigration desks where special arrangements had been made for them to be processed *en masse*, then they should collect their luggage from the reclaim area, and then all reassemble there.

While this was going on, the other three of the meet-and-greeters were milling around, but seemingly making sly comments about the state of the new guys with their rounded collars, flared trousers, whiskers and long hair, and pissed AV off immediately by pointing and sneering at his three inch-heeled blue platform shoes, the jealous bastards, which were probably in retrospect a small man's attempt to make up for his three inch blue dick, which in itself was *no* laughing matter.

No one had a clue if they were senior officers or not, until one of them, later learned to be a Welshman, Tommy Allcock, (very aptly nicknamed 'Two Dicks' in view of his very soon-to-be-revealed obsession with the opposite sex), cockily and beamingly went amongst everyone, introducing himself, proffering the hand of friendship and bonhomie, and informing them that he had joined the RHKP locally and would be a member of their intake from thereon in.

He reminded a few of the more rock and roll-orientated and rather nervous new recruits of Jocko Marcellino, the moustachioed drummer out of Sha Na Na, with his swarthy good looks, tash and curly black hair, but it became quickly apparent that Tommy had gotten a few beers 'under his belt' at, or before arriving at, the airport, probably because of the two hours' delay in the aircraft reaching Kai Tak.

Nerves can do that to people.

In fact, he looked like a 'Welsh wop', more so than the wonderful Victor Spinetti, who had absolutely gloried in that self-appointed title.

One other of the three was also spiritedly introducing himself, a Senior Inspector called Keith Franks, whom Tommy had followed out to HK from their Mid Wales town of Llandiddleme, or some such unpronounceable place (to the non-Welsh, anyway) who was a rep for the Expatriate Inspectors' Association.

He was attached to CID Wanchai and in truth turned out to be one of the nicest chaps one could ever wish to meet, although he appeared to have a beam and real glow about him that night too.

It must have been the weather. Either that or the air-conditioning wasn't working inside the terminal, or perhaps it was a peculiar trait of the Welsh, come to think of it.

The last of the three, though, a very tall, thin and balding chap in a two-piece blue suit, but without a tie, was hanging around like a spare prick at a wedding, with an all-knowing, superior grin, grimace and sneer in turn, his expression alternating with each sip of beer from the pint glass in his right hand.

He then sparked into life, by loudly bellowing in a very broad Northern accent, 'Are any of you sprogs from God's Own County of Yorkshire?'

No reply. Obviously not, then. A general embarrassed looking around at one another, until one of the group put his hand up and gently ventured, 'I'm from Manchester, if that helps!' only to be met with an extremely rude rejoinder of, 'Manchester! That's of fuck all help to anyone!'

Then this 'Yorkie' Bill Towser, unable to find a soulmate amongst the new recruits, and obviously not wanting to dip his hand in his pocket to buy a drink for any outsiders, took himself off and sat alone on a stool, just glaring at everyone, having been 'whispered-to' by Mr Snyder.

The new arrivals just took it as a joke - what else could they have done? - as Mr Towser had obviously become 'tired and emotional' while waiting so long for the aircraft to finally arrive.

He was a confirmed Inspector of three years' service, and thus had two metaphorical pips - and obviously some chips - on each shoulder, working in the CID, somewhere in North Kowloon. But, in any case, he doesn't figure in any more of these tales, killing himself in a car crash a year or so down the line.

So it goes.

Once the bags had been collected, another police officer arrived on the scene, obviously this time, though, aiming to impress them as he was dressed in the RHKP summer uniform of light green tunic and shorts, cap, highly polished black shoes, fawn socks and Sam Browne belt, resplendent with a holstered revolver attached to it, and bright silver accoutrements to his shoulders and cap.

Yes, their first real glance of a uniformed, one-pip *'Bon Baan'* (or Probationary Inspector to you.) The number of shoulder pips represented one's rank as an Inspector.

And very impressive he looked too, not only in his uniform but obviously with himself.

Chief Inspector Snyder pointedly turned to the now gathered throng and told them all that *that* was how they'd have to turn out in the not-too-distant future.

Some hopes, thought Bottomley, an 'Oxo cube' man, while Bob Yates, one of the 'cigar-shaped' men, thought he'd have no problems, which in fact he didn't.

The Inspector's name was Ron McFyffer, yes another Scot, attached to the Uniform Branch of the Airport Division of the RHKP, whose wind was then taken out of his sails, somewhat, by the stocky young 'sack of spuds' they'd seen back at Heathrow bidding a tearful goodbye to his grandmother, when he turned to no one in particular and commented, 'Body of a Greek god, but probably with the mind of a Greek goat,' which, as it turned out in respect of Mr McFyffer, proved to be not too far off the mark.

A bit unwise, though, as quite a few heard it, including Snyder, and Martin 'Dog's' Dinner, as he was, on his first moments in Hong Kong, hadn't yet had time to learn that one of the first important lessons to 'get on' in the RHKP was: Don't upset people who can either help you or harm you.

But there would be *so* much like that to learn in due course.

And now that the darling bags of May, well April really, had been safely gathered in, it was time to breeze through customs inspection, which was cursory (because if you can't trust a policeman, then just who *can* you trust?), gathering once more to board a large blue police bus to travel to the Police Training School.

Luckily, at about 8pm, it wasn't too hot, as the party travelled from Kai Tak Airport along the East Kowloon coastal road, getting its first magnificent view across to the bright sparkling lights of Hong Kong Island and harbour, then through the Cross Harbour Tunnel, up through a very busy Wong Nei Chong Gap, on the island's hilly spine, and down to Aberdeen on the south coast, all the while sneaking glances at one another to try, even at that early stage, to determine who were the likely competition, trouble-makers, big mouths, braggards and bullshitters, with just a few defensive snippets of comment and conversation entered into, with even the Scottish clique temporarily partially silenced.

Off the main road, then down a much smaller one past a shacked village set amongst a largish body of water, then through the PTS main gate and guardhouse and into the Training School itself, past office and accommodation blocks and then finally the large blue bus stopped just at the cusp of a fully lit parade square dead ahead.

Then the proverbial shit hit the fan as everyone was ordered off the vehicle and to drop their luggage nearby, then form into two lines.

But just what was going on over on the opposite side of the square itself?

Half-naked what appeared to be male Chinese officers being apparently assaulted by local youths with sticks and hitting back with truncheons, batons and wicker shields, making one hell of a commotion.

While that was occurring, there were a few grumbles from those standing to attention, especially after they had been marched about the square for fifteen minutes, drill instructions being shouted at them by some young Sergeant Major, or whatever.

Then some tall, blokeish looking woman doctor, a Mary Normalington, gave a very short warning about sexual diseases and informed everyone that their penises would be inspected by her on the following Monday, and every Monday thereafter!

(Well, AV's three inch blue one won't be, that's for sure, madam!)

Then a dog-collared vicar, a Bill Robinson, who incredibly seemed to be well pissed, gave a brief talk about going to him with any personal problems, in a rather gayish way, although the term back then was in a 'queer' manner.

Still in two lines, a tall, moustachioed, officious, loud-mouthed, arrogant, disdainful uniformed officer named Blake Piggard, nicknamed 'Motor Mouth', started strutting up and down the rows, briefly interrogating, and in many cases, insulting those on parade whilst waving his swagger stick around threateningly.

AV was worrying about what would be thrown at himself, but Piggard merely glanced once and strode past (thank you, baby Jesus) probably not thinking a bloke of his size was worth bothering with, although AV had built himself into attack mode just in case Mr Piggard felt like giving his generous buttocks a thwack with his cane.

However, perhaps Piggard had a long memory, or was just plain stupid, or possibly had been influenced by the film *Conduct Unbecoming* set in Victorian times, where the subalterns ran around on an Indian Army Mess Night trying to stick a stuffed wild pig up the bum with sabres. Because back to the story - at a PTS Officers' Mess barbecue some three months later, he had sought Bottomley out and had stabbed him in the arse several times with a double-pronged barbecue fork, drawing blood, at which juncture there were several options, which were : to kick him in the cods, as dad Geoff had advised him at London Heathrow, nut him, or report him for Assault Occasioning Actual Bodily Harm or Wounding, Section 19.

Common sense prevailed, though, thanks to the intervention

of Steady Eddie and Tommy Allcock who were the sole witnesses, and Piggard came to his senses and realised all could be up with his career, forcing an apology which AV accepted with what good grace he could muster.

In fact, had it not been for his new friends' intercession and presence, and that he wasn't half drunk, AV would have surely gone the other way, never believing that the RHKP was a long-term proposition for him, and living by the adage that it's perfectly fine to throw the baby out with the bath water if all you ever wanted was the plug.

Thus scandal was averted and 'Motor Mouth' saved his career, rising in due course to very dizzy heights indeed, despite being a back and arse-stabbing tosser.

Back to those interrogations on the parade square, however, where Steady Eddie was asked quite a few simple non-contentious questions, and gave short, sharp, reasoned replies, his experiences with Seamus O'Stropley back in Luanshya teaching him not to answer back or annoy the '*bwanas*'. Piggard gave up in frustration that he couldn't get a 'rise' out of his intended victim, so well done that man!

Yes, we have no *bwanas*, as the war-time song pronounced.

One chap behind though wasn't quite so fortunate, his first and only question being, 'Would you sleep with a man if ordered to by a senior officer?'

The reply? 'Yes, sir, I would.'

Then countered by Piggard's scathing and venomous repost of, 'Then you, sir, are a POOF!'

Several intakes of shocked breath, and some mysterious sounds of loud, cackling laughter coming from somewhere behind, and then… then… called to attention, and 'FALL OUT!'

Fall out? AV and Steady Eddie damned near fell over, never mind falling out, to then discover the whole of the fighting, the marching, the lady doctor, Reverend Robinson's open invitation to go up and see him some time, and the inquisition from Piggard had been nothing other than a staged wind-up of the new recruits by other recruits in training, who'd been at the school maybe four months ahead of the poor new bunch of very naïve suckers.

They'd been similarly wound-up on their arrival, and it would be the new intake's job to do the same to another fresh intake in another few months.

Then out came the first trays of San Miguel beer in the adjacent Officers' Mess, and thereafter the ice had been well and truly broken, although a few *did* think the induction a bit over the top, until, that is, the beer started to flow even more freely.

Even the bloke who'd claimed he'd sleep with another man if ordered to gradually felt better about things, and claimed he knew it was a wind-up all along and just had said it for comedic affect and for its shock value.

Maybe he *had* known, as he was standing next to Tommy 'Two Dicks' who may have told him, as he, himself, had been previously informed of the planned Induction Ceremony, and had gone along with it just to show solidarity with his new playmates.

Damn it! Let's be generous and say he *did* know.

Then suddenly someone realised that the baggage was still where it had been dumped, and no one had yet shown the by now half-pissed new arrivals their quarters, a fault soon remedied by taking them across to a barrack-style dormitory, four beds to a compartment, in an opposite block.

Unfortunately, housing them in single quarters adjacent to the Officers' Mess had to be delayed a few weeks as those rooms would not be available until two senior squads finished their courses and exams, and then had been posted to various police formations throughout the Colony.

The two married recruits who'd brought their wives along fared a little better as they were in hotel accommodation downtown, and in due course would be provided with quite spacious flats.

Common sense should have dictated that their bags be placed by the beds, they dump themselves in those beds and a good night's sleep had by all, but the wine was *in* and the wit was most definitely *out*, with the senior squads, those responsible for the wind-up, insisting that they take the sprogs down to 'The Wanch', or Wanchai, the main bar area on Hong Kong Island, which they'd heard about at the seminar earlier that month.

And there were very few dissenters, so much so that several taxis were summoned from outside the main gates and people just bundled in, AV being hosted by the now unfrocked vicar (a pity, because as frocks went, it was a very nice one), Bill Robinson, and joined by a few of his mates and one or two new colleagues.

Hong Kong taxis in the main were red Datsuns and Nissans, and could take up to five passengers, two in front, three in the rear, the best position being in front as, in the absence of air-conditioning, they usually had a small, high-speed rotating fan attached to the dashboard.

And the first bit of Chinese vocabulary was learnt, but in many cases forgotten, too, that first balmy night, namely that a Hong Kong taxi was a '*Heung Gong dik si.*'

So back up to the top of Wong Nei Chong Gap and what a view, looking ahead and down on Hong Kong Harbour, across to Kowloon, with seemingly endless, well-lit ships at anchor, and the bright, brash lights of the mainland itself. Even the Old China Hands of four months in AV's cab commented on the glory of what lay spread out before them.

Another thing then learnt was that trams plied along the north side of Hong Kong Island only, back and forth from Western to Eastern, mainly along Hennessy Road, which was one road further back from the sea front than Lockhart Road, and the Wanchai bar area.

Just so the lads had their bearings.

Then out of the cabs, and straight into a series of bars, all fronted by large neon signs, in English and Chinese, curtained off at the entrances, with sexily clad, late teen Chinese girls waiting on tables or at the bar counter and trying to inveigle highly priced cups of cold tea from customers, though offered up as a lady's drink. Beer was cheap enough though and just as well.

Bill, a generous and very personable host, it transpired, was from Gloucester, and in fact went to the Crypt School there, and blow me down, it seemed AV and he must have played rugby against each other several times in their schooldays.

Very quickly that night, given the way he obviously knew many of the girls around the place, the people who had only met Bill a few hours previously were reassured that his 'homosexual vicar act' was indeed a wind-up, which was quite a relief to some.

The smell of joss sticks in the bars was very evident and loads of other expats were on the town that night apart from the PTS mob, many obviously being policemen known to the senior squad, and a fair proportion of off-duty soldiers and sailors.

The décor and types of bar varied a lot too, with some having a live local band, some with jukeboxes, another with only young ladies and beer being the main attraction, and one even with a local girl singer accompanied by a piano player and violinist. Most were quite dimly lit, with disgusting toiletry facilities, maybe a reason for the joss sticks and incense.

The names of those bars? The Neptune Bar, Washington Bar, Popeye's Bar, San Francisco Bar (known also as the SanFran), Panda Bar, An An Bar, Side Door Bar, Back Door Bar, Lucky Star Bar and the Limelight Bar, and *that* list compiled from what the whole gang could collectively remember of them the following day.

The rest of the crowd with AV and Bill had moseyed off to other watering holes, but the travel, tiredness, the lack of local currency and not wanting to get too drunk on the first night, hit Bottomley who was a little overwhelmed by it all, and thus Bill had accompanied him back to the PTS and thankfully guided him to his designated sleeping block, where he damned near collapsed into immediate unconsciousness.

Neither he nor Bill could later recall who the rest of the initial party were or had been.

Yes, tiredness can do that to a person.

Now while AV had had a pleasant enough time of it, poor old Bob Yates had been really struggling to keep up with most of the others in the rounds of drinks consumed, lemonade being, back then, his preferred tipple. But, encouraged by the hospitality, the bonhomie, perceived required manners, and peer pressure, even he had manfully gotten a real bellyful of San Miguel beer down his gullet. And wasn't he suffering!

Apart from in the first two or three bars, he'd kept it down, but in everyone thereafter he'd been violently sick, projectile vomiting like Regan in *The Exorcist*, although she had the Devil inside of her, while Bob only had to cope with the demon drink. He thought he was dying and then prayed he would as he felt so awful.

('Oh thou invisible spirit of wine, if thou hast no name to be known by, let us call thee Devil.')

He had been hosted by a Ross Hillman and a Phillip Martins, and a few other chaps on the intake immediately before his own, but he couldn't later remember how he had managed to return to PTS, let alone how he'd found the accommodation block or even his designated bed.

Yes, once again, tiredness does funny things with one's head.

(The strange thing was that neither Hillman nor Martins, nor any of their squad, ever again seemed to cut loose, as it were, and were never again seen by Steady Eddie, Bottomley, Allcock or by any of the soon-to-be-introduced remainder of 'The Cast', crawling, trawling or falling around 'The Wanch').

Nevertheless, what a night! But never again! Thank God it was over!

The following day, 20th April, was a Sunday and the new recruits had a day off to sort themselves out, recover from jet lag, and, if they felt like it, take a trip into town and explore.

Most of the PTS staff of instructors, administrators and ancillary helpers, plus the hundreds of Chinese rank and file PCs and WPCs currently under training, customarily had their day off on Sundays, and thus the school was almost in skeleton staff mode.

But not many of the shell-shocked, (or San Miguel beer-shocked rather) wanted to do much of anything until about midday, when the stragglers shook themselves into being human again, and awoke in barrack accommodation with a ceiling fan clunk clunking above them.

AV was feeling poorly, desperately needing a hair of the dog, while Bob Yates was still feeling wretched. Several of their colleagues were milling around, making the most of the first real opportunities they'd had to get to know each other, while their mentors of the previous evening were probably sleeping it off in their single rooms opposite.

One thing *not* explained had been how ordering food was done, meal times and payment method, so a few lads went across to the Mess and returned with the good news that it was open at 6am and shut at 10pm, with a full menu a la carte or set meals of the day, as required, and signed food and beverage chits, with monthly billing, the accepted practice.

The bar was always open during those times but the thought of food and drink was presently anathema to many, including Bottomley and Yates, although a few hours later AV would be gasping for a pint but didn't want to go to the Mess and be seen having his hair of the dog by supping it up through a straw, just in case he had the hippy hippy shakes, and if early drinking was frowned upon.

There were quite a few inquests taking place on what had happened, and to whom, the previous evening, but the consensus was that a jolly good time had been had by all, even though most memories were rather hazy, it being agreed that it would take some time, and remaining relatively sober, to explore 'The Wanch' properly, and at leisure.

Some initial friendships were being formed, while some instant dislikes became obvious and would last as long as those friendships would. Never mind, you can't like everyone, and not everyone likes everyone else or, in some cases, even themselves.

A small gathering of brave souls decided to take a trip up to the Peak Tower, overlooking the north side of Hong Kong Island and the whole of Kowloon and beyond, whilst the remainder just milled around a while longer, in a sort of confused stupor.

AV, though, felt quite isolated, thinking that he didn't see himself as an officer and a gentlemen, after all, if he ever had, being more of Richard Gere's dissolute, low, able-bodied seaman of a father, as played by Robert Loggia, rather than Gere's aspiring *Officer and a Gentleman* in the later film of the same name. Particularly so when comparing himself to most of his intake again, and those senior squad people he'd met so far, though admittedly he hadn't yet come across any blatant NSTs, apart from Piggard that is. (Remember those, anyone?)

However, he should have reminded himself that looks can be deceptive, and that 'there's no art to find the mind's construction in the face.' In plain English, bullshit baffles brains.

Bob Y busied himself, chatting away to a couple of lads who were lounging on their neatly-rowed beds, and the three of them then decided to have a look around PTS as it was relatively quiet and because, not yet in uniform, they'd not be required to march everywhere within its precincts, or return salutes from the rank and file, or give them to senior officers, of which there would prove to be many, both Chinese and Expatriates.

PTS then showed itself to be a well-established and fairly large training establishment, for both the rank and file, and officer recruits, also providing ad hoc management, firearms and specialist in-house and refresher training, as required, to officers of all ranks.

Located along from the fishing town of Aberdeen and the village island of Aplichau, as earlier noted, on both a flat and sloping, terraced site, the most dominating feature was the very distinctive, highly and heavily foliaged, Brick Hill, immediately to the east, this having steep paths and trails up to its 1,000 feet high summit and, as the recruits were to later learn, sometimes featured in the physical exercise routine to be required of them, and as punishment for minor disciplinary infractions.

Debilitating, energy-sapping, exhausting and knackering do not even begin to describe a scrambling scurry to the top or the careful, perilous descent, particularly when considering the often prevailing and sultry heat and humidity, or even the heavy rains. No, there were no 'passes' for the weather... up they had to go, regardless.

Mind you, the view from the top was tremendous, apparently, spanning Deep Water and Repulse Bays on one side, and way back across to Western District on the other, incorporating PTS and up the Wong Nei Chong Gap. *If* one could draw in enough breath to actually look up and appreciate it.

(It is an unknown blessing for current day recruits that Brick Hill is now part of the Ocean Park Oceanarium and Theme Park's cable car complex, and thus is out of bounds to trespassers and members of the public except to those using the cable cars themselves.)

The parade square, now on closer inspection, was fringed by a raised dais on the middle of its right side, where march-pasts were focused and salutes taken, with a canon placed either side (for effect, not as a threat to the policemen on parade) and behind the dais was a covered area where guests were seated during formal functions such as Passing Out Parades.

And behind that was a three-quarter-sized, tarmacked football pitch; more of that later.

Steady Eddie and the two others slowly walked around the office block, the rank and file classrooms and their living quarter blocks and canteen, then the senior officer and instructors housing block, to the assault course (another horror story!) down to the firing ranges, and the armoury, leaving with the thought that the school was very well appointed indeed.

So just bring it on gentlemen and do your worst!

They then followed the through-road on the level above the parade square and exited via the rear guardhouse to the large multi-towered resettlement estate of Wong Chuk Hang, where thousands of the local people were housed, crammed together in what, on initial sight to the very wet-behind-the-ears Westerners, seemed almost slum conditions, only to discover later that the small apartments in those tower blocks were generally exceedingly clean, tidy and well maintained, despite how many people lived in each room.

At the base of the building was an open market, selling fish, crabs, prawns, frogs, chicken, ducks, geese, beef, pork and some meats and offal that could not be easily identified, along with all kinds of general household items and provisions, much of the poultry still alive and various strange varieties of fish swimming in tanks and buckets, to be killed on purchase. Talk about fresh!

Bob Y, in fact, who must have eaten in his eleven years in Africa a veritable shoal of exotic seafood, well outside of the standard MacFisheries fare, was the only one amongst them who could appreciate that a Red Snapper was a fish and not a sexual disease.

Two stalls sold roast duck, roast chicken and roast pork, and some ridiculously small roast birds which didn't seem worth the bother of eating at all.

The fruit and vegetable stalls displayed a plethora of colourful and exotic fare and Bob Y's day and condition improved dramatically when he spotted mangoes and groundnuts for sale, items he hadn't tasted since his Luanshya days. What joy and although he couldn't work out what the vendor was telling him on price, a few Hong Kong ten dollar notes thrust across to her seemed to do the trick, and thus his first purchases in Hong Kong, apart from beer, had been made.

There was also a small supermarket in situ, plus a restaurant and a barber's shop, with two of these featuring in a later narrative.

The place was absolutely bustling with people, and the noise of the haggling and the strange, new smells, colours and overall 'orderly chaos' were absolutely enthralling, with very few of the local people batting an eyelid at foreigners walking in their midst.

For AV though the day had been quite 'dead' and a bore, only somewhat brightened up by slinking across to the Mess with a few lads at about 5pm and getting a feed down himself, with just a single beer out of politeness.

Well, perhaps two, then; he was nothing but polite when he wanted to be, and his hangover had subsided since he'd earlier been to the ablutions room at the end of the block house's corridor and had managed a bloody good spew, a blunderbuss of a crap, and a cold shower, but not necessarily in that order, making it seem more like a normal Sunday 'back-home.'

Then all of the new blokes returned early to their dorm in dribs and drabs, and settled down for a good night's sleep, with quite a week awaiting them, although before AV entered 'the Land of Nod', negativity and resignation were very much on his mind and had to be wrestled with overnight.

Good night, sweet princes, good night!

Chapter Six

That Was the Week That Was[3]

And so good morning to Monday April 21st 1975, the start of a familiarisation week for the new intake, who found from the noticeboard near the Officers' Mess that they had been split into two groups, being courses number 101 and 102, and although this delineation was probably completely haphazard, the character of each course seemed to be, it later transpired, very different.

In fact, the split between squads had already started on the Saturday night on arrival as 101 were on one side of the dormitory while 102 had been placed on the other.

Both had also been allocated course instructors, namely Chief Inspector Frank Topley for course 101 and Chief Inspector Frick Jacobs for the other, both of whom would introduce themselves the following afternoon, when a 'Meet and Greet' in the Officers' Mess was scheduled.

No more threatening to look at our dicks, one hopes, thought AV,

---

3   © Copyright BBC

while Steady Eddie was dreading to have to go, or thinking he had to go, and throw ten pints down his neck again.

But as the day commenced, the Bucket was feeling quite chirpy and most of his negativity had dispersed, with thoughts of resigning put to the back of his mind, not least because he simply didn't have sufficient funds to pay back the Hong Kong Government for the airfare to get to Hong Kong, let alone afford the fare back to the UK.

Not only that, but he had found the three other lads in his bed area to be decent enough fellows on first appearances; on his opposite left side was, yes, it had to be, of course, Punjab Pete Spicer, 'King of the Khyber Rifles', he of 'Pater in India' fame, who was a tall, thin, dark-skinned, moustachioed cove of nineteen, straight out of school with three A levels, and although he spoke like a public-school pudding, he was quite an amiable and humorous chap.

He could recall AV from his bank days but had no inkling whatsoever that he'd been duped into thinking he had no inward remittances, and AV was quite happy to let him continue to believe that. Obviously.

Immediately to his left, and again it just had to be, was none other than the second bag of spuds, Martin 'Dogs' Dinner, aged nineteen but the youngest of all the recruits on both courses, again with A levels, who hailed from Somerset, so another West Country lad to join AV.

Although palpably a little immature, especially after a few beers, he was harmless enough, especially once he had settled down into the course, and he'd giggle away at anything. Just as well, or the poor sod could have developed a complex about his very thick limbs, which seemed not to possess much elasticity at the knees or elbows.

He was a bit of a dreamer, or fantasist, though, toying with the idea of either becoming a mercenary or a fur trapper in Venezuela once his three year stint came to an end.

And to complete the section, directly opposite, was Maurice 'Plod' Smiley, so nicknamed because he was an ex-UK policeman, plodding a former beat in Loughborough, a bit of a ten-stone lightweight with a pot belly and a daft grin always on his face, although to tell the truth he wasn't grinning too much on Wednesday of the first week after he and 'Dogs' had a few beers, and good old Martin had waited until Maurice fell asleep, and then tried to pee in his ear.

He would have managed it, too, but he couldn't get a flow going as he was laughing so much, but not when Maurice awoke and tried to brain him with his size 12 marching boot while stark-bollock naked.

(Remember the question about size 12 boots at the seminar?)

All part of settling in, and it amused AV no end at the time, causing everyone to remember that: 'Single men in barracks, don't turn to plastered saints.'

Yes, even saints can get out of line when plastered. Allegedly.

Bob Yates was sharing an alcove with a young Scottish fellow named Sadler Wells, an ex-Inland Revenue officer, and another Scot named Mungo McMee, (much more on him shortly), along with a quiet English chap called Miles Farquharson, yet another ex-banker, who'd worked for Barclays, who was only in the dorm for a few weeks, as he later brought his wife across from England to join him.

That morning started at 07.00 hours (yes, we're on police time now) bright and breezy, to find space in the ablution room, then down to breakfast in the Mess by 07.25 hours, where there was quite a commotion as the senior squads were rushing around getting ready for the morning parade, which commenced at 08.00 hours sharp.

The new mob were then herded to the top road opposite the parade square to watch, but where had all the people come from? Whereas PTS the previous day had seemed dead quiet, it was now chock-a-block with rank and file squads forming up, the junior squads being directed by what were obviously Drill Sergeants, while the senior ones were being directed by one bare-chested male Inspector, a little forward from three or four of their squad mates.

The parade square was full of them, with a marching band (where had *that* come from, then, as Bob Y hadn't seen it the during his pleasant walk round on Sunday afternoon?) beating 'time' and playing military tunes to accompany the inspection.

So off those squads marched in turn, with the new kids on the block marvelling at the precision and symmetry exhibited and performed by everyone there, although admittedly there must have been some cock-ups not within their experience to spot.

Many of the new trainees, virgin policemen in fact, were a trifle worried in case they couldn't reach that level, which seemed damned complicated to the untrained.

And then it was to the PTS barber's shop (the sheep-shearing shed more like), where the flowing locks, beards and sideboards just had to go, exactly like the opening sequence of the Vietnam War film, *'Full Metal Jacket,'* but without the music. Short back and sides for everyone, with laughs and chuckles when as one by one the 'victims' returned to coyly display their almost bald pates. And they had to pay for the privilege too!

Then it was the 'swearing-in' and the Oath of Office, administered by the Commandant, and more on him later, as he was also to address them at the Tuesday afternoon function.

Then it was photographs for all, necessary to produce blue PTS identity cards, to show that they were all police officers under training and, presumably, with the Chinese writing underneath, asking kind taxi drivers, ladies of the night and anyone else who may find them walking around lost and unable to get their bearings, to pat them on the head, give them a few bob and send them back to the Training School.

Bless!

Well, it just went on and on, that day, with a visit from the kind people at the Hong Kong and Shanghai Bank to open up bank accounts, and to grant everyone overdrafts until the first month's pay had been received, and why not? Guaranteed business for life, and once again, if you can't trust a policeman, then just who *can* you trust?

And so that was about it for the day, just nodding to a few now-familiar faces and writing post-cards home to let the folks know how they were doing, PTS operating a postal service.

The following day it was the same routine in the morning, again watching the morning parade and once again, how impressive, with some squads of PCs even performing drill whilst carrying rifles.

And then, what a malarkey, when kit was issued to them by the Barrack Sergeant, a Clarence Chong, and his merry men, most of them fellow Sergeants.

Obviously, the new blokes had no idea of the power of the post of Barrack Sergeant especially in Divisions when, 'in the old days' not only were they apparently responsible for kit, and fixtures and fittings in the police stations, but also for collection and distribution of corrupt 'extras' which all the instructors and senior officers would assure the lads was well and truly over.

But what a '*si fat*' or real arse that fat Chinese 'Barrack' was, with a quick measure of the tape, and then barking out gruff orders to his staff to fetch a hat, four pairs of khaki shorts and shirts, a pair of boots and shoes, a white belt, a PT kit, a lanyard, a Sam Browne belt, a whistle and a cuddly toy, almost, and then a pack of silver (shoulder) pips and bits and pieces, both arms full, then away to try it all on.

No complaints entertained either!

Bob Yates, as mentioned, was one of the many members of the 'cigar set', and a standard size saw his PTS uniform fit well, but AV and Dogs Dinner had to go back and work hard and long to obtain better-fitting gear, greeted with derision that they were too, shall we say, portly, for their height and that there was no one like them in Hong Kong. Yes, two sacks of spuds, admittedly, but persistence paid off.

Neither incidentally were as bulky as that damned Sergeant Chong, who probably enjoyed having a dig at Probationary Inspectors knowing that it was the one time every two months that he could get away with abusing some and not be up on disciplinary charges for insubordination.

However, the Bucket still resembled a cross between Don Estelle, or Gunner 'Lofty' Sugden, out of *'It Ain't Half Hot, Mum!'* and Eric Morecambe in spoof tropical gear. All it would have taken to top it off would have been an oversized pith helmet!

But didn't AV enjoy himself a year or more later when Chong's time in the cushy post of Barrack Sergeant at PTS was over and the 'ex-Barrack' was sent to Divisions, and then one evening was caught by AV and his team from Yaumatei Special Duty Squad (near 'Chimsy' - remember that one?) inside an illegal and large Chinese casino and was thus statutorily presumed to have been gambling therein. Oh joy! Remember me, Sergeant?

AV's own Sergeant was red with embarrassment when AV informed him that Sergeant Chong, the ex-Barrack, was to be arrested with the hundred or so other gamblers, and carted back to the police station with them, AV refusing to believe that he, both living in Police Married Quarters and working in Central Division, was merely gathering gambling information whilst off duty and across the harbour.

Eventually, though, after having made him confess he *was* there for gambling, and after much pressure on a young Inspector by a vastly more experienced Sergeant, the fat bastard was released, although his request for reimbursement of gambling losses from the monies seized was treated with the contempt it and he deserved.

But yes, AV had made a mistake, but wouldn't be so 'soft' in future, not even with officers in similar or worse positions. Oh no!

Now back to the main story.

After lunch, which was a crowded, rushed affair and hardly relaxing, it was time to meet the PTS Senior Command and

Administrative Staff, luckily still in mufti, the new uniforms not needing to be worn until the following week (nor the PT kit as the morning work-outs wouldn't start until then, either).

It was such a high-powered meeting that AV had even forsworn his three inch, blue platform shoes, having had enough of the jealousy they'd engendered, and besides, even he, with sod-all style really, had realised that they didn't look at all trendy on a bloke now with hair and bonce like the rear end of a badly plucked chicken, the Number One haircut fad not yet quite coming into fashion. Especially not for anyone under sixty five.

Luckily, he had brought his 'National Westminster' brown brogues.

And what a crowd had gathered in the Mess, apart from the recruits, with more (shoulder) pips on display that at a Lemon Squash factory, and more crowns than at Queen Victoria's Silver Jubilee and at a busy dental technician's combined.

AV had exchanged a few words with a tall, wiry chap called Neville 'Nev' Tenspeed, the one referred to much earlier as 'Ginger', who'd been bobbing and weaving during the past few days, to find they were on the same course, that he had worked in Lloyd's bank before joining, hailed from Jersey in the Channel Islands and was mad keen on soccer.

He was twenty, leaving school with GCE O levels and seemed as bright as a button, with a spark about him that was both infectious and very compelling, and with a sense of humour, and of the ridiculous, that could leave one in stitches and awe.

It transpired he was a fellow film and television comedy buff, although his musical tastes differed somewhat from AV's, an avid Beatles fan, while he was a Clapton man. He had the hots for Suzy Quatro and Tina Turner, while AV was a Ronnie Bennett (of the Ronettes) and Three Degrees fancier but of course that had bugger-all to do with music. He also proved to have a constitution of an ox and a liver made of steel.

He mentioned in passing that it took two Jews to catch a Jerseyman in terms of business acumen and commercial skills, with AV hoping it was just a statement, not a warning, but even after almost fifty years he's still not too sure.

Conversations ceased on the arrival of the Commandant, a Chief Superintendent of twenty five years' service, a quietly spoken English fellow named Keith Churches who was retiring in a few months to join the clergy, having seen 'The Light', or who had had a conversion somewhere along the line. Funny though, he didn't look like a rugby player, although his surname certainly echoed his intended future vocation.

He welcomed them to Hong Kong and explained that the following week they'd embark on a two month Colloquial Cantonese Course and the successful conclusion of that would start them on a six month intensive course on learning to be a policeman in the Colony, incorporating plenty of law, procedure, drill, musketry, physical training and practical exercises.

There would be examinations every fortnight, with one failure resulting in an immediate retake of another paper, with two failures resulting in probable dismissal (faces fell!). He did add though that very few had ever failed consecutive papers.

He explained the concept of 'face' as far as the local populace interpreted it and that the expatriates were referred to as '*Gwailo*' or, collectively, '*Gwailos*', meaning white ghosts or devils, with no one to take offence at it as the Chinese even called the Japanese that, and to consider it a friendly, passive term though context must be considered.

'Monsieur' to the French or maybe 'bastard' to the Aussies could maybe help modify it if anyone should want to take umbrage.

At the successful end of the six months' training and passing a series of 'Finals' they would be granted their Standard 1 Police Professional qualification, with further self-study exams required to qualify them to be considered confirmed Inspectors after three years and qualify them to wear two pips.

Again, a reiteration that there had been corrupt officers in the past, but things had been rectified (My! Didn't they continually drone on about former corruption?) and then he passed them on to his designated replacement, an Irishman named Paddy Loughlin, who more or less said the same things, except that he taught them their third little snippet of Chinese (after *Heung Gong dik si* and *Gwailo*) being my '*May Gwok tai tai*' or 'my American wife,' referring to *his* American wife, whom he'd introduce to them later.

Finally, he reminded them that they were officers and gentlemen and to always keep that in mind. (*Oh dear*, thought AV, shuffling on both feet.)

Then it was the turn of the King of the Parade Square, the Chief Drill and Musketry Instructor, a Chief Inspector named Morgan Effin-Jones, a former Welsh Guards Regimental Sergeant Major known as 'Taff' to his friends.

He'd retired from his Regiment to take up the position and how he loved the power he had over hundreds of recruits who hung on his every word, actually admitting it when he dropped all pretences after a few beers with the lads, especially following a game of football with them. In fact, he sometimes dropped them so much he became downright abusive about it, maybe envying the youthfulness of most, or bored with churning out the same 'bloody sausages' time after time.

He had even wanted to take up a Divisional Chief Inspector's post but was immediately knocked back on the grounds that he'd be required to go through exactly the same training as those he claimed, when pissed, to despise.

He could be very amusing though and when courses 101 and 102 finally *did* have their Dining Out Night in December, he had one of the new, fully qualified 'one-pip *Bon Baans*' in absolute stitches. More on that later.

This day, however, he gave an outline of weapons to be used, and studied, along with drill requirements. He also advised on keeping fit in hot climes to stave off sluggishness and concluded with the wonderfully inviting phrase. 'Gentlemen, the bar is open. Please be our guests!'

Zoom!!

AV had been seated with Tenspeed throughout and slithered up to the bar to do the honours, only to be approached by a tall, fresh-faced, cheerful chappie who rubbed his hands together and said, in an obvious South African-ish accent, 'Hello chaps. I'm Bob Yates. Can I buy you lads a soda pop?'

Nev glanced at AV, who glanced back at Nev, and they both glanced at an obvious Steady Eddie with, if not pity or outrage, a 'No thanks, mate, but a beer would do very nicely!'

And you've all probably heard of the Temperance Seven, the Sharpeville Six, the Renault Five and the Guildford Four? Well, at that exact moment the San Miguel Three (the SM3) were formed, and although it took a little while for poor old Bob Yates to become a fully-fledged member, the Bucket and Tenspeed could not have asked or have wished for a more willing or apt pupil.

Even though he *was* on course 101, the 'rival' course to 102, as it were.

Admittedly, it did take a while for him to get the final seal of approval, mind you, being a little unkindly temporarily referred to as, 'The Soda Pop Kid', but he was also a fellow footballer and that was good enough for starters.

Two others who drifted in, out and around the SM3 were also 102 squad members, the first being the already mentioned Tommy 'Two Dicks' Allcock, aged twenty five and thus a bit older than the rest, who had already spent a lot of time in trying to make himself popular, although probably one of only a very few Welshmen *ever* who couldn't either play rugby or sing a note.

He had the least educational qualifications of anyone in the two squads, probably helped into the RHKP under the recommendations of his mate, Keith Franks, although it must be said he did pass the selection interviews and subsequent examinations off his own bat.

He had been in Hong Kong for a few months prior to that, having photos of himself modelling underpants (one of his part-time jobs on first arrival) and most people in squad 102 initially tended to listen to his advice on where to go, and what to do.

He took great pride in the reputation of being a Jack the Lad and a louche, but admittedly he *did* seem to know women wherever the squad went on a night out, but he wasn't the sort of bloke to get them to introduce their friends to the lads, and certainly was not beyond trying to chat up any women his new friends might later snare.

Whilst not being much of a sportsman, he did possess a motorbike and had been an ace off-road scrambler when back in the UK (so he said) again with photos carried with him to show anyone, at the drop of a hat.

He had a boyish charm, although he would vent his opinion to all and sundry if he thought he had a point to make, even when he should have realised it would have been more politic to rein himself in.

He actually managed to curb his nature and attitude many years later, when he realised that he'd never be promoted to a high level, and thus busied himself with using his government accommodation, and Masonic, police and family contacts, to engage in various entrepreneurial schemes and scams.

However, in those early days he seemed a fellow one could trust, although perhaps not at the dinner table as he was an absolute gannet where food was concerned, greedily eating leftover scraps of meat and gristle off his new mates' plates in the Mess, and when eating outside in restaurants. (He must have been making up for all that laverbread he had been force fed down in the valleys when he was younger.)

Another one who liked a drink. Or ten.

Then last, but by no means least, there was Laurence 'Lats' Latimer, a monster of a man at 6ft 5ins in old currency, aged twenty three, who was an East Anglian lad, who'd been a teacher after studying geology at the University of Sheffield. He'd been a public-school boy, a boarder at Ipswich Grammar, which was a far cry from Punjab Pete's pampered life at Wycherly College, harking somewhat back to *Tom Brown's School Days*. (Yes, Seamus O'Stropley would have fitted in very well there.)

Lats was a gentle giant, though, a real toff, and was a fine sportsman who excelled at rugby and soon proved to be a stalwart of the Police First XV, and thus spent a good deal of time away from the SM3, mixing out of PTS with his rugger friends, many of whom were senior officers.

For his size, he was a surprisingly nimble and skilled footballer, with one hell of a stamina honed by regular jogging, his fitness levels the envy of many.

It is very much to their credit that AV Bucket Bottomley *never* heard a single bad word spoken about Lats or Steady Eddie, and please believe me, dear readers, if any had been flying around, he most definitely would have gotten wind of them, having quickly developed an acute situational awareness, that rather sadly, years later, began to verge on the edges of paranoia.

Laurence was yet another, along with Steady Eddie and Two Dicks, who enjoyed his food and, with Nev, Two Dicks and the Bucket, also appreciated a beer, even though the local pale San Miguel Pilsen did take some getting used to.

But there again, where there's a will, there's a way, and there soon proved to be very many ways indeed! Especially for the weak-willed.

Yes, pissheads find each other as easily as do Freemasons and persons of genius, although for most of the group it was merely 'sowing wild oats' rather than being true devotees of Dionysus or

Bacchus (with neither incidentally having anything whatsoever to do with Dion and the Belmonts, 'Runaround Sue' or Mr. Magoo.)

But the die was cast, the scene was set, and some long-lasting friendships forged, although those relationships were sometimes strained, and could be up and down like a dock-side gobbler's head when the fleet is in town.

Then the squad instructors broke the gang up by calling for respective pupils to report to them for a quick briefing in the Mess ante rooms, with Frank Topley, aged thirty two, being a tall, slightly balding, dark-haired Chief Inspector of some twelve years' service, having previously been employed by the Met Office back in the UK.

He seemed very gung-ho, but the squad members were to find that the instructors very seldom let their hair down in front of their squads, even though neither were strict disciplinarians. His previous posting, prior to becoming 101's course instructor, was with the Anti-Corruption Unit, probably sent to PTS as corruption was finished, according to what everyone to date had claimed.

Frick Jacobs, about thirty three, also had more than ten years in the Force, mostly in uniformed branch, last as a Sub Divisional Inspector (SDI) in Kowloon, and was a slightly built, softly spoken South African who'd been a former professional jockey back in Durban, and who had also ridden in Kitwe, Zambia, a fact that immediately pricked up Bob Y's ears. He'd ridden as an amateur in Hong Kong as well. He had a quiet demeanour about him, but would take no nonsense, as AV and Nev would learn to their cost a while later.

He'd also represented Hong Kong at the 1964 Tokyo Olympics in the 880 yards race, a fact that one would not have believed when first meeting him.

For the first two months, they'd merely monitor the squads each morning, then have no more contact until the Cantonese course was almost over, unless there were personal or disciplinary problems that required them to speak to their charges.

'And with that, goodbye and enjoy the first week. The hard work will start on the following Monday. Be warned. Now back to the bar!'

But not quite so fast, because just *who* was that sturdy, balding, dark-haired Scottish bloke guffawing with obviously false laughter, standing there with his head slightly uplifted, with a grimace more than a smile on his face, who AV had spotted 'working' the room, looking around for someone more interesting or of more potential use to him than his own squad members, and who had the biggest mouth amongst all of the new intake?

He'd been the one at the seminar and on the flight to Hong Kong who'd seemed to be the most 'gobby' Scotsman amongst the whole clan.

Steady Eddie enlightened them that he was in his squad, and in the next dormitory bed (well thanks for small mercies, *not* part of 102 squad) and was Mungo McMee, an ex-Glaswegian policeman, aged about thirty, who obviously had much ambition about him, and a fervent desire, or even a need, to impress and push himself forward, presumably, at his age, having almost run out of fresh career opportunities, let alone any chance of a lifetime.

One to watch out for and to avoid, two of the SM3 agreed, who laughed their cocks off after McMee (McMee by name, *all* me by nature) had tried chatting up a late-twenties, blonde-haired, white European female who'd been standing alone at the Mess bar, not knowing she was the wife of Terry Carpenter, the Deputy Commandant of PTS, who'd been called to the office to answer a phone call.

She complained to her husband on his return, who gave Mr McMee a dressing-down and how dare he tell his wife that her husband shouldn't neglect her or leave her alone!

It didn't faze Mungo, though, who was obviously a thick-skinned individual, as he just looked for someone else of use, this time spotting a bloke with three pips on his shoulders talking to another with a crown on his and took his forced smile and blatant bullshit across to the other side of the room to try and worm his way into their good grace.

It transpired however he was a good, if ageing, rugby lock, and would occasionally team up with Lats Latimer in the RHKP First XV, but who would more or less 'run' or control the more impressionable younger lads in 101 squad, through his age, police experience and overwhelming bullshit and ego.

No wonder the courses had a completely different 'feel' to one another, as 102 squad was much more relaxed, with everyone having an equal say as to what went on.

As far as AV was concerned, McMee was an enemy for life, with the enmity reciprocated, and expressed many times during their RHKP careers, although luckily, they never had to serve with or under one another.

But to be fair, AV didn't like the 'in-your-face' Billy Connolly either. Still doesn't, in fact.

Anyway, despite that, the SM3 exchanged backgrounds, learning more about each other and it was part of their instant rapport that they could freely exchange such information, and more personal stuff, without feeling the need to be on their guard, or at all defensive.

The following day, it was a trip out by police bus escorted by Dick Snyder and Richard 'Clusterfuck' Clutterbuck, who had returned to Hong Kong, travelling out to Wong Tai Sin and the hills above East Kowloon to stop and gaze down at the masses of tower blocks within the many resettlement estates located there, and then the many widely spread wooden squatter hut villages perched on hilltops.

Over the years these wooden townships were decimated by fires, which could be seen glowing redly from Hong Kong Island, with Snyder commenting that despite how Westerners might decry how they imagined life was inside the resettlement estates, it was far better than how it was inside those flimsy shacks with hardly any protection from the elements or any utilities at all.

Then it was through the Lion Rock tunnel to the village of Shatin (these days a modern city in itself, hosting and boasting the second Jockey Club racecourse) and through the then very rural New Territories, right up to the Chinese border, where uniformed communist Chinese soldiers could be seen on patrol on the Chinese side. The return leg included a stop at Police Headquarters on Hong Kong Island for a late curry lunch on the twentieth floor, Officers' Mess, curry lunches, they subsequently learnt, being a regular feature of Mess life in 'the real world' outside of PTS, with invariably an extended meal time and, of course, washed down with copious amounts of San Miguel beer.

Next, a visit to pick up their chequebooks from the Hong Kong and Shanghai Bank in Central, with its magnificent, rounded, muralled ceiling, opposite the cricket ground, right in the heart of the city's business hub, taking in the colonial buildings of the Hong Kong Club, and the Post Office.

How the SM3 later wished they could have attended cricket matches there, or even played, but by the time they had passed out from PTS, it had been demolished and moved up to Wong Nei Chong Gap, the area now renamed Public Square, and is a favourite gathering venue on a Sunday for countless Filipina domestic helpers enjoying their day off. (And the tales a few of those poor girls told about their treatment at the hands of some expatriate and Asian families for whom they worked, and the abuse endured, would perhaps have mirrored those of some badly mistreated Luanyshan house and garden servants. People! Ye Gods!)

But what a day and what a place Hong Kong was proving to be!

The next day, though, was even better, with a voyage out on the Commissioner of Police's launch, from the Star Ferry Pier to Lantau, the biggest of the islands, on the way being told by Snyder why San Miguel beer in brown bottles is better than San Miguel beer stored in green bottles, something to do with how sunlight reacts with brown, better than green, apparently.

Anyway, there had been several crates of both chilled green and brown bottles placed on board for the journey there and back, while Bob Y started to think something was wrong, somewhere, about how he'd been drinking now for three days in a row, although a good sign was that he hadn't spewed up since their first night in Hong Kong.

A wonderful forty minute journey, taking in the sights and sounds of ships all around, and the pleasant sea vistas looking back on Hong Kong Island toward Western District, and the mainland of West Kowloon leading up to Kwai Chung and Tsun Wan.

Then being met by a police lorry at Silvermine Bay on Lantau Island and being driven to a small police-favoured restaurant at Cheung Sha, or Long Beach, for yet another curry lunch with, yes, you've guessed it, several bottles each of San Mig.

Lunch over, a continued drive to the very picturesque fishing village of Tai O on the west coast of the island, then a return voyage directly back to Aberdeen where the weary and somewhat bleary Recruit Inspectors were shown the typhoon shelter and boat people there, crammed tight together, with some people on board allegedly living there full-time and never putting to sea. It was a boiling hot day, however, and the stench was quite sickening.

Must have been the green bottled beer.

Again, a later fire decimated the local fishing vessels there, destroying a lot of the character of the place, but admittedly Aberdeen smelled a darned sight better once the masses of boats and people had been somewhat cleared.

Finally, a trip out to the magnificently ornate Jumbo and Tai Pak floating restaurants, moored between Aberdeen and the island of Aplichau, but no time for a feed this time, and only one beer each, then to the Police Marine Base where a lorry took them back to PTS.

All in all, yes, quite a week, with Bob Y progressing well in the 'beer-drinking stakes' under carefully arranged tutelage, and Bottomley so pleased that he'd not jacked it in, especially now with a few people he seemed to get on with.

It seemed that not only was Nev quite a sportsman, who appreciated a social beverington, but he liked the opposite sex as well and had *quite* a turn of phrase when talking about them, and the sex act itself.

For example, his charming expression of 'taking it up the dirt track' so confused poor Steady Eddie that, because he knew Two Dicks had a motorbike and claimed to be an off-road scrambler, on hearing such a delightful expression, he understood that Nev must be an off-road enthusiast as well.

Mind you, another wag in their burgeoning group of colleagues came out with a couple of quite unambiguous phrases, such as 'I don't mind batting on a sticky wicket!' (no Bob, *not* cricket). They rather eclipsed AV's rather jolly ditty of 'You'll wonder where the yellow went, when you brush your teeth with black cement.'

Gazumped! Bottomley would have to try harder to keep up!

While Tenspeed claimed to have a girlfriend of sorts at Lloyd's bank back in Jersey, the lovely Rita, AV and Yates reckoned he was still a randy little devil, confirmed a tad later when it was clear that, if and when the chance arose, he was 'like a rat up a pump'.

Yes, another of his expressions, as if you hadn't guessed.

Mind you, the words kettle, pot and black come to mind on that sort of activity, one must say.

But it's a great pity he had never been to Stroud, where AV could have passed Maggie on to him much more willingly than to the Perve, and then they could have compared notes.

One more but politer expression, however, was, 'I've got a mouth like a dead dingo's donger,' meaning his mouth was exceeding dry through a bit of drink-induced dehydration, old chap, such phrase immediately picked up by the others in the SM3 but shortened to 'Dead Dingo's!' so he was certainly a trendsetter in that regard.

But it was approaching time for the Commandant's Parade on Saturday morning after which they'd be free until their first PT lesson at 06.30 hours on Monday. Which meant of course they could go out by themselves on Saturday night and explore 'The Wanch' alone, without being directed here, there and everywhere by the senior squad.

Bugger it! With new mates in tow, why wait until the evening? Let's go out in the afternoon! Which was exactly what they did!

However, you'll find they couldn't and didn't even wait until Saturday afternoon, but sneaked out on Friday afternoon first, merely shopping, of course.

So don't miss the next exciting episode in this series, where more squad members are met, the lads explore Wong Chuk Hang, get roped into a soccer match and go shopping.

You'll regret it if you do!

Chapter Seven

Finding Their Feet

Well no more day trips out, unfortunately, just back to the routine of watching the morning parade on the Friday, followed by a visit from the contracted PTS tailor, whose helpers would measure everyone for two full summer and two full winter uniforms (the ones they'd wear when assigned to Divisions, depending on relevant seasons and postings of course), along with Mess Kits, essential for formal Mess functions such as 'Dining In' and 'Dining Out' of squads, one of which was due to be held two weeks hence, with the new intake being the ones 'Dining In'.

Obviously, the uniforms were free, but the lads had to pay for the Mess Kits, which seemed a bit unfair, especially as they had little knowledge of what 'Dining In' actually was, and what it entailed. They needn't have worried, though, as it was nothing other than a good old piss-up and fancy food followed by speeches, then Mess games, or so the defrocked Bill Robinson succinctly advised.

Twenty three expats plus four local chaps being measured took quite some time, and what with becoming acquainted and arranging 'terms' with the room boys who'd launder and iron their civvy clothes, uniforms and bedding, and polish their boots, gaiters and Sam Browne's, the morning was soon enough over. So, time for grub.

However, the Mess seemed to be busier than usual, the reason being that all the other squads had been taking their fortnightly exams that morning, and there was nothing else required of them that day other than to wait for the results to be posted, the papers marked by the same RHKP Training Officers who had also set the questions.

There was definitely a strange atmosphere around the place, apprehension mixed with expectation, and thus the bar area was busier that lunchtime than AV and Bob Y had hitherto seen it.

Rather than waiting until the place quietened down, it was somehow suggested that the SM3 of Steady Eddie, Nev Tenspeed and Bucket Bottomley, along with Tommy Two Dicks and Lats Latimer take a stroll into the adjacent Wong Chuk Hang Estate and see what they could forage, with to date only Steady Eddie having ventured there.

So off they went, but just as they exited the rear guardhouse, there was a deflated plastic football lying to one side and without any apparent second thought, or a break in his stride, Nev flicked it up with his left foot and chipped it into a rubbish skip with his right, about twenty feet away, and carried on as if it was just a normal occurrence.

Not only that, but there was a playing card face down on the ground, and quick as a flash he pronounced, 'Eight of Diamonds,' which - knock me down with a feather - it was.

AV and Steady Eddie just nodded at each other, both realising here was a special chap indeed, but never thought to boost his ego by commenting.

Anyway, the sights, sounds and smells were just as fascinating to the four who hadn't been there previously as they had been and still were to Bob Y, and they had a good old poke around the market, and yes, Recruit Inspector Yates bought more groundnuts and mangoes, while AV purchased a plastic football.

They thought about buying some beer, cold meats, salad and bread from the small supermarket and having an al fresco picnic at one of the grassy sitting-out areas, but eventually decided to try the restaurant instead, on the way there having a butchers at the barber's shop which seemed a darned sight better proposition in future than submitting themselves to the butchery of the PTS hacker.

The eatery was a smallish place, and surprisingly so, bearing in mind the size of the estate, with about twenty booth-type tables, but just not enough room to accommodate five people at one of them, until an extra chair was shoved on the end.

The waiter came across and gave them menus, but everything was in Chinese. Never mind, first things first, and Two Dicks had been in Hong Kong long enough to know how to order beer and thus five large San Migs were demanded, ('ng ji daai San Lik bei jau, m'goi,' in case you are interested) and they arrived very promptly, being opened even more quickly. Well, it had been hot, thirsty work, walking around that market.

But how to order food, as the waiter, then his boss, spoke no English. However, the fellow knew enough to suggest fried rice. Yes, Manuel, we'll have a big plate of that. And chicken? No, he couldn't understand chicken, even though they shouted louder and louder, thinking it must be an auditory problem rather than the language barrier.

However, Steady Eddie was a problem solver, if nothing else, and began flapping his arms as if they were wings, while someone else started clucking, and another walked his two fingers on the tabletop. They couldn't have done any more apart from either producing a few feathers or laying an egg.

But obviously charades isn't a popular party game up in Wong Chuk Hang, and the lads were on the point of giving up, as pretending you're a chicken was thirsty work, until - *yes!* - a glint of understanding and jubilation came into the owner's eyes, and he smacked the menus shut in triumph and off he happily toddled.

In the meanwhile, as there were several racks of glistening roast pork hanging in the display window, an order was made for two of them by pointing, and the waiter busied himself with slicing them onto a large plate, so there were the lads, looking forward to a meal, the beer giving them quite an appetite.

Then the boss came through the swing doors from the kitchen, smiling his head off, carrying a large plate on which was an obvious mound of steaming food, and then the question that has worried philosophers and scientists through the ages - when is a chicken not a chicken? - was answered:

When it's a plateful of steamed ducks' webbed feet, with oyster sauce on top!

There was a pregnant silence and then they all had a good old laugh about it, hoping the boss hadn't spotted their initial shock and disappointment.

Mind you, Two Dicks was delighted; he'd eat any damned thing, and he had a whole plate of duck webs to himself with everyone chipping in to pay for it.

Never mind, garçon; they were on a Cantonese course from Monday and just you wait a week or two. They'll be back!

But the fried rice and roast pork were spot on, as were the five more ice-cold long necks to follow.

AV had been left to ponder, though, having eaten at half a dozen local places to date, why he hadn't yet found a *proper* Chinese restaurant, one with red flock wallpaper like they all have back in England, even at the Oi Kwan in Stroud?

But he'd actually now fulfilled one of his ambitions in going out there, in that he was becoming pretty nifty with a pair of chopsticks; the other, though, looked like it would be a long time in coming, as he hadn't yet spotted even one single suitable banister.

And he realised that he'd been eating Chinese food the wrong way back home for years, having previously maybe ordered chow mein, chicken and cashew nuts, beef with black bean sauce and fried rice, and had dumped them all out onto the same plate, mixed them up, and then spooned it up as it came, wondering how in hell the Chinese could possibly have such disgusting eating habits.

The way of course was to eat a little from each dish with rice or noodles as a separate accompaniment.

Hell, he'd better write home to Gina and his sisters. Fast!

And also tell them that you don't have to have ten pints inside you to eat Chinese food, and that it's perfectly acceptable to eat it outside of Friday and Saturday nights.

Boy, aren't they in for a shock!

So it was back to PTS to find that everyone from each course had passed their respective exams, though it would have been surprising had anyone failed.

The throng had thinned out, many going to their rooms to grab some sleep, a few remaining to have a quiet beer, some just sitting inside, contemplating their standing within their group, as someone always has to be first, and someone has to be last, obviously.

Friday was not usually a heavy drinking day or evening, as the Commandant's Parade on a Saturday was quite a big deal, with Passing Out Parades held on that day as well, and no one could afford to make a fool of themselves on those occasions, needing to have their full wits about them. However, there were always exceptions, of course.

Some of the new intake were lolling about outside the Mess, on Alan wicker chairs and settees, and passed a few friendly comments seeing the return of the gang from Wong Chuk Hang, with some shaking of hands and fresh acquaintances made.

One such was a squat, light ginger/sandy-haired, slightly pock-mark-faced, fair-skinned, twenty eight year old Scot named Norman

'Norrie' Pinkney, very aptly so because even mild exposure to the sun turned his face pink.

Mind you, so did the drink.

Whilst having a gruff, growling Highland accent, he was actually extremely good humoured, was a former Bermudan and Aberdonian copper and was so laid-back he was almost the antithesis of Mungo McMee, often stopping Mungo's bullshit with a cutting phrase or quip, his obviously having gone around the block a few times being even respected by him.

Not a sportsman, but even so AV thought it a pity he was not in 102 squad, but in 101 along with Steady Eddie.

Another new friend was twenty three year old David Kensington, from Richmond, another ex-National Westminster bank clerk, but one who was extremely well spoken, cultured and mannered, almost effete, who wore a smoking jacket and slippers in the dorm, while sucking thoughtfully on a pipe. He was a slightly built chap with not much muscle tone to him, and it seemed a good puff of wind would blow him over.

However, he had brought with him the largest array of different kinds of contraceptives, of all shapes, sizes and colours, that any of the lads had ever seen, which of course immediately shot him way up the totem pole of respect in many quarters, especially in the eyes of Tommy 'Two Dicks' Allcock.

The two of them, with others looking on, one afternoon had a teacher-pupil session on types of condom, flavours, how some dissolved, which best suited the woman and which best suited the man, then rambled on about sexual prowess and technique.

No one though thought to ask Dave how in the world he planned to use his supply out there, when they'd just arrived and didn't know even one potential 'playmate'.

Nev had been watching this, as had AV, but after listening to the sex instruction lesson, (and back then Tenspeed was oh so intolerant of bullshit and pretension), he burst out with, 'Load of bollocks! All you do is put it in, waggle it around, and come yer cocoa!' then off he stormed.

That's my boy!

AV had thought exactly the same thing, but in the Gloucestershire-speak of, 'Wop it in, wop it out, wipe it!'

Steady Eddie just supped on his glass of San Mig and looked on. After all, he *was* out there to learn, although how he wished AV or Nev had still been around to explain to him what Two Dicks and Kensington had been on about when discussing, 'the little man in the boat' and 'yodelling in the valley'.

Was it something to do with canoeing in Switzerland, for some obscure reason?

Yes, Two Dicks had found a kindred spirit, and Dave a disciple.

And then there was a real Walter Mitty character in the shape of a well-built, bronzed, rather pompous twenty three year old Scot (there were actually eight Scots out of twenty three expats) named Iain Douglas Bullingham, who was prone to rush into things and make statements and claims, without first engaging his brain.

He was ostensibly a fish farmer, but supposedly, before that, had done everything that an action man, ex-commando type could possibly do, such as - so his new mates deduced - climbing the North Face of the Eiger, supervising the Irish navvies who had dug the Mariana Trench, and single-handedly sailing the seven seas, non-stop, in a Glasgow City Corporation Sports and Leisure Services rowing boat!

Despite that, he was quite a kind and generous bloke, who wouldn't knowingly do anyone any harm and mixed well with the rest of the lads in 102 squad.

Two Dicks played around with the initials of his Christian names, Iain Douglas, being I and D, rhyming it with the Cantonese for 'quicker' or 'faster' being 'Faai Dee', and thus forever he was known to the squad, and later, wherever he went in police circles, as 'Faai Dee (or Faidi) Aidi'.

So with the PTS relatively quiet, the PCs and WPCs also having taken exams that morning, not fancying boozing or lying around aimlessly on their beds, and with AV having bought a plastic football, someone amongst the group suggested a kick-around on the tarmacked soccer pitch, which to that date they'd never seen used.

Was it allowed? Well, yes it was, but not for the rank and file unless supervised, but officers and gentlemen were a different kettle of fish as they knew how to conduct themselves and behave responsibly. Ha!

It was 14.30 hours and it was agreed that anyone fancying it should make their way across behind the drill square for 15.00 hours, giving the newly named Wong Chuk Hang Five (WCH5), and those who'd been in and outside the Mess, a little time to digest their food and drink.

It was reckoned they'd best be attired in correct PTS sports gear too, which was bare-topped, with only white shorts and plimsols. Yes plimsols, or daps to you, with none of those fancy running shoes that came into vogue about ten years later.

And so it came to pass that ten of the new boys turned up; the WCH5 and Dogs Dinner, Faai Dee Aidi, Sadler Wells, Plod and Punjab Pete.

Bearing in mind the hard surface and hot weather, no one wanted to exert themselves too much, so they formed a circle and passed the ball to and fro, and then took it in turns being 'piggy in the middle' to try and intercept those passes, then throwing the ball at one another, playing 'Catch'.

All very basic stuff, but one by one a few senior squad members drifted across, then more, led by a balding Phillip Johns from Doncaster, who, although not too tall, was a muscular little sod, and who proved himself to be a very competent right back, but a bad drunk, always bursting into tears when even half pissed, and a gannet to almost equal Two Dicks in respect of food.

Then the Chief Drill and Musketry Instructor, Morgan Effin-Jones, strode manfully across with the Deputy Commandant, Terry Carpenter in tow. Whoops! Now for a bollocking!

But no! 'Do you mind if we join in, gentlemen? How about a game then, lads!'

And so, before they even knew it, they were involved in a fiercely competitive match, the ten new lads against the rest, with a few other assorted bods later arriving and just fitting into whatever team seemed to have the least men at the time.

The rank and file saw this going on as they finished drill practice on the square, and quickly formed an audience, with over a hundred or so cheering or jeering, in turns, probably desperate to see the CDMI get floored, and enormously amused to see expatriate officers kicking the crap out of each other.

The new blokes were more than a little hampered, what with everyone being bare-chested, and in hardly knowing who was who, let alone who was on which side, but the ginger-haired Nev, and the giant Lats, were targets they could *not* miss.

Tenspeed proved to be as good as they thought he'd be. Yates could seemingly eat up the ground and chase anyone down; Lats proved a revelation, feeding off Nev's corner kicks to power in two bullet headers, while AV confirmed himself a nutter in goal by throwing himself along the concrete and tarmac without a thought for his own safety (or anyone else's, actually).

Mind you, the difference between the sides was not the good players, but how good or adequate the roped-in occasional and the usual non-players were, and theirs were better than the new intake's, but at least Plod, Punjab Pete, Sadler Wells and Tommy Allcock had given it a go, which is more than Mungo McMee managed. He'd hurried down to see if anything was going on that he thought he should be part of, from which he could make gain or push himself to the fore.

He didn't even have the balls to step onto the pitch to at least take up space at the back so people would have to run round him, thus helping to relieve the ceaseless mid-field efforts of Steady Eddie.

He did however shout plenty of sarcastic and pointed comments from the side-line, about it not being a man's game, and how he'd bring a rugby team to play them if they'd like.

A stare and a word from Terry Carpenter, whose wife he'd earlier pestered, soon saw him drift back to his lair.

There were some crunching tackles and revenge scythings, and things could easily have gotten out of hand if the two senior officers hadn't been present and giving as good as they got. Nevertheless, it had been quite enjoyable and honour and respect had been earned and given by all.

Some early positive points had been made, obviously.

The result? Who knew? If they'd have had a willing, committed goalie instead of changing around every five minutes, the opposition would have won easily, but every time twinkle-toed Nev got a shot on target, he seemed to score.

The game came to a premature end when someone hoofed the ball out of play into a large fenced-off drainage and flood overspill nullah about twenty yards beyond the pitch, and no bastard was going to wade into *that* slime and shite to retrieve it, not even Bottomley, whose ball it was.

It was the start of regular Friday afternoon games, looked forward to by everyone involved, and word spread so much that Nev quite often had selection problems over what was the best team to put out, depending on the strength of the opposition, which varied week to week.

(The status of each game could actually be judged by whether it had a referee or not, or whether it would be yet another increasingly heated slanging match about fouls, over the line, in or out, numbers of players on each side, and so on, and so forth.)

Back to the dorm, and then sluicing off the sweat and tending to cuts, scrapes and bruises from the tarmac, such things not thought about at the time, with AV particularly scraped about the hips and elbows.

So it goes.

Anyway, what to do next?

So, as a general discussion took place, it struck them that *this* was the only Friday when they wouldn't have to worry about being either on parade or having to attend lessons the following day. Further, they needed to buy some bedside lamps so as to be able to study at night, and needed exercise books and pens, pencils and the such for the following week.

Two Dicks then told them that the China Products store in Causeway Bay, the area next along from Wanchai, would be best for those items.

Would they be open? Of course they would!

Could we go now then? Of course they could!

Should we have just a 'few' bevvies, while out, as our final opportunity?

You're tootin' right we should!

And so the Wong Chuk Hang Five, along with Spicer, Dogs Dinner and yet another fellow from 101 squad, a Richard Short (yes, another Dick, who was to become a good buddy of Laurence 'Lats' Latimer) boarded taxis, agreeing they'd meet outside the Hilton Hotel in Central, just along and up from the Hong Kong and Shanghai Bank, the taxis likely to be separated as the traffic was horrendous at rush hour, especially on a Friday.

When gathered outside the Hilton, it was subsequently decided to try a couple of sophisticated beers inside the hotel's lounge bar (ostensibly to steel themselves against the dangers of crossing the busy road) in what was thought to be happy hour, and so they entered the hushed, and plushed luxury of its décor and ambience, where a pianist was tinkling out nondescript tunes of the day.

They ordered eight bottled Heinekens, ogling the beautifully uniformed Chinese waitresses in the semi-tonal darkness, and rabbited on about the football and whatnot, until the beers came, nibbling on the salted peanuts and wondering how and where they could possibly meet or even date such beautiful women.

A second round of drinks arrived, and with shopping still to be done, these were quickly quaffed with about half an hour having been spent inside the obviously well-appointed and classy hostelry.

Having called for the bill, the lads had their wallets out, ready to divvy up, until it actually arrived and was handed to them by the most stunning girl one could have imagined, when they incredulously realised that it came to over 90 Hong Kong dollars each.

90 Hong Kong dollars! (At a set conversion rate of 7.80 HK dollars to the US dollar.)

Now 90 dollars was a lot of dosh back in 1975, when their salary was about 2,400 Hong Kong dollars a month, so sod the ambience, the piano player, the beautiful girls, and the salted peanuts, and a foutra to the Hong Kong Hilton too!

Fair enough, caveat emptor and all that, and so what if it hadn't been happy hour as they had thought, or if the bill included tax and service charge, that's still one hell of a lot!

Well, what with the export-strength beer taking effect, and some quite strong characters in the group, there was a considerable amount of chat on what to do next, but AV and Bob Yates were taken aback, and obviously *must* have missed something, as the other six blokes stood up and walked out of the bar, into the lobby and into the streets.

Gone! Skipped! Offski! Made off without payment!

'*Surely not!*' thought both Steady Eddie and the Bucket, as they sat amongst the empty Heineken bottles, though not worrying too much as they had enough money between them to settle the tab and could presumably reclaim it from the skippers at PTS, but just as they were sorting through their as yet unfamiliar currency, so returned their colleagues, looking it must be said extremely sheepish.

Lats, like the gent he was, and is, apologised while Two Dicks and Nev started to berate them for not showing solidarity, although of course they were only joking, and in any case, they were told to belt up by the others, just in case they weren't.

Never mind; it was a lesson learnt, as, let's face it, it was not as if they were rugby club pissheads playing away in a town they wouldn't come to again for another two years, was it? No, they were bright young men on the cusp of careers in a town where any serious fuck-up could see their futures take a drastic reversal.

So, the bill was paid, with a generous tip given just in case the staff had twigged what had happened, and away they went, with a hey nonny no, and not a care in the world.

They managed to cross the road without being run over, via a pedestrian bridge over the main thoroughfare, turning left and into the Jockey Pub on the first floor of some skyscraper or other, where a Tony Carpio Trio were doing a good job of banging out some pleasing and familiar pop songs.

Tony was a very accomplished guitarist, and the brother of a famous Filipina songstress called Teresa Carpio, who was extremely popular in Hong Kong, back then. They were from a musical family and on Sunday afternoons he performed modern jazz in the Excelsior Hotel's basement bar, opposite the Hong Kong Yacht Club and Noon Day Gun.

That genre of music was not to either AV's or Bob Y's taste, but the half-priced beer all Sunday afternoon more than made up for it, such venue being discovered after they'd been in Hong Kong several months and were getting to know their way around quite nicely.

The Jockey Pub was a pleasant enough place, although a bit of a plastic replica of a British tavern, mainly frequented by expat businessmen from the literally hundreds of offices and companies in Central District, and busiest at lunchtimes and early evenings.

It became the regular starting place for the SM3 on Saturday nights, a place to prime the livers for the flash flood they would have to endure later, once they were down 'The Wanch'. Mind you, they didn't go there quite so often after AV was set upon in the toilet one night, three months later, and had to have three stitches in his chin as a consequence.

Never mind; we all need a slap now and again, and with his cockiness and sardonic sense of humour coming to the fore when under the influence, he probably deserved it.

And what were three more stitches to the ones he already had?

Anyway, Two Dicks then insisted they pop across to the Bull and Bear pub, adjacent to the cricket ground, and as they walked the 200 yards to where it was, they could hear the noise emanating from it, well before they reached it.

As they pushed through the sturdy doors, they could see the place was heaving, with mainly dark-suited expats, noisily engaged in the Friday night swill, with people three deep at the several bar counters pushing their way forward to try and get served.

It was the drinking hole not only of business people, but of government and private lawyers, policemen, soldiers, ICAC operatives from their nearby headquarters, plus the occasional, desperate tourist. Again, it was modelled on an English pub, but the atmosphere was not at all relaxed and AV thought it would be an ideal place to take the piss out of pampered expat executives, although it could probably lead to 'handbags at ten paces'.

The manageress was a late-middle-aged, fearsome, gargantuan, behemoth English harpy called Hortense, assisted by her equally corpulent and ill-tempered husband Cyril, and AV imagined her running a Blackpool boarding house or a wing at Holloway Prison with the same rod of iron as she used at the Bull and Bear.

No personal contact at all with the customers, unless they misbehaved, just employing a succession of busty European and Antipodean girls who were staying in Hong Kong for a while on the Far East experience 'bit' and primed to smile, show their tits and pull the pints.

AV had a run-in with her over her refusal to give a statement some years later, when a British Army soldier broke a top lawyer's leg in the main bar, in a furious and sustained attack, right before her fat-enfolded eyes. Another story, for another day, obviously.

Oh no, not a place for any of the SM3, thank you very much, the sort of place they'd left the UK to get away from, not go running back to in order to pretend they were back there, if you get the drift, even though they did sell English beer.

But by now time was pressing, and it was becoming obvious that the shopping would be soon forgotten if they didn't make a move, and so they reluctantly jumped into taxis and sped off down Hennessy Road (along which the trams ran, remember?) to Causeway Bay, a main shopping area, with cinemas, nightclubs, many restaurants and some major department stores, it being an extremely busy place at night.

Now China Products store did exactly what it said on the tin, in that it marketed goods manufactured in mainland China, and was state-owned and operated. Hence, drab grey two-piece uniformed store assistants, no smiles and no customer service to talk of.

It was the flagship for cheap, practical and long-lasting, woven woollen and cotton clothes and bedding, plus silk jackets, nightgowns, kimonos and the such, as well as communist propaganda books and postcards. It offered all manner of general household items and consumables, along with, it must be said, some wonderfully crafted pottery, paintings, carvings, screens, camphorwood chests and sets of rosewood furniture.

But even on a Friday night, at what was a peak shopping period elsewhere, the place was hardly busy, so the lads had a good old browse, and as well as each buying a bedside lamp, they bought some 1940s-looking tailored shorts, which were extremely hardy, although, along with the shirts and towels some also bought, stank of mothballs, as, incidentally, did the sales assistants and cashier.

They'd also stocked up with loads of blank exercise books and writing equipment, anticipating having to scribble loads of notes in the coming months. Boy! How right they were.

But how times have changed, for the China Products chain are now luxury stores, the drab Chairman Mao uniforms of the staff long gone, with a complete makeover modernising the business ethic and marketing strategy out of all recognition.

There were no qualms at all about subsidising the communist regime across the border by purchasing their products, and in any case such an attitude would have been hypocritical as they had tried, and had enjoyed, a few bottles of China's Tsingtao beer, the brewery being another state-owned entity.

It was then 21.00 hours and make-your-mind-up time; back straightaway to PTS, go down 'The Wanch' for a quick one (but they all knew where *that* would lead), or find a place to eat and have a beer before heading back?

For once, common sense ruled, as it was the third option that won out, the deciding factor being that they'd look pretty damned stupid flopping and staggering around the bars, carrying electric table lamps, with shorts, shirts and towels in plastic bags, and all of them stinking of mothballs, and they'd probably end up losing or dropping the lot somewhere along the line. No 'probably' about it, in truth.

And how fortunate they were in finding, one street down and across from China Products, a small eatery called Ming's Café, surprisingly not busy for that time of night, with an English menu, Chinese and European dishes available, reasonable prices and a staff member who spoke excellent English. Oh joy!

Again, tables in booths were the order of the day, so they plonked themselves in two of them, their shopping in an empty third, got the beers sorted, and pored over the menu, AV ordering the egg curry, a dish he always thereafter ate at Ming's which became one of his favourite places to call.

Bob Yates ordered up a rice dish (and why not, as he fully

agreed with the Lemon Piper's song that 'Rice is Nice'), Lats a steak and Tenspeed a chicken cutlet, the other table similarly sorting themselves out, although Two Dicks surprisingly just ordered a salad, the thirty or so ducks' webbed feet he'd consumed at lunchtime, somewhat repeating on him, and the football had left him a bit quackered!

Anyway, he was probably banking on polishing off what the others left, if he was running true to form.

So then it was taxis straight back to the Police Training School, the '*Ging Chat Hok Tong*' (please try and remember that one; you'll be asked later) and the dorm, where their bedside lamps, clothes and stationery were much admired and asked about, prompting one or two of the revellers to query themselves as to why they hadn't bought a few more of each item to sell to the others at twice the price.

After all, it's no sin to make a profit, is it?

And on that note, it was off to bed for the lot of them, the weekend promising adventures new, but with the Phil spectre of having to buckle down and work their little cotton socks off as from Monday, with the Colloquial Cantonese Course beckoning, looming, threatening.

Catch you all later…

Chapter Eight

Stepping Out but Hardly Up

Well, come Saturday morning at 06.30 hours, my oh my, weren't there more than a few aches and pains from the previous day's football, and an uncomfortable night having been spent in trying not to let the scrapes and grazes stick to the bedsheets.

There was even some talk about visiting the PTS doctor who was due to arrive at 08.00 hours, but the thought was in some minds that if he or she turned out to be to the medical profession what the school barber obviously was to hairdressing, it would probably be best to give it a miss and just apply iodine and plasters themselves.

Then all assembled to watch their first Saturday or Commandant's Parade on the drill square and this proved to be a notch above the morning parades, both in requirement, and certainly in length.

The PC and WPC squads under training and the Recruit Inspectors, without the obvious participation of courses 101 and 102, marched into positions accompanied by the full RHKP band, bagpipes and all, but, while awaiting the delayed arrival of the Commandant, under the hot sun, several of all ranks collapsed.

And there they lay - no medical team, or even First Aiders on hand to rush on to take care of them - until there was a suitable pause in the proceedings, for either someone to break ranks and carry them off, or instructors, viewing from the top embankment, summoned a room boy or two to drag them away so as not to ruin the symmetry of what was taking place on the 'dancefloor'. In fact, those stricken would not have expected otherwise; yes, it was certainly a more stoical time, when men were men, and sheep were wary.

But blimey! Note taken! Moderate yourselves on Friday nights, chaps! Indeed, several of the new boys were already feeling a trifle 'Heady Lamarr', with mouths like the proverbial 'Dead Dingo's Donger' from their final sluice at Ming's Café, and obviously the cruelly clement weather.

The band was in fine form, dishing out Dawn's 'Tie A Yellow Ribbon Round the Old Oak Tree', and Sousa's 'The Liberty Bell' (probably better known to you as the theme to *Monty Python's Flying Circus*') while the inspection was taking place, and drums beating time to the set drill moves, and the march past the dais itself.

The boys were impressed but couldn't make out what one local Superintendent was playing at while inspecting a full squad of WPCs. He was slowly walking up and down the two rows of them, moving their shoulders, changing their feet positions and all but groping them. They hadn't seen him before and he certainly wasn't at the Meet and Greet afternoon, but it transpired this squat, bespectacled fortyish fellow was the Deputy Commandant, whom Terry Carpenter had been relieving while he was on leave, although it appeared this David Man, as he was named, was close to relieving himself that morning and he wanted no help from anyone else either, the way he was going about it.

Apparently, he was well known for his penchant in rearranging the uniforms and stances of the WPCs, and for sitting in his Mercedes

Benz, watching squads of them pass by, seemingly transfixed by thirty female bottoms swinging side-to-side in unison, encased in either green uniform trousers or white cotton shorts, after both formal and informal inspections, sometimes visiting their quarters unannounced, just to keep them on their toes, you understand.

He was nicknamed, (and pay attention as it's yet more vocabulary for you to learn) as Ham Sap Man, '*ham sap*' meaning full of salt, so he was being called, basically, a dirty old man.

Well, it was more of a Half-Cut Barracks than Deep-Cut Barracks, but, even so, many of the WPCs must have been distressed by this, fearing for their futures if they complained.

When AV was the PTS Duty Officer some months later, such post explained in a subsequent section, he naively thought that Mr Man's vehicle had broken down near the main gate where it had stopped, and went across to see if he could assist, most annoyed to receive a bollocking as it transpired that the Deputy Commandant had merely stopped his car to view the passing WPC squad in his rear-view mirror.

Manners cost nothing, you know, even if he may or may not have had his dick out, although back then AV would not even have thought to check! However, more on Ham Sap Man in due course, and how he got his partial comeuppance.

It's a great pity that the morning PT and the drill weren't set to a strident-hollering-out of military-type cadences, as portrayed in films about the US marines training on 'The Island', or Fort Bragg, or wherever.

You know, the instructor calls out a verse and the recruit marines shout it back as they run to its rhythm.

AV could have produced some wonderful ones, such as:

'Hide now ladies, while you can,
Here comes 'Ham Sap' David Man.'
Or:

'Oh Drill Sergeant I must spew,
Cos last night I sank a few!'

Yes, quite the little charmer, was AV. I sometimes wonder whatever *did* happen to him?

Maybe he should have written to the USMC. Or maybe the YMCA; they are extremely liberal these days, apparently.

Now despite most at PTS being under instruction, there was very little, if any, contact between the Recruit rank and file and the Recruit Inspectors, except on one bush camp (more later) and, when proficient enough, drilling the junior ranks' squads. Obviously, there must have been interaction between PCs and WPCs, the latter quite shapeless in their normal day-to-day gear of white PT shirts, shorts and daps, and baggy marching gear when the occasion arose.

In all probability, everyone would have been too busy to fraternise anyway, with the amount of study required and the competitiveness of examinations. And the Chinese concept of 'face', desperate to do well for themselves and their family.

But when the WPCs left to go home on Saturday afternoons, or returned on Sunday evenings, in their normal civvy clothes, most revealed themselves as very beautiful young women indeed, some, as Yates commented, 'Like little song birds!'

AV agreed, but never forgot that even the most beautiful song birds can crap on you from a great height.

Tenspeed, however, was a little more direct in his comments, with a 'Where the hell can we meet them when they are off duty'? He never did get an answer, though.

Anyway, the parade was over after about an hour and a half and basically that was it for the day, although the officers mainly headed back to their quarters to shower and get out of those sticky uniforms. Standing all that time with swagger sticks under their left armpit seemed damned hard work and it was perhaps lucky that they were no longer to be issued or carried, although they would, some imagined, be handy little weapons in case of any annoyances, to make a point or to end an argument with.

Long batons or truncheons were only ordinarily issued to the rank and file as standard.

Never mind, swizzle sticks were far more practical, bearing in mind the obvious, often rampant, drinking culture within the officer corps. More later, but just a taster for now.

In a later setting, ICAC operatives went to one Divisional Police Station at 07.00 hours one morning to arrest one of 'Faai Dee Aidi' Bullingham's former police Constables for alleged corruption offences, but he wasn't due on shift for another hour. The ICAC staff were told by a uniformed Sergeant to wait in the Station's Officers' Mess, but where, unfortunately, the Divisional Superintendent was enjoying his bacon and eggs, with three pints of draft San Mig beside him on the table, his normal daily heart starter.

Boy! Didn't the Superintendent or '*Ging Si*' bollock the poor young Sergeant who'd caused him so much embarrassment when a gang of people unexpectedly burst through the Mess door, ruining his digestion and causing him to damned near spit out a mouthful of ale and eggs, which he invariably consumed alone!

And not only that, but another bollocking for allowing ICAC personnel to have access to the Officers' Mess when the leader of the party only had the equivalent rank of police Sergeant, not even of Detective Sergeant, and thus no right to Officers' Mess facilities whatsoever.

Another Divisional Superintendent, Harry Silverman, who for some reason was called 'Hymie' instead of Harry, but only behind his back, was in the habit of trying to drive home late at night when well pissed, but as he couldn't always manage to focus enough to put the key in the ignition, he sometimes slumped under the steering wheel and would sleep the whole night like that.

Unfortunately, his car was parked in the area of the station where the duty Sub Unit paraded before hitting the streets, and the sight of Hymie crawling out of his car on all fours, and the Station Sergeant calling his squad to attention on seeing who it was, was terribly embarrassing for all concerned.

Another time, some headquarter units were using Divisional CID squads where Hymie was in charge to execute a series of search warrants, the briefing being given in the DDI's (Divisional Detective Inspector's) office where Hymie was fast asleep in a chair in the corner, having had a hard day, obviously.

The squads reassembled some three hours later to report on results and to be debriefed, and there was Hymie, still fast asleep, and 'sawing off logs', snoring fit to burst.

But what with the raised voices after the excitement of the raids, the kerfuffle woke him up, and he somewhat came to his senses and, slowly realising where he was, Hymie asked, 'What time are we off then, lads?'

It was rather sad, and in no way endearing or praiseworthy, to find that on leaving Silverman's office, he had a life-sized coloured poster of the TV '*Sweeney*'s' Jack Regan, revolver drawn, in the crouched 'Stop or I'll fire!' position, stuck on the back of the door. What the hell? Where were the ones of *'Dixon of Dock Green'* under the blue lamp, or *'Kojak'* sucking on a lollipop?

Never mind; it must have impressed someone, as Hymie was awarded a Colonial Police Medal sometime later.

Coincidentally, four ex-UK coppers, who joined Hymie's Division after passing out of PTS around 1978, and despite being in one of the most dynamic, vibrant, colourful and crime-varied cities in the world, would all rush out of the Mess to cram into the TV Room to religiously watch *The Sweeney*, with Hymie sitting alongside them. They'd learn!

And it was quickly found that not all ex-UK coppers could forget UK Regional Police Force rivalries, resentments and jealousies, with a Wanchai Divisional Detective Inspector having to intervene to prevent a chap called Jones, from a Welsh Force, and a John Walsh from the Merseyside Force, coming to blows over the merits or otherwise of their former Constabularies.

And, finally for now, yet other Divisional Superintendent used to gather his flock around him after office hours and stand behind the Mess bar with a bucket next to him so he could pee in it without missing a drink, a bit of scandal or a rumour. He still managed to occasionally pee himself, though.

Now it's time to introduce a few more people within the squad back at PTS, some more noteworthy than others.

One on the parade square, the right marker, taller even than Lats Latimer, and from whom the sizing commenced and around whom the squad would form, was an ex-private soldier named Nigel Bland, hailing from Basingstoke, who indeed was so nondescript and humourless that he certainly lived up to his surname.

But while taller than Lats, he was in no way bigger as a person, and it was pointedly observed that he could seldom read without simultaneously moving his lips.

He seemed to be in a little world of his own, hardly mixing at all except with the self-sufficient Plod (Maurice Smiley), with neither apparently too interested in sports, or in the often madcap 'nocturnal prowlings' of their squad mates. Maybe he was struggling with the study regime, adjusting to PTS, or whatever, but who is to say he was wrong in living in his own head and maybe, perhaps, he had a very rich and fulfilling inner life?

Let's hope so for his sake.

From some of Bottomley's later experiences, a few people can be quite content in toddling along like that.

Secondly, there was an ex-Kirkaldy bobby, aged twenty eight, named Billy 'Whizzer' Nairn, a married man who brought his wife Morag out with him along with their ten year old son, and thus lived outside PTS in the Lee Gardens Hotel in Causeway Bay, not too far from Ming's Café.

He would apply for and be given married accommodation, a large flat within a private development, in due course.

Unfortunately, he was not at all sociable, and wanted to head-butt anyone at the drop of a whisky, having a mass of simian-like bodily hair, if indeed it wasn't fur. No one apart from his wife wanted to get near enough to find out which.

He claimed to have played football for the Scottish police and once was thus persuaded by Nev to stay behind after lessons one Friday to show his talent against what was probably the best team they faced while at the Training School, Phillip Johns picking from squads above him, and staff, to try and make a point. Tenspeed was stuck with the usual suspects, with one or two ringers joining as the game progressed, admittedly.

Whizzer certainly showed what skills he had, all right!

Losing by a single goal, and everyone in Tenspeed's team playing their little China Products socks off, he found himself in possession on the six yard box directly in front of the goal, clear, with plenty of time, but he somehow contrived to slice the ball and put it out of play a foot from the opposition's corner flag for a throw in! Mind you, the rest of his inept performance indicated that he was something of a legend, soccer wise, only in his own mind and that something like that *was* on the cards.

He wasn't asked to play again, particularly as he shopped some of his own squad over alleged cheating on the firing range. More later.

And then there was another Scot, Callum 'Sunny Boy' Colgate, aged twenty four, and a very nice chap. An ex-casino worker who was great in class, both for Cantonese language and the law studies, as he'd be the first to put his hand up and volunteer an answer.

Dullards and lazy bastards need a bloke like Callum in their midst to keep the attention off themselves. Well done that man!

He was nicknamed 'Sunny Boy' because he loved the sun, and would be invariably found, 'catching the rays' at every opportunity he could find.

Then there was Paul 'Clicker' Cannon, yet another ex-Nat West banker (yes, there must have been a job lot of bank clerks on offer to the RHKP), though he'd been brought up in Singapore, and was a quiet, polite and softly spoken sophisticate, who was thought a bit 'suss' to begin with as he casually walked around the dorm in a flower-patterned sarong, insisting it *was* a sarong and *not* a bloody dress!

Somewhere along the line, when younger, he'd become an expert shot with a revolver and was asked by the CDMI, Morgan Effin-Jones of course, if he wanted to join the PTS shooting team? One drawback with him, though. He didn't often drink. Yes, he was a dead-eyed dick with a revolver, while the San Miguel Three were often dicks with dead eyes.

There *is* a difference, you know.

Anyway, after lunch, with Lats heading off for a try-out with the Police First XV rugby team, and Two Dicks visiting one of his girlfriends in hospital, it was decided that the SM3, with Dogs Dinner, Clicker Cannon and Dave Kensington, would take a taxi ride up to the Peak Tower, starting a little deception at worst and a tradition at best.

You'll remember that taxis were only licensed to take five passengers, so when the taxis arrived someone would distract the driver whilst AV, the smallest but not of course the thinnest, would dive onto the floor in the back, while three others would take the rear seat, disguising him with their legs. Two would occupy the front seat next to the driver and away they sped. A perfectly reasonable procedure one would have thought to avoid paying for two taxis.

Two things often thwarted this arrangement, though; one was the driver being annoyed if he spotted the ruse, and secondly was the occasional good kicking AV would get from the three passengers almost sitting on top of him, but always in fun, or so they claimed.

It was quite fortunate though that dogs roaming the streets of Hong Kong were usually quite rare and thus at least there was an absence of dog poo from people's shoes that he had to contend with.

Unfortunately, it took quite a good while to get to the Peak early that Saturday afternoon and by the time they arrived, poor old Bottomley's bones and football grazes were playing up a bit, which evinced not one hint of sympathy from the others, as, after all, a saved cab fare was a saved cab fare.

But the view from the top of the Peak, up around the hill to the left of the Peak Tower that the normal or usual tourists don't know about, was wonderful, way up there, enjoying the tremendous panorama stretching to the North and South of Hong Kong Island, way across to encompass the outlying islands and West and East Kowloon, way past Kai Tak International Airport where they had landed just seven days before.

Seven days! It seemed like seven weeks.

They took a walk around the pathway atop of the Peak, to get views of Aberdeen and Brick Hill over the South China Sea, then doubled back to where they had started, with Clicker Cannon, who'd bought some expensive camera equipment during the week, and whose nick-name was 'Clicker' because of his fondness for photography, setting up a tripod on the slope to get some time-lapse pictures with his brand-new Olympus camera.

Yates and Nev made their way to a mobile, motorcycled ice cream vendor, and bought some Nutty Nibbles, being ice cream cones, and some beers (they always carry some beer deep down in the ice boxes, just in case!) and passed them around, AV petulantly not paying in view of the taxi kicking.

But something went wrong, a gust of wind or something, as Clicker's tripod tipped over, thus smashing the side of the camera lens, denting it badly. Naturally, that put a damper on the afternoon, as some photography had been planned in the Central District and near the Star Ferry Terminal with a suggested trip across the Victoria Harbour to Tsimshatsui (Chimsy) for the first time.

Paul, in a foul mood about the damaged lens, sarcastically suggested they go and help drown his sorrows in the Hilton Hotel, probably to try and get a rise out of his companions, obviously having heard about the previous 'skipping' incident, but none of them reacted, understanding his frustration.

The Hilton Hotel, however, was definitely out of bounds as far as they were concerned, anyway, as once bitten twice shy, or as the Chinese say, once you see a ghost you become scared of the dark, or '*Gin Gwoh Gwai, Pa Haak*!' (Don't worry; that's a hard one, as the actress said to the bishop.)

But it was a bit early for the Tony Carpio Trio, and the Bull and Bear was definitely out, so how about the China Fleet Club, where they heard they could relax in almost private club-like surroundings, at reasonable prices too?

And that started another tradition - gin and tonics at the China Fleet Club - amongst both the Wong Chuk Hang Five and the SM3, with them often becoming confused over which group they were currently part of. Even Nigel Bland was part of the WCH5 for a couple of hours very early on, until he went all deep and serious on them and never snapped out of it the whole eight months at PTS. None of them saw him again after that, disappearing into the depths of a Kowloon Police Station, presumably.

(Some of the more caring souls *did* wonder whether Bland ever recovered from being wound-up so much by Piggard at the PTS arrival induction, so as to admit he'd sleep with a man if ordered to, but the subject was never openly broached.)

So they caught the Peak Tram, the funicular tram-cum-rail system providing transport up the Peak, to and from Central, and what fun that was with tremendous views on the way down, leaning back on reclining seats to combat the slope.

AV was dreading another taxi ride, and hence they walked along Hennessy Road, found their way to Police Head Quarters and almost opposite was the China Fleet Club (CFC), having been established in the early 1900s by the Royal Navy to provide a place for their matelots to go to for cheap food and drink, unmolested by the general hustle and bustle outside, and down 'The Wanch', just a short swagger and stagger away.

The location had been changed a few times over the years, with the one there in 1975 being relocated later in 1982. Its upstairs lounge actually *did* have the air of a 1950s colonial club, with waiter service, large ceiling fans and where bad behaviour was frowned upon.

The riff-raff, or the ratings, used the bottom bar and discotheque, very rarely venturing into the inner sanctum, as it were, and the clientele seemed to respect their surrounding and themselves.

It was as much a famous venue for members of the police, army and navy, both visitors and personnel posted to Hong Kong, as the Mariner's Club in Tsimshatsui (Chimsy) was to merchant seamen, or the Red Lips Bar, again just across the water, was to everyone. More later.

Nev had wanted to get to 'the Wanch's' action itself, of course, but it was far too early at 16.30 hours on a Saturday for much to ordinarily be open. Paul wanted to get back to PTS to sort out the receipt for his camera so he could go to the shop the following day and have them contact an authorised repair agent, and so off the worried chap went, with Dogs and Dave Kensington seeming set fair for the duration with the SM3, although Dave was a little later shocked on how long that would prove to be.

It was now about 18.30 hours, with probably eight gin and tonics inside each of them, maybe slightly fewer in Dave, as they walked out of the CFC and along Lockhart Road to surprisingly find it was actually 'heaving', because two US Navy ships were in port, as well as an Australian vessel paying a visit, and one British Army Battalion was in the process of taking over from another.

The United States military still, at that time, used Hong Kong as one of its favourite locations for Rest and Recreation, the Vietnam War coming to a close that very next week with the fall of Saigon.

British army MPs were patrolling the streets, bolstered by the US Navy's own Shore Patrol contingent.

What a difference a week makes because they hadn't been there the previous week!

In fact, they might very well have been, but the new arrivals had been too 'jet lagged' to actually realise what was going on around them.

So, as they staggered up the street, pondering on just which bar to choose, two drably dressed old women, both at least sixty years old, slinked up to the now new Wong Chuk Hang Five and asked if they'd like a young girl?

One crone they came to know as May Ling and the other as Ah Cheung, and they were Hong Kong's equivalent of Liverpool's Maggie May, but had the lads singly, or all together, chosen to follow these ladies up some staircase to a dingy apartment, they'd have had the shock of their lives to find that the 'young girls' were actually the old harridans who'd been touting themselves as such.

Dream on, crazy momma!

To some people, though, it wouldn't have made a bit of difference, but they'd probably have been robbed of their cash as their trousers were down, pockets being rifled by experienced hands, while the blokes were in the paroxysm of delight, delusion and delirium.

There were many such side lane whores and 'short-time' gobblers plying their trade that night, though the scruffy, straggly-haired May Ling and Ah Cheung were the most regular common sights on the bar area's street corners, and in the Wanchai Police Station and then Causeway Bay Magistracy for Soliciting for Immoral Purposes.

Who said love is a many splendoured thing? But, there again, what exactly had love to do with such sordid, base and demeaning transactions? Nothing whatsoever, is the simple answer.

There were sly, cunning pick-pockets preying on the drunken revellers too, those parasites of the festal (celebratory) hour, and in fact Yates and Two Dicks later once had a task in pretending they were drunk (pretending?) trying to entice a pickpocket or two to try and 'dip' them, an operation set up by Keith Franks, one of the chaps who'd met them at the airport, who was working in CID/Wanchai.

As they were laughing at the openness and cheek of the two old harlots, they were standing outside of Bob's Oriental Tailors, with Bob himself framed in the open doorway, who introduced himself and called them in for a beer. Why not? The premises had air conditioning and they could sort out their next moves.

Bob in fact was an experienced and wily entrepreneur, and after the first beer, he ordered up five bowls of roast pork and duck, with thin noodle soup (*'Char siu, siu awe, lai fan'*) for the lads, from the large street restaurant, or '*Die Pie Dong*' the next side street up, a dish he'd been eating as he spotted them, and very tasty it had looked too.

He commented unflatteringly on their China Products shirts and shorts, and then out came his various bolts of cloth for shirts, trousers and suits, and even leather samples for shoes, and yes, with Bob now their mate, why not order a few shirts and a trouser or two?

To which they agreed, as it seemed a good idea at the time, so Bob like a flash whipped out his tape measure and away he went about his business, the whole collective order secured with a deposit of less than ten quid.

But hell, why not, as they'd surely quaffed more than ten quid's worth of booze inside his shop already, and a load more had just been pulled out of the fridge.

Luckily, he provided a receipt and an order number, though, or they may very well have forgotten all about it the next day.

He had access to HMS Tamar, the base of the British armed forces in Hong Kong, and to Stanley Barracks where the incumbent battalions were located, and was also both well-known and well-patronised by many United States military personnel, and to the US Naval vessels.

He was a nice chap and even if they didn't always buy something, he'd invariably spring for a beer or two for the lads.

There were in fact tailors like that spread far and wide, all over the place, especially in Chimsy, where another favourite of the lads was an Indian bloke called, strangely enough, Sam the Tailor, famous all over, and whose obituary many years later, was in both *The Times* and the *Telegraph*. He was another one who'd load the beer on board, and sometimes bear the cost of a good few bevvies as a loss leader, often paying for a meal out too, in what of course was a cut-throat business, with a fast turnover needed, especially for tourists who were there and gone in a few days.

So yes, how they liked their 'regulars'.

Bottomley and Dinner in fact took their summer and winter uniforms, and Mess Kits, which had been measured at PTS by obviously half-blind lackeys who liked taking the mickey, to be re-tailored by Oriental Bob, and he did a splendid job too.

On leaving Bob's, the first bar they tried, the Washington, had some MPs standing outside it, and they were informed that it was out of bounds to military personnel.

'Well, it isn't to us then!' was the immediate rejoinder, but when the curtain was drawn back to let the lads enter, they found no one at all inside except for a very miserable old Chinese chappie behind the counter. They never found or asked the reason for it being Out of Bounds, but what a good idea for a shake down when the strip was heaving. 'Give us a thousand dollars or we'll shut you down!'

Still, they couldn't imagine that sort of thing went on. This wasn't Chicago in the twenties, after all.

So it was to be the Side Door Bar first for a beer but which was jam-packed with people, and hence then to the Back Door Bar, which was in a basement, run by a Chinese fellow called Georgie

Luk who somehow sussed they were police (well, of sorts) and then found them a table.

The local Chinese house band were the Wynners, a well-known group at the time, who did a great rendition of 'Soldier of Fortune' by Deep Purple, and played mainly rock covers, a few years before the local music scene changed to Canto Pop, original songs in Chinese to cater for modern, local youngsters.

A group of white and obviously British soldiers were seated at the next table, and while the biggest of them moved off to the toilet, his apparent wife, a portly, busty 'round-eye', was approached by a very large black American sailor, in his very smart whites, who said something to her and she accompanied him to the dance floor.

Back came the squaddie who slumped down, obviously noticing his wife was missing, and then incredulously spotted her gyrating to Van McCoy's 'Do the Hustle' with her new friend. So up the irate hubby stood, announcing to his mates, 'I ain't having my wife dance with a n****r' and then strode across and... chinned her, sending her back across the table from whence she'd came, but much quicker than when she'd left it.

And then it kicked off, but Georgie Luk was no fool, as he'd called in the Shore Patrol at the first sign of trouble.

(They were different times in 1975, and to mention the N word in such a context today would rightly result in absolute total mayhem.)

Georgie though wasn't too smart some four years later when he obviously wasn't either paying someone off, or not paying enough, as two snakes were released onto the dancefloor, when it was packed, causing a mass, panicked exodus and a very large number of unpaid tabs.

And so the lads changed bars with some haste and ended up in Popeye's, where they happily met up with the unfrocked vicar, Bill Robinson, with another bloke from his PTS course named Denny 'Mad Dog' Browning, who was a big fellow, but one in whom drink set off a fury he hardly ever exhibited when sober, and after which he became a real bloody handful, particularly dangerous as he had some martial arts skills.

Bill, though, in those days, could handle him. About the only one who could, although they had a mighty falling out a few years later, never talking again thereafter.

So it goes.

The SM3 also met a very nice English gentleman in there, an immaculately suited Eddie Edwards, an English teacher, in his mid-fifties, shortish, with a gruff but hail-fellow-well-met demeanour, and he was around the bars for many years after, AV visiting him in hospital just before his death. A fine Old China Hand.

The music on the hi-fi system wasn't great, though, mainly disco stuff such as 'Kung Fu Fighting' by Carl Douglas, 'Shame, Shame, Shame' by Shirley and Co, 'That's the Way (I Like It)' by K C and the Sunshine Band, 'Lady Bump' by Penny McLean, and the ubiquitous 'Do the Hustle' by Van McCoy.

Popeye's was known as a policeman's bar, where the manager, another George, would cash cheques, pass on messages to police friends and even give loans.

He had a dozen or so girls working for him, and all were tremendously busy selling cups of tea as ladies' drinks at extortionate prices to the British and American squaddies, plus to the many wild colonial boys who were weaving their ways in and out of the bars looking for the next thrill. Any thrill.

Then suddenly a huge fracas developed, with punches thrown, and nine or ten people were suddenly rolling on the floor in a heap, like a collapsed scrum, a tangle of arms and legs with no one able to give a blow. A Shore Patrol job of course and George had sent the word out they were needed, but suddenly a bold knight on a white charger galloped across, intent on sorting it out most chivalrously in the form of… Dave Kensington, his blue PTS identity card raised above his head like a Knights Templar's cross!

How it happened or where exactly he'd been sitting before it happened, who the hell knew?

But what was poor Dave thinking of, his brain obviously stirred into judicial hero mode by an overindulgence of gin and tonic, and San Mig beer.

'Stop it, you chaps! Stop it! I'm a policeman!' he politely intonated, in what was a shout to him, but not heard by the would-be combatants, in the manner of Mr Barrowclough, the mild-mannered prison warder as played by Brian Wilde in *'Porridge'*, or the dithering Sergeant Wilson as acted by John Le Mesurier in *'Dad's Army.'*

The Shore Patrol came in immediately thereafter, and the pressed rats and warthogs within that squashed group were untangled and dragged off, presumably to the brig. Another lesson learnt, with the others congratulating Dave on his noble actions, although deep down thanking baby Jesus that it hadn't been a knife fight or something worse.

So, it was offski from there into the San Francisco Bar, the 'San Fran', where, despite what you cynics might think about love at first sight, (as earlier spoken about in relation to Pigswill and the Perve), the Bucket, Nev and Steady Eddie witnessed it that night when Dogs Dinner, well-pissed, admittedly, clapped eyes on a girl named Lilly and was immediately and totally smitten. (Dave would have seen it too, had he not been feeling so 'poorly' after his previous exertions.)

Yes, Lilly, and he was chasing her for the rest of his time at PTS. Again, more later.

A couple more beers, then time to have a mooch about, some climbing up stairs to massage parlours, which were merely fronts for brothels, where many blokes were queuing, and then in one place with some chaps each inside what appeared to be a cross between an industrial washing machine and an iron lung, just their heads showing, and steam venting out of an exhaust pipe. A sort of portable massage machine-cum-steam bath apparently.

Only Nev and the Bucket wanted to have a *qui vive* at as much as they possibly could, with Dogs going back to the 'San Fran' to stare with unrequited love at Lilly, while some great big Aussie was trying to strike a deal with her for the night.

Dave had had enough and was desperate to finish the evening, while Bob Y bought a can of San Mig from one of the many brightly lit open fruit stalls-cum-grocery shops and leant against some railings and watched the world go by in all its sordid pageantry, in total amazement, with 'Sir Galahad' propped up alongside him.

Meanwhile, Tenspeed and AV hit yet another staircase to an actual brothel where hard-faced doxies, fresh from douching, probably, dully and woodenly asked if they wanted 'a short time', i.e., a quick shag. Mind you, they'd have to join the queue, and the best time estimate was two hours hence.

A bit like queuing at a theme park, or being given a ticket and number at the cheese counter in Tesco! (Queue four hours, to reach the Towers! On your knees, it's time for cheese!)

No bloody thank you, madam!

'Would they like some tattoos?' some tout asked as they went up yet another alley, then disturbing some bloke and a woman having a knee trembler against the wall in the dim light.

'No need to salute, son. As you were!' And if that didn't confuse him, it may at least have put him off the vinegar strokes.

Back into the street, where - guess what? - sparsely haired May Ling sidled across and asked if they'd like a young girl. Well, she still didn't look any better than when they'd seen her earlier that evening, so the answer remained the same, but more vociferously so. And as she sloped off to try her luck somewhere else, they spied Ah Cheung leading a tall, young, fresh-faced expat soldier off along the opposite side of the road and then disappear down a side lane.

Best of luck, mate; you *are* in for a shock!

And so, for the second week in a row, it was decided that it was best to explore 'The Wanch' when it wasn't quite so busy and when completely sober, initially, anyway. Hence the WCH5 reassembled and pondered on all that had transpired. But at least they'd met a few characters and been to a couple of places where they knew they'd be welcome, even though the girls, (apart from May Ling and Ah Cheung) hadn't had any time at all to pay them attention.

And so it was time to call it a day, and head back for a good night's kip at… where? Yes, *'Ging Chat Hok Tong'*. I told you I'd ask! It's also known as *'Ging Chat Hok How'*, if that is easier for you to remember.

And heading back there was exactly what the Wong Chuk Hang Five did, having had quite a fine time of it all.

Dogs Dinner though had wanted to stay alone and continue his courtship of Lilly, but common sense prevailed and he saw the wisdom in not remaining out by himself.

So, let's see how things stand when they awake the next day, and what they made of their first night out alone in 'The Wanch', for it wasn't only Steady Eddie's innocence and incredulity that had been tested. Certainly not.

Good night, all!

Chapter Nine

Up and Running

Well, on Sunday they certainly had Monday on their minds, and it was collectively thought advisable to have a quiet, alcohol-free day and just hang loose, as much as they could in a shared accommodation environment.

Several senior squads were away on a three day camping exercise, while others were on attachment at various police formations, to gain experience of exactly what policing was like outside of PTS, and perhaps give them some idea of where they would like to be posted.

And so it came to pass that the new blokes pretty much had the Officers' Mess and outside tables and lounge area to themselves, and indeed most of PTS as the recruit rank and file were on weekly leave, of course.

It was time to check out and prepare their PTS day-to-day uniforms, which would consist of boots, gaiters, shorts, blanco belt, and cap with badge, wearing no shirts but with a blue flash on black-backed plastic wristbands, to signify that they were the lowest of the low amongst the Recruit Inspector squads.

As they progressed throughout their course, the flash would be changed to grey, then yellow and finally to white, when they'd be top dogs, kings of the dung heap, and rulers of the roost. Thus, at a glance, the whole school could easily identify what stage they were at.

The room boys had whitened their belts, pressed their shorts and polished their boots and gaiters, and had attached metal studs to the soles so as to make a satisfying click when on the drill square, but otherwise more difficult to walk around in, not that they could do much walking as they had to march everywhere within the school precincts, even if alone.

But one thing became blatantly obvious! Instead of going on the piss, or playing football, or Bunburying off to Wong Chuk Hang, or wherever, they should have spent some time walking around in their new boots to try and break them in.

My oh my, there *would* be a few blistered feet and toes in the next fortnight, you mark my words!

Too late now.

Now that the squads more or less knew each other, despite some difficulty when on a crowded football pitch when they were all bare-chested, some cliques had already formed, and the posers had not been able to conceal themselves, while the unofficial pecking order would find its own level in due course.

It's fair to say that Nev and Bottomley, who were bumping along together quite well, found the openness, friendliness and apparent lack of any guile in Steady Eddie, obviously the product of a wonderfully free upbringing in Africa, refreshing, (a mangenue amongst the parvenu) and knew from the start that he would 'walk the walk' without bothering to talk much about it beforehand, while it was quite equally evident that a few others had already been tagged as blowhards or 'choccos' who would melt, or put blame for their faults or mistakes on others, and prove to be jealous, gossiping backstabbers.

Lats was obviously a man you could metaphorically bet your house on, while Two Dicks, despite all his bluster, which some said would probably embolden him to try and talk away a sunburn, seemed someone worth having as a buddy.

The SM3 and the proper WCH5, then, seemed to be a well-matched 'team'.

But yes, in truth, the twenty three expats and eight locals seemed a fair cross section of people in general, but with San Miguel beer being the lowest common denominator that enabled some of them to even nod at one another.

So, after the uniforms were readied, many squad members made their way to the Alan wicker chairs and sofas outside the Mess, generally chatting away about the past week and finding out how they had all variously fared when roaming around by themselves.

Some had gone to Kowloon for a night out, so 'Wanch' stories were swapped with 'Chimsy' stories, and it was very clear that no one had even come remotely close to finding the fabled 'hooker with a heart of gold'. (Mind you, it was a good few years before Sean Fitzpatrick even started playing for the All Blacks and even then, he could be a mean, antagonistic, provocative bastard when the mood took him.)

No, all they'd encountered in the bars were just gaggles of mean-faced and hard-hearted scrubbers (probably more surly than normal because of the large number of drunken foreign visitors in town) and not a single (or married) potential Suzy Wong, as portrayed by Nancy Kwan in that 1960 film, amongst them.

Most certainly, there was a disappointing absence of any ladies who could be considered as potential 'Mrs Rights', but even if they had come across any, it is doubtful if they would have recognised those women as such, and, in any case, they'd probably be married to their 'Mr Rights' already.

In fact, they hadn't even encountered any who could have been merely a 'Miss Right Now!' apart from May Ling and Ah Cheung, and they of course were totally out of the question.

Mind you, it had to be admitted that none of 101 or 102 squad members even came close to being a William Holden, Nancy Kwan's co-star, though that good old boy in real life was infamous for drunken binges with his Hollywood buddies. Good on yer, mate!

Never mind! Better luck next time! Maybe! (Or *'Wak jeh'*, as the locals would have it.)

It became clearer that Norrie Pinkney, even though in 101, was a hell of a nice bloke, and told them he'd gone into Aberdeen with a couple of the others trying to find some 'Sampan girls', who were allegedly young ladies offering their individual services from small, covered boats which were normally used to ferry people to and from larger vessels, or to and from shore, when not otherwise converted into, let's face it, floating brothels.

Poor Inspector Pinkney! He found he was about fifteen years too late, as they had long ceased operating, and the closest he would ever get to seeing one would be in the 1955 film '*Soldier of Fortune*,' starring Clark 'Frankly I don't give a damn' Gable, as that soldier, and Michael Rennie as a RHKP one-pipper. (Remember that pips were worn on shoulder epaulettes to distinguish the various Inspectorate ranks, one pip for a Probationary Inspector, post PTS, rising to three pips as worn by uniformed Chief Inspectors.)

All that damned camera equipment he'd brought with him from Scotland, too! Not that anyone actually believed his story that he went out taking photos on his first night 'solo' in Hong Kong, but no one dared to challenge him on it.

Incidentally, if anyone is interested, '*Soldier of Fortune*' has some wonderful views of a comparatively barren and uncluttered Hong Kong, before it became so very urbanised, and densely populated.

Norrie was much amused by Dave Kensington's righteous if ill-advised attempt to break up the previous evening's fracas in

Popeye's, but bollocked the SM3 for not stopping him, which in fact they would have tried to do had he not metamorphised from 'King of the Condoms' to 'King Cop' quite so unexpectedly and so quickly.

Point taken, though, even if begrudgingly. 'Look after each other when out!' was certainly a motto well worth keeping in mind.

Nev, Yates and the Bucket had been surprised to find deposit receipts from Bob's Oriental Tailors in their pockets amongst the crumpled banknotes and snotty hankies, and it would be amusing to go back at the weekend and see just exactly what the apparent shirts and trousers they'd ordered actually looked like? Still, it did guarantee a few free beers at Bob's.

Lats Latimer was well pleased with himself as his place in the RHKP rugby team had been secured and he'd remain a stalwart there for many years, even later in 1975 going back to the UK with them on an official tour. Yates also had a couple of games with the police rugby team later in his time at PTS.

Consequently, Lats was happy to '*cheng*' (which meant he'd invite them to, and pay for) a lunch down in Aberdeen, so it was bollocks to the increasingly sarcastic banter and ironic invective amongst the chaps, particularly with the arrival of 'Mouthy' McMee and some of the senior people who'd remained, and thus the WCH5 bid their farewells and exited the rear gate into the estate, and took a cream coloured, fourteen seater Public Light Bus, commonly called a PLB, into *'Heung Gong Jai'*, which means Little Hong Kong, which was Aberdeen.

Paul Cannon was invited but was taking his broken lens to 'Palysound' in Chimsy from where he'd bought it, and where they very kindly took it back and gave him a new one for about twenty quid extra, which was a good deal. The shop would send it for repair themselves. They would be rewarded with the custom of AV, Nev, Yates and Co. in a week or so.

Dogs declined, too, as he was going back to the San Fran later that afternoon to hopefully see Lilly, if she had escaped from that

Antipodean she'd last been sat with when Nev and AV had dragged him through the bar's curtain, back into the street, and 'home'.

Dave Kensington just wanted to remain alone in his smoking jacket and slippers, puffing on his pipe, counting his contraceptives, and getting over a hangover, having a severe case of the 'Never Agains!'

But what a fine lunch they had in Aberdeen, although they'd had to stand over a table of diners until enough space had been cleared for them to be seated, such was the crush on Sundays and as was the custom. They consumed a large variety of dim sum, just pointing at what they fancied from trolleys pushed around the restaurant by old ladies, and even though some of the small dishes weren't to their fancy, such as steamed chickens' feet in aniseed sauce (a change from ducks' webbed feet!) and tripe, there was always Two Dicks to polish them off.

They were amazed that seated Chinese customers were allowed to write on the large white tablecloths, as many seemed to be doing, although it wasn't a proper restaurant according to Bottomley as it didn't have red flocked wallpaper. However, he was now slowly cottoning on to the fact that what counted as a Chinese restaurant in Blighty, may *not* perhaps be kosher after all. The food most certainly wasn't, and the fare provided at the Oi Kwan in Stroud was a pale imitation of real Chinese food, with so many different regional varieties yet to be sampled and voraciously enjoyed.

Only a couple of bottles of beer each, too, and they resisted the temptation to hop on a bus from Aberdeen and head off to Central via the Western Road, not cutting through Wong Nei Chong Gap, but another very picturesque route albeit the traffic could be horrendous at times. But where in Hong Kong wasn't the traffic horrendous, to be truthful?

The reason why so many people seemed to be writing on tablecloths was evident a bit later when, on leaving the restaurant, they saw crowds of people crammed in and around a Hong Kong

Jockey Club betting office. It was horse racing day at the Happy Valley Racecourse, and some diners had been working on their picks.

Nev fancied himself as a bit of a punter, and fortunately for him the six race card of runners and riders was bilingually posted in the betting office window, plus there was a pretty girl in a smart uniform at the inside reception desk to help. Thus it was that he had a 'win or place' bet, a quinella, a double quinella, a multiple and a six up, different ticks in different boxes for each, run through a betting terminal, and 120 Hong Kong dollars please, the girl then pushing through the crowds and passing across the cards to the cashier and it was all so very simple. He'd find out the results on the morrow.

A quick walk around the town, some groceries bought, then back to PTS, and much self-restraint shown in no more beer until the following day.

A late afternoon, very gentle kick-around with a ball bought by Yates, a salad in the Mess, a chin-wag and early to bed, only for AV to be jolted awake from his slumbers at about 22.00 hours by a rather incomprehensible Martin Dinner tripping over his kit and falling on the floor while trying to slump onto his adjacent bed. He was giggling to himself, so it was presumed he'd had a successful sojourn in town. No harm done. Good night! Now shut up!

Plod also shot awake on hearing the kerfuffle Dogs was making, probably fearful that he'd be getting an earful of piddle, the same as Dogs had tried to do just a few days earlier, if you remember.

Up at six. The programme for the day? PT, Cantonese, drill, lunch, Cantonese, drill, but not necessarily in that order.

And so, by 06.30 hours, with a combined 101 and 102 squad drill formation not yet organised, they had moseyed down to the gymnasium, a little along from their dorm, all dressed in their white PT gear, where they were met by a small, but well-muscled Chinese Sergeant named Bill Wong, about mid-twenties, who proved to be a very nice fellow, with no one ever disrespecting him or giving him any lip.

He called them to attention, made a roll call, put them into a line, and with another Sergeant assisting, began putting the squad through an indoor circuit of exercises, consisting of push-ups, pull-ups, sit-ups, some damned near throw-ups, vaults, rolls, touchy toes and who knows what! And he was marking down success or otherwise on his clipboard too.

Now it was obvious that some of the lads were struggling, and AV had had a few jibes thrown at him about his physique, which a little belied his dexterity and actual residual fitness, so he had decided to give it his all as a 'Fuck You!' and to lay down a marker, particularly as two who'd thrown taunts, Nairn (what??) and Plod (even more what???), were making a right pig's ear of their circuits.

'You've got to work harder than the others, son,' were, if you remember, some of the last words his mother had spoken to him at London Heathrow.

But after he'd shimmied up a rope and touched the ceiling, and then went at it hell-for-leather in running twenty yards and back to see how many he could manage in two minutes, a growling Scottish voice rumbled behind him, and a Highland hand was clasped on his right shoulder as Norman Pinkney let out a, 'For fuck's sake son! Calm doon! They'll test us again before we leave and we'll be expected to do better than what we do today.'

Oh Christ! Wise words from an old hand at this! And AV hadn't remembered how he'd antagonised the big kids at Whiteshill Primary School when he'd solved that simple long division problem that they couldn't.

And so it was back down into second gear, but perchance a trifle late? Never mind; we'll see.

Anyway, that was the first PT session over with, but some points had been made and scored, with Mungo McMee loudly letting it be known, to no one in particular, that just because some of them could shimmy up the ropes whilst he couldn't, or do more pull-ups, or vault when he couldn't, it didn't mean that they were stronger than him, it was just a case of body-weight ratios.

Norrie caught AV's eye and gave a raised look up at the ceiling and a wry, conspiratorial smile, which Bottomley certainly caught the meaning of.

Tenspeed and Steady Eddie had sailed through it, Lats was fine with most of it, bearing in mind his size, and Two Dicks would improve drastically by December.

However, poor old Dave Kensington had struggled badly on almost every exercise, while Dogs Dinner should have considered it a major achievement to have completed it without fainting or puking, what with two heavy sessions just behind him.

When questioned about his afternoon out alone, he proudly informed them that he'd taken Lilly out from the bar, treated her to a meal at one of the many '*Die Pie Dongs*', or open-cooked food stalls (remember?) then into Popeye's, which was almost next door, until she had to report back for work at seven.

He'd met two policemen in Popeye's, one a Senior Inspector called Jack Claymore, who seemed a good fellow, and another much stranger bloke who was an Englishman, but with a German father, whom they called the Kaiser. They both lived at Western Police Station Officers' Mess, apparently, and he'd been invited by Der Kaiser to attend a small party, or rather a wake, at their place on the evening of the 30th April, to mark Hitler's death, complete with bratwurst, sauerkraut and German beer, with Nazi marching tunes he'd play from a cassette tape.

He'd been mainly with Claymore, as 'Kaiser' Wolfgang Sheitzer, to give him his full name, had to go and get ready for duty somewhere, then the two of them sloped across to the San Fran for a couple of hours to keep an eye on Lilly.

Obviously, none of his new classmates would allow Dogs to attend that party, as surely there was 'something' not quite right in a policeman in HK with such blatantly fascist leanings, even if merely historical and even if Martin had been sorely tempted.

But the following day, with squad formation in place, and for many subsequent days thereafter, it was a jog down and back the maybe two miles to Deep Water Bay, sometimes incorporating a swim out to the end of the roped-off, designated swimming area, with the only saving grace being that Nigel Bland was the right marker, the pace set by him on Bill Wong's prompting, and not the super-fit Lats Latimer, who'd have had most of them dropping out on the way there, never mind on the return slog.

Occasionally, there'd alternatively be gym circuits or basketball instead, but the fallback was invariably the trot to Deep Water Bay. It could have been worse, though; there was always the thought of a Brick Hill run or even attacking the assault course to quell even a hint of dissent.

To be fair to Sgt Wong, he never really over-extended anyone, and everyone on those squads, allied with the drill training, became much fitter after two months under his watchful eye, and the majority of them actually came to enjoy those PT sessions.

(As an aside, the squad were under Bill Wong's control again between say 23rd December and 1st January 1976 as, whilst the squad members who'd lasted the course had passed their final examinations by then, it was not felt in their best interests for them to be sent to police formations when, basically, no one would have much time for them over the festive period, and thus different programmes, additional training and diversions were laid on, including PT. And yes, they still had to run down in squad formation to Deep Water Bay, but this time with a few slight differences; it usually was at mid-morning, and they stayed at the beach for a couple of hours with no supervision by Sergeant Bill, and most plonked themselves at the beachside café and got quietly 'merry' - well it was Christmas - with a gentle jog back, only interrupted by a couple of comfort stops to allow some of the lads to pee in the bushes.)

So whilst the rest of the Recruit Inspectors busied themselves with the Monday morning parade, squads 101 and 102, after a shower and a hearty breakfast as befits the condemned, donned their PTS uniforms in anger for the first time and hap-hazardly marched to Room 25 within classroom block C, which was kitted out with chairs and desks as per any training establishment, anywhere in the world, for the start of their Cantonese course.

Nev incidentally had a 'pig on', as he'd eagerly checked the *South China Morning Post* newspaper that had been delivered to the Mess to find that none of his bets had been successful, and he also had the equally self-deceptive 'Never Agains!' as Mr Kensington.

(There were actually several expatriate police officers who got themselves into heavy debt over illegal betting on the horses, two of whom lost their jobs over it.)

A Doctor Hugh Baker addressed them on the Colloquial Cantonese Course ahead in such an ebullient manner that even the most cynical and pessimistic of them began to think that they could manage the basic complexities of the Cantonese dialect, with the good doctor telling them it was a wonderful language for anyone who loved to pun, as the same apparent word, but in up to six tones, could have very different meanings.

He introduced them to the government language teachers who would be with the squads for the whole two months, finally stating that he was an outside consultant who would be conducting their examinations in due course and wished them the best of luck and '*joi geen*', or goodbye.

The instructors were: a Mr Lau, who seemed to be the head man, a squat, black-hair-dyed, middle-aged, humourless chap who was a stickler in trying to obtain the right tone for the right word but often from the wrong pupil.

A David Lam, in his thirties and a real keenie, who couldn't believe that most of the course couldn't identify the English-language subject, verb, object or the conditional or imperative, for example, in what they were saying, or in what English grammatical construction he wrote on the blackboard. In fact, this was probably a red herring just to show how damned clever he was, and thus everyone should do what he said because he knew more than them in both languages.

A Mr Pooi ('Poo-ee') a nice, gentle, bespectacled old chap who looked as if he'd just stepped out of the Shaolin temple on the set of the then-popular *'Kung Fu'* television series, having each week poured out words of ancient wisdom on the trainee monk, Kane, played by David Carradine.

He became an instant 'hit' with 102 squad when, after trying to get one of them to pronounce a word, which he tried, but obviously in the wrong tone, he sat back and with a huge grin said, 'Ah! *That* means "fuck"!' Loud bursts of laughter all round, including from Mr Pooi. A hero had been born.

Right, grasshoppers! Back to the Cantonese for 'hotel' (*'jau deem'*, by the way).

Then there was Joyce Cheung, a plump, bespectacled girl with acne and prominent teeth, but a jolly soul, who was determined to get everyone through the examination at all costs, but a bit manic, up and down like a rapist's bum.

Next was Hatti Wildskirts, a lovely woman, married, but not for much longer, to allegedly one of the RHKP's top European detectives, with a truly bubbling personality and a lovely giggling way about her, with a real command of colloquial English.

And finally, a real beauty, a Mrs Chaumbrier, married to an Italian, who again could speak very colloquially, beyond the often staccato English of those many Chinese people who had been taught English by other Chinese people who'd also been taught by other Chinese, etc., etc.

And so, then the intake split into their two squads again, and were plonked into adjacent classrooms, and away they went.

Firstly, the word *'Ngoh'* or 'I', pronounced 'Naw' and the class had to practise it in the six tones by following what the teacher recited. Frankly, initially, and to the tone deaf, they all sounded exactly the same, but gradually, yes, there was a difference, but it was very hard to discern it in sentences. It was all about context.

And almost impossible to speak it in the right tone so as to satisfy the teachers.

It soon became very evident, as the days wore on, that there were very few, if any, real linguists in either class, with Steady Eddie having dropped French lessons after three years of study, and AV having failed French O Level (more later), Nev presumably had passed his French, living in Jersey and, being a pilot (again, more later) who had flown several times to St Malo in France on boozy jaunts with his mates. Lats surely had one or two languages under his belt being a public-school swot, while Dave Kensington seemed the sort to have studied hard at his school.

It was a pretty sure bet, too, that Dogs Dinner and Tommy Two Dicks didn't have any languages behind them.

Not that it mattered, because whatever their level of linguistic ability, if any at all, this was new to all of them.

The teaching method was to hammer out a load of vocabulary, and then seek to put it into set phrases in such a repetitive manner that it should have been ingrained. The level of difficulty, and the complexity of those patterns, increased as the course went by.

Lesson five, as they'd already been warned by Bill Robinson and crew, was the hardest as it was concerned with classifiers; simply, for example, one person was '*Yat GOH yan*', two bottles of beer were '*Leung JI San Lik bei jau*', three taxis were '*Saam GA aik si*', and four houses were '*Sei GAAN uk*', and thus it was a question of matching up the right classifier, of which there were many, with the corresponding noun.

In fact, lesson five was a watershed and a Eureka moment, because once it was over and grasped, then the sentences and patterns to be learnt made a lot more sense because they were practical, more expansive and could be tried out in Wong Chuk Hang Market, at Ming's café, the bars and everywhere else really, and all it took was confidence.

Now while there were no stage tests or examinations before the 'Big One' after the full two months, there must obviously have been some reports sent back to the Senior Training Office because one or two lads were called in and talked to about their progress.

Again, poor old Dave Kensington was one, and he could just not seem to get his tongue around the words, and while no one in class liked to be 'on the spot' or asked to recite difficult bits and pieces (except for 'Sunny Boy' Colgate, who was always volunteering) there was a lot of concern for him as he did seem to occupy a lot of the teachers' time.

But as a distraction, some class comedians took the stage in a few lessons, which lightened up the mood considerably, and a couple of the teachers (*not* Mr Lau or David) joined in, giving out little phrases to help chat up women, or how to tell people to sod off, for example.

There was a lot of private study needed at night time, too, which was quite difficult in dormitory conditions, with no privacy at all, although it was quite handy for testing one another, the new vocabulary to be learned always a challenge.

Things though improved considerably after a month or so when two of the senior squads finished their training and were posted to Divisions, thus 101 and 102 moved into the Officers' single quarters next to the Mess, and thus could study uninterrupted.

Well, ostensibly they could study undisturbed, but Two Dicks could be a bloody nuisance when coming back from the bar, quite refreshed, and banging on the door of anyone and everyone who still had their lights on and who were studying, and then coming in for a chat, probably a bit guilty that he hadn't been doing the same.

Similarly with Callum Colgate, the keenie, who probably went back to his room and studied for hours after such a visit, thinking or worrying that 'someone' may have stolen a march on him.

Even Steady Eddie Yates once, after the Cantonese course, admittedly, paid a late-night visit to a few people, as he and some colleagues had been to Chimsy, and he had lost a false tooth down a toilet in some bar or other, which seemed a daft place to have dropped it.

The poor lad was after sympathy, obviously, as it was impossible that any of his course mates had found it, and certainly at that hour wouldn't form a posse to return to Chimsy and try and help him find it, even if he could have remembered which bars he had been to. Besides, what's another lost tooth – it would only 'complement' a front tooth he had recently partially sheared when his head collided with the tarmac football pitch at PTS.

Of course, the Cantonese course was run in tandem with drill lessons and practice, with more of that in the following chapters, but having the physical exercise of PT and drill, combined with the Chinese course, made it more bearable for those whose forte or bent was on the more physical than the cerebral side of things. But everyone knew that it was essential to get the thing done and dusted and out of the way, to concentrate on the nitty gritty, not realising how valuable it would be to have a real command of the language to get a feel for what was happening around them post PTS, and not to have the wool pulled over their eyes, as far a possible anyway.

It was a pity that no one couched it in those terms.

Well, '*tempus fugit*,' or time flies, and it was almost time for their Colloquial Cantonese Exam, and what progress they had made!

They'd gone from 'hot', which was '*yit*', to 'very hot', which was '*ho yit*', to 'extremely hot', which was '*sap fan yit*', to 'fucking hot', which was '*ho lan yit*', to 'absolutely fucking, boiling hot', which was '*ho lan chat yit*'!

They could cuss in the most common local vernacular, which was '*Dew lay la mo!*' or 'Screw your mother!' There are some further, stronger variations on this, which we shan't go into here.

They could use classifiers and identify which ones pertained to which noun, pretty much without error, and mess around with the meanings of words, with different tones, even if inadvertently sometimes messing up.

For example, *'yat'* was the number 'one', *'luk'* was the number 'six', *'sei'* was the number 'four' and *'chat'* was the number 'seven', giving 1647.

But put them together, using different tones, and obviously writing different Chinese characters, which *was* beyond them, then you have *yat luk sei chat*, but this time *not* 1647.

'Yat' still meant 'one'. The classifier was *'luk'* and then with a different *sei* and *chat* you have *One dead dick!*

(About three years later, Bottomley was being driven around in a CID/Wanchai Ford Cortina with the numberplate AM 1647, and in his case the 'dead dick' version was certainly the most appropriate. Just ask his ex-wife.)

They could order booze, impress some bar girls who would no longer think them squaddies, and no bastard would ever give them ducks' webbed feet again *unless* it was really what they intended to order.

Yes, they could do all this and more, but could they pass their Colloquial Cantonese Exam?

It was held at the Lee Gardens Hotel in Causeway Bay in June 1975, and the advice from Mr Lau of all people was, so as not to get nervous, and to loosen their tongues, it would be best if they had a beer while waiting to be called in.

Well, that was fine if you were number one to maybe six, but pity the poor blokes numbered, say, fifteen to twenty four. One beer wasn't gonna cut it during that long, nervous wait, certainly not if it had been Two Dicks, Bucket Bottomley, Tenspeed or - and he *was* coming on very nicely - even Steady Eddie.

But in the end, what was all the fuss about, as everyone passed.

And what a collective sigh of relief, although the formal results were only announced on Monday by the Commandant in person, on the first day of them studying the vagaries of Hong Kong's Judicial system and the laws holding the fabric of its society together.

Joyce, however, had tipped a few of them the wink, most likely with the tacit approval of Hugh Baker and Mr Lau.

It was particularly satisfying for AV the Bucket Bottomley as he had failed O Level French by a whisker, by being kicked out of the oral part of his exam for not being able to recall the French for Wales (le Pays de Galles!) and had been reported to his teacher who shamed him in front of the whole school, and who wouldn't let him re-sit.

And so, being the generous-spirited and forgiving chap he was back then, he sent a postcard to that teacher, Mr Michael Granger-Smythe, care of his old Alma Cogan, telling of his passing the Cantonese Exam, with the admonition that, 'You should have given me a beer first!' Oh, and a French phrase in capitals which surely pleased that double-barrelled tosser even more:

'*VA TE FAIRE FOUTRE!!*'

Anyway, despite the results being unconfirmed, the lads were feeling mightily pleased with themselves, and with Hong Kong now very much their adopted home from home, off they toddled to celebrate at some of their many favourite watering holes on both sides of the harbour.

But now, with that over with, it's time to catch up with what else had been taking place in tandem with the Cantonese course and, boy oh boy, weren't they having some wonderful experiences.

I'll catch you all again shortly… *joi geen!*

Chapter Ten

Learning the Drill

Immediately after the first Cantonese lesson, both squads assembled outside the administration block and were 'ushered' down to the otherwise empty drill square by a Chinese Senior Inspector (SIP) named Tony Ho, a stentorian-voiced, lantern-jawed bronzed chap, in a very serious tone indeed, one of their two Drill and Musketry Instructors (DMIs) for the whole eight months at PTS.

There they came face to face with the other, a round-faced, more rotund fellow named Franny Fong, another SIP, and although they never showed it on the square, both were actually quite pleasant blokes, in their mid-twenties, only displaying that side of their characters once the lads had attained some kind of proficiency at what they had been ordered to teach.

These two Senior Inspectors were under the direction of a Chief Inspector (CIP) Gerry Hong, a Christopher Lee-as-Dracula look-alike, who never smiled and gave off an air of menace, and of one not to be messed with or taken lightly. He in turn was directly under the CDMI, Morgan Effin-Jones, although they were of equal rank, and was responsible not only for 101 and 102, plus the other Recruit

Inspector squads, but for the training of the rank and file also, and thus for the mainly Sergeant DMIs square-bashing those PCs and WPCs.

The ultimate aim was to train the lads so they would be able to drill a squad of rank and file themselves and move them around the drill square in a professional and orderly manner, not only at Passing Out Parades, but to a standard acceptable to the CDMI, with an examination to be held at the end of their course.

But first, obviously, they themselves had to be trained in drill and musketry, and so it was 'sizing' first, right to left, tallest to smallest.

AV thankfully was no longer the shortest, as eight local officers had joined them, four to each squad, two women and two male officers, five of the eight having risen from the ranks and three via direct entry. While the expats learnt Cantonese, the locals were being groomed on their English to better equip them for the Law and practical courses.

And then three ranks or lines were formed and that would remain the combined squad formation for the duration, subject to resignations, of course. More later, sadly.

But first things first. How to salute and return a salute. Importantly too, just exactly *who* to salute? Basically, nearly every bastard in PTS who didn't seem to be a trainee. This resulted in a few mishaps, with Inspectors occasionally saluting Sergeants and even recruit PCs by mistake, but they soon got the hang of it.

AV received a bollocking from another course's instructor, a Kevin 'Tits' Monkman, not nicknamed 'Tits' because of any ornithological leanings but because he did have a fine set of what appeared to be mammary glands on him, which in fact were fat deposits. The infraction? Saluting him without a cap on. Oh dearie me, didn't he deserve excoriation!

And what an officious, petty ponce Monkman was, apparently in the greater world outside of PTS known as 'The Little Drain' for some as then unknown reason, but not for peeing his money down one apparently. More on him later.

And then it was learning how to march, so they split into pairs, and had to hop about on one leg, then the other and then conduct left turns, right turns, about turns and mark time. AV was paired with Nev but, unfortunately, much akin to tittering in church, once they started laughing, they couldn't seem to stop for some reason that neither of them could put a finger on.

But as good old Ringo Starr sang, 'It don't come easy!' and it certainly didn't, but twice-daily practice sessions ensured it *did* eventually come, with the squad then being reformed and guided (well, ordered and driven, actually) around the drill square, with a left wheel and right wheel, and left turn, right turn, about turn, mark time, eyes right, and, amazingly, after a few weeks, they seemed to be getting the hang of it.

Even Dogs Dinner, whose limbs when marching seemed not to belong to him as he couldn't bend too well at the knee or elbow, and who resembled Robocop in his movements, as if he had an invisible roll of carpet under each armpit and had to go to the end of the street to turn round.

Never mind, he like the others was doing his best, although uniformity was what the instructors were demanding.

Punjab Pete fell afoul of Franny Fong one hot afternoon as his boxers were hanging below the bottom of his PTS khaki shorts, with the SIP bellowing out a vociferous, 'Mr. Spicer. I can see your underwear! It's disgusting!' and thus the King of the Khyber Rifles had to leave the drill square and change into his Y-fronts.

Another time, Yates was messing with his cap, during a 'stand easy' break, drying the sweat from the band inside it, and temporarily turned it inside out. Nev similarly did this, as did most of the squad, then placing it on their heads like that. The drill instructor was confused; everything seemed uniform and he couldn't immediately spot what was amiss. Not for long, though.

Unfortunately, Claudinella Leung, one of the local ladies who'd joined, was class prefect for the day and because of her perceived lack of control over the squad, she was gated on Saturday, not allowed to leave PTS to presumably go back home to visit her family. Some felt guilty at that, even as they were quaffing their third gin and tonics in the China Fleet Club, the tonic because the quinine helped to fight malaria, and the gin to combat the boredom and loneliness of those long, tropical evenings, according to the caddish Terry Thomas, in *'Spanish Fly',* anyway.

Another time, after Two Dicks had a spill on his motorbike (more later) and had put a bandage on his elbow, he was on the drill square when the CDMI was putting squads 101 and 102 through their paces. He smartly snapped to attention and asked if he could pick up his dressing, which in Effin-Jones's world was to check his distance, arm's length, fist to shoulder with the man immediately on his right.

Two Dicks though broke ranks and sprinted across the square being immediately challenged by the CDMI as to what the hell he was playing at, with Tommy triumphantly bending down and with his bandage held above his head, replying, 'Picking up my dressing, sir!!'

The CDMI didn't know whether to laugh or cry, whether Tommy was being facetious, insubordinate or truthful, but had no choice but to allow him to return to the ranks in silence.

Just a brief word on some of the apparent peculiar English names that some locals chose for themselves. Their given Chinese names were something like CHAN Wing-fat, or WONG Tim-tim, CHAN and WONG being family names, with Wing-fat and Tim-tim being given names. The individual, in the main, when at junior school, chose an English 'Christian name' for themselves, not really understanding the meaning or connotation in some cases.

Thus, you may have an Igor YIP Chun-man, for example or, leaving out the given names, a Fondle Pang, a Carrot Lee, a Lassie

Leung, a Hitler Auyeung, a Hampton Wang, a Labia Dong, a Wimpy Chu, or a Lavi Pong.

Still, back home in Butterrow there was Zed Victor One and Zed Victor Two, so I guess horses for courses. Anyway, returning to the main programme.

Once the marching concept had been absorbed, it was time for complicated stuff like forming two ranks, mainly for inspection purposes, which consisted of a movement of two diagonal steps from the two of the three rear ranks, but when executed correctly was very impressive indeed.

And then there was advancing in review order, which was a thirteen-step movement forward of all squads to the beating of drums, but if one lost count or became confused, there was a danger of making a complete fool of yourself as you'd be carrying on a step or two after everyone else had come to a halt.

But several of the new intake including - almost unbelievably - one or two of the WCH5, suffered that embarrassment, and the ribald ribbing in the Mess just had to be endured, although most of it was from people who were mightily relieved, indeed lucky, that they, on that day at least, had got things right.

Obviously, all of it took a great deal of practice, very often in extremely hot conditions, with most of the lads and lasses drenched with sweat after a lengthy session, especially if punishment drills had been applied, such as marking time for a few minutes to an increased pace as bawled out by Tony Ho or Franny Fong.

The most dreaded order on the parade square was an 'As you were!', which meant an exercise or a manoeuvre had to be repeated as many times as was required to get it right.

It was sometimes the case that they wished they could get back to the Cantonese course as soon as possible, to have a breather, although the end of day drill session was an almost open-ended affair.

After drill, and being marched to and dismissed opposite the

Officers' Mess, there was a rush to purchase Cokes, Fantas and cream sodas from the bar outside the Alan wicker lounge area, with no one even thinking to purchase bottled water, not even sure if it was on offer. Conversely, though, no one ever thought of ordering a beer either, particularly at the drill session immediately before lunch. Progress indeed.

However, there was always a large tub of salt tablets placed on the bar counter, which everyone downed like Smarties, as they thought it'd do them good, which maybe it would have in small doses, but handfuls at a time? Still, no one presented with any adverse symptoms, so one presumes they got away with it, as it were, all being increasingly fit young people back then.

So, with the drill up to that point going swimmingly, it's time to return to the first Wednesday of the Cantonese course, 30th April 1975, with AV, Yates and Nev inside the TV room just adjacent to the Officers' Mess, on the ground floor of the single accommodation block, at about 18.00 hours.

There were two English television stations, no satellite or cable back then, and the room was quite full, being able to take about twenty people.

The hot news was the fall of Saigon, with those iconic pictures from the roof of the American Embassy of the clamouring to board helicopters, and one being pushed off that roof so the communists couldn't use it.

But the second hot item of the day was the arrest of eighty, yes eighty, Hong Kong police officers from a Sub Division called Bay View, for alleged corruption offences with no one in the room exactly knowing where it was, apart from somewhere near Causeway Bay, Hong Kong Island.

(Actually, it was a Sub Division of Eastern Division, the next area along from Wanchai Division and just past Causeway Bay, with quite a small police station, as it turned out, bearing in mind the numbers 'lifted')

The news presenter also intimated that ICAC were stepping up action against the police, and that it was the third such mass arrests since ICAC was formed in 1974.

The SM3 were a little nonplussed as they'd obviously been informed that corruption was a thing of the past and didn't then actually know what 'corruption offences' meant, although they'd learn soon enough.

Back to the dormitory to pass on both pieces of news, Dogs pacing up and down wondering whether to attend 'Hitler's' forthcoming commemoration party or not, when, after about ten minutes, the day's Duty Officer, Recruit Inspector Jerry Makepeace, came from the guardhouse looking for Dogs Dinner and Eddie Yates and informing them that they had two people from Western Division Mess visiting them, and waiting in the bar.

Wondering what the hell it was all about, and being nosey bastards, Nev, Bottomley and Two Dicks accompanied the two lads to the bar, where Jack Claymore, the chap he'd met the previous Sunday, was waiting for Dogs.

No, *not* to take him to the Fuhrer's party, but to advise him *not* to attend, which was jolly good of him.

While Martin did the decent thing and got some beers organised, a Steve Greening, on finding out who he was, introduced himself to Yates as an ex-Luanshya High School lad and had heard of Bob Y through Frick Jacobs, the 102 course instructor, a South African of course.

It transpired he was the elder brother of that snotty, stuck-up David Greening who had resented Bob Y's arrival at Luanshya's junior school, but who had subsequently been sent to boarding school in Cape Town. Unfortunately, his elder brother seemed a real ponce, full of himself, talking down to the newly arrived Bob as if he was God's gift to law and order, living in Western Mess, Hong Kong Island and working in an Emergency Unit, West Kowloon, responding to 999 calls and as directed through his area command.

He'd also been bunged off to school in Cape Town, so hadn't known Bob in Luanshya, his parents being ex-Rhodesian colonial administrators and it was eminently clear that Steve had been brought up with a total sense of entitlement and of his own superiority.

Not Yates's cup of beer at all, but probably exactly what young David Greening had also become. And good luck to them.

AV and Nev had sidled off to the bar, keeping a watching brief, wondering just how Steady Eddie had so much patience.

Dogs seemed to be getting on like a house of fire with Jack Claymore and called people across to meet him. He'd been in RHKP for about six years and was currently a court prosecutor at South Kowloon Magistracy, awaiting an Assistant Sub Divisional Inspector's (ASDI's) post, which would be a quicker path to promotion, or so he reckoned.

He was maybe twenty seven, blond, stocky and chain-smoked in the manner of Dwight D 'Ike' Eisenhower, closing his whole hand across his face as he puffed on his cigarettes, and mumbled rather than talked.

He was an ex-public school swot, although one would never have guessed it, and a very tough rugby player, rumoured to have once been found with his teeth gripped on the laces of a rugby ball when a collapsed scrum was disentangled. And no, he and Lats had not yet become teammates, although they soon would be.

He had a finger missing on his right hand, and informed them that when performing his party piece, a few years back, balancing his whole weight on two bottles of San Mig, one of them had broken, resulting in a huge gash. That hadn't severed his finger, though, but he'd been making such a drunken pest of himself in the ambulance to go for a pee, that the ambulance men pulled up on a slope, and in trying to get out of the vehicle, he fell down the hill, and that was the last he ever saw of *that* particular finger.

Thereafter, he was known as 'Fingers' Claymore, but if you are to be saddled with a nickname, then 'Fingers' wasn't a bad one to have.

'Must have been a green bottle,' somebody chirped, and that really broke the ice.

Greening had left to chat with someone he allegedly knew at the bar, and while the SM3 were sitting with Claymore, someone asked about corruption, and what *was* the score, with those eighty Bay View policemen being arrested so recently?

He wouldn't be drawn, except to say that while at PTS they would be told the 'party line' but would find out the truth when they were sent to Divisions, *if* they wanted to know the truth. And in any case, he added that the PTS bar wasn't a suitable venue to discuss such matters, with so many eager listeners and perhaps spies, just at the very same moment as Mungo McMee poked his head round the door to presumably see if he was missing anything or should make himself known to persons of potential use. He wasn't and didn't, luckily.

Claymore did though mention that many senior officers were totally paranoid about ICAC and their own pasts, scared almost witless that they'd lose their pensions, child-education subsidies and indeed their livelihoods, let alone being incarcerated, and *that* paranoia would be bound to get worse if and when any of them were arrested. Beyond that, he wouldn't elucidate.

However, he hadn't been happy about the apparent fascist goings-on at Western Mess that evening and thought it best to head off young Martin in case he be implicated by association, even though it was meant to be a jolly jape. Some might not see it like that.

With that, and with Greening chomping at the bit to be off, away he went, telling them that he was usually in Popeye's on Saturday nights, the long weekends one big bonus of being a nine-to-five, Monday-to-Friday court prosecutor.

And yes, they would all meet with Senior Inspector Claymore

many times, over the years, and especially when they all worked and drank together in Yaumatei Division starting some eight months later.

As for Steve Greening, well, hardly, although he was apparently annoyed, or jealous, when AV became friendly, on occasions, with Debbie or Dee Dee, one of the girls who worked in Popeye's Bar, as he was also pally with her. But if he was jealous of AV, then he must have been fit to be tied when she upped and married another Inspector named J B Farrier, with AV merely thanking her for her previous friendship and for trying to settle the 'sliding down a banister' issue for him.

Oh yes, and asking for a quick one, for old times' sake!

The banister result? Inconclusive, as AV had never seen an expat woman sliding down one, so he actually had nothing to compare Dee Dee's efforts with.

Still, he could leave Hong Kong at any time, with a clear conscience, now that he knew how to use chopsticks, and also that the banister issue was impossible to resolve.

Now while the squad still observed the Saturday morning parades, they didn't get off lightly anymore, because at its conclusion, as soon as the last squad had marched off, *they* were marched on for an hour or so of practice.

It was so unfair, but they were definitely improving.

Saturday 3rd May. Cup Final day. Fulham against Bob's West Ham United, so it was a few social gin and tonics in the China Fleet Club, one beer in Popeye's and another in a new place, the Godown at the basement of Central's Furama Hotel, which was actually quite a 'spit and sawdust' bar, despite the Furama connection, well patronised by squaddies and underage schoolkids from Hong Kong's two international grammar schools.

Of course, they'd visited Bob at Oriental Tailors and picked up the clothes they'd somehow ordered the previous week, highly delighted with the shirts and trousers they'd bought. And after a couple of beers each, they ordered more, AV and Nev even ordering made-to-measure shoes.

AV! Made-to-measure shoes! Just *what* would Geoff Bottomley make of that?

Then back to PTS to listen to the live footie broadcast on the BBC World Service, presented by Paddy Feeney. No live TV broadcast back then. Sorry. But Yates was pleased, as West Ham won 2-0, AV a bit nostalgic as he'd been at the 1974 final where Liverpool hammered Newcastle 3-0, having won tickets awarded to Bond Worth FC by the FA and then raffled.

However, he hadn't been too pleased at being thumped on the train home by Newcastle supporters from Cardiff, but it did teach him two lessons which should have stood him in good stead: hide your colours, and don't, whatever you do, display your rosette unless you're either a winning horse or a jockey.

The following week was even more special. Yes, fair enough, the Queen was visiting Hong Kong and it was all pomp and ceremony as she paraded along Nathan Road, the main spine through the centre of Kowloon from Chimsy through Yaumatei to Mongkok, thousands upon thousands lining the route including, briefly, the WCH5, none of them previously having visited Chimsy apart from Tommy Two Dicks.

But what made it a real red-letter day, after the Queen regaled by, was their first visit to the Red Lips Bar, along Peking Road, near the Hyatt Hotel, set back a little down an alley and curtained off.

It was a dark, pokey little place, with seating at the small bar for maybe five or six people, with four or five booths, and it employed some of the oldest bar girls you've ever seen, Chinese or otherwise. But, notwithstanding their ages, Bonnie, Connie, Amy, Shirley, and the four or five others were kind enough 'girls' who wouldn't try to rip off the customers, while thin, bespectacled, middle-aged Charlie behind the bar looked more like a harassed solicitor's clerk than a barman. No music, thankfully, and if you couldn't find any policemen in Popeye's then you could bet your bottom dollar you'd find some in the Red Lips.

One day, some months later, in the road just outside the Red Lips, Nev spotted a crowd of about fifty Japanese tourists being dragged by a flag-wielding courier into the opposite Duty Free Shoppers store, obviously on commission, and grabbed her long-poled flag and scurried off to the bar, sheepishly followed by at least thirty elderly Japanese who pushed through the curtain and turned circles in the place until their eyes became accustomed to the dark interior, probably wondering just on what level of hell they'd arrived at?

The courier was not amused. But why not? Charlie would have allowed her at least two Hong Kong dollars on every beer sold. She wouldn't get that at Duty Free, now would she?

More on Chimsy later.

The following day, lessons started late as Prince Philip was arriving by road to PTS after having visited the Army Battalion at Stanley and was flying a Wessex helicopter someone had very carelessly left on the parade square, back to the naval base at HMS Tamar, just across the road from Police Headquarters in Wanchai, to meet up with his missus, who was probably out at Sam the Tailor's having a few gowns knocked up.

Hopefully, Sam gave her a beer or two. And in a glass!

It was drizzling, but all of PTS had to turn out in little black, plastic macs, as if they actually liked, respected or had forgiven the Queen's husband and consort for, in 1961, so rudely urging the British worker (whomever 'he' might have been), to pull his finger out. Full of pomposity and indeed velocity, he strode straight past the Commandant, who had saluted him grandly, without even a glance, and off he flew.

There's gratitude for you!

So, bearing in mind that Philip was not only a Prince of Greece, but also one of Denmark, there would be no more ouzo,

Danish bacon or Hamlet cigars for the San Miguel Three after *that* discourteous behaviour, no siree!

He hitherto had taken great pains to make out he was an officer and a gentleman, after all! But perhaps away from his wife he was a different chap, a case of '*Saan go, wong dai yuen*,' literally, 'The hills are tall and the king is far away,' meaning simply that 'While the cat's away, the mice will play,' or 'What the eye doesn't see, the heart doesn't grieve over.'

That being so, surely 'someone' should have gone across and demanded to see his chopper pilot's licence, and the helicopter's MOT certificate, after such dashed bad manners, what?

Nevertheless, they had to don those little macs again a little later when it rained extremely heavily, and the recruits were on standby, just in case the village outside the main PTS gates became flooded out, which luckily it didn't.

All good experience, though, and an early rehearsal for those typhoon parties when so many officers were trapped in police Messes until the typhoons passed, and there was nothing else to do except get pissed or slip upstairs for sex with whomever they were 'knocking off' at the same station, such often illicit relationships generally being very well-known open secrets. More later.

Now back to the parade square, where the squad had improved out of all recognition, and practised and practised the Saturday and morning parade drills, and, with the passing out of two squads, they were actually allowed onto the dancefloor, as it were, but how would they fare with the real deal?

They actually got round very well the first few times, when a Drill and Musketry Instructor was barking out the commands, but poor Dave Kensington was chosen to lead them around the very first time on their own. It was very unfortunate that, being the junior squad, and stuck at the back, quite a few senior and intermediate squads had completed their circuits before they started off, and thus witnessed the debacle to come.

Not only did Mr Kensington struggle with blasting out the commands, but his lack of coordination, hidden somewhat when inside the formation itself, found him floundering when his quiet voice and lack of authority resulted in chaos, and the formation fracturing at the very first left wheel, which had been left three paces too late.

As a consequence, the squad were too far right to negotiate the dais, display canons and potted plants, and thus they stumbled and tripped over the lot, and then each other. And so, with the left and right commands out of sync, the next left wheel was ballsed up as well, the right flank of the squad marching, or rather splashing along in the laundry and rain - overspill gutter running down the extreme right of the parade square.

Frantically, the deep-voiced Tony Ho was bellowing out instructions to try and put them back on an even keel, which he managed to do, about ten yards before they should have been halted, but Dave couldn't even get that right. The squad then had to fall out and reform, and whilst the SM3 had initially thought it hilarious, the seriousness of it all hit home, as did the awful embarrassment.

It didn't reflect at all well on the squad, the instructors or Dave, of course, and it was fortunate that they weren't collectively gated.

AV had a similar experience maybe a week before their Passing Out Parade, when a Woman Inspector named Bandy Yat-ding Lam froze when leading a platoon of recruit Women Police Constables around the square, Bottomley part of its officer contingent. Fortunately, another Recruit Inspector, a former rank and file fellow named Phillip Yip, had the presence of mind to take over and restore order in a timely fashion.

Yes, she'd chosen the name 'Bandy' and, to add to that, '*yat ding*' in Cantonese, depending on tones, *can* mean 'sure thing', or 'certainly', and she certainly was a 'sure thing', if one chose to believe some of the obviously jealous and bitter lascivious lechers in the Mess, the truth actually being that she'd rejected the sexual advances of one or two of them, in favour of a senior Chinese training officer who could be of more use to her.

Hell hath no fury like a male Recruit Inspector scorned, and so Bandy was subjected to a veritable maelstrom of malicious scuttlebutt.

'*Yat ding*, sure thing!' as the full phrase went!

(And spare a thought for the single British, Canadian, South African and Antipodean Recruit Women Inspectors passing through the Training School, and into the great beyond, for the rumours they had to endure were positively legion, and totally unfounded in most cases.)

Bandy incidentally had formerly been a Ground Hostess with Lufthansa Airlines, but never let on just who she'd been grinding, and initially on the parade square, had the annoying Teutonic habit of clicking her heels together when the squads were ordered to 'Attention!' as if she was still with them. Several sessions of private and punishment drill soon cured her of that, though.

A little previously, on a Sunday, with Nev buying a car (again, more later) and Tommy owning a motorbike, a gang of them, including Yates, AV, Kensington, Plod, Spicer, and Faidi Aidi, all jollied off to Kam Tin in the New Territories, on the road to Yuen Long, ostensibly to have a decko at the walled village belonging to the Hakka people, whose young folk had mainly moved either overseas or to the urban areas for work.

The real reason for most though was to explore the several bars opposite that village which allegedly serviced the Army units in the area, although most specialist servicemen up there were married.

So straight to the bars, which were a wash-out, not getting lively until the evening.

Never mind, a pleasant afternoon in the country, but Dave was as miffed as hell. If he had wanted to get pissed, he declared rather haughtily, he would have stayed at PTS.

But Nev, another very plain speaker, who had to take it easy on the booze because he was driving, pointedly told him to go across and have a shufti at the walled village if he wanted some culture, and then come back and tell them all about it.

So off he went, crunching on the stem of his pipe, presumably with his blue PTS identity card at the ready should he spot any malfeasance.

But poor Dave was obviously under pressure, with the Cantonese and Drill getting to him, with the balls-up as described above probably the final straw.

Some of you may have wondered how everyone passed their Cantonese exam, if Dave was struggling so badly? Well, everyone who took the exam passed but Dave Kensington sadly resigned before then, even though his fellow squad members tried to ta.k him out of it on the grounds that things would become better for him as drill progressed, and when the Law course started.

Even if he failed the Cantonese exam, they'd make special arrangements for him to be privately tutored, surely, as the HK Government had spent a lot of money in getting him to Hong Kong and training him.

But no! He was implacable, and so within a week he was off, 'johnnies' and all, followed shortly afterwards by Paul 'Clicker' Cannon and a fellow member of 101 squad called Simon 'Slam Dunk' Crossley, an ace badminton and basketball player, both of whom very unexpectedly threw in their cards.

Come on, chaps, it's not that bad! But again, they wouldn't change their minds, so away they went as well.

Perhaps AV was *not* the only one, then, whose ambition stopped at chopsticks and banisters.

Dave re-joined Nat West Bank, where he remained for a couple of years, until Aids, very fortuitously for him, reared its annihilistic head, and spotting a niche in the burgeoning 'Safe Sex Industry', not least because of his familiarity with all types of condoms then on the market, he became very big in latex, and manufactured and exported containers of condoms all over the world, particularly to Third World countries after having been contracted by the World Health Organisation to do so, buying several 'condominiums' on the strength of it.

He eventually sold out to a major American prophylactic company and retired at forty, living out a life of sophisticated luxury until it was unfortunately cut short at forty eight by some 'Johnny' in Jamaica, during a home invasion robbery which got out of hand.

'Clicker' Cannon returned to his Singaporean roots, having gone into partnership with Hong Kong's Palysound, and opened up outlets inside the Duty Free shopping areas at Hong Kong, Singapore and Kuala Lumpur Airports, selling watches, cameras, video recorders, radio cassette players and the like, making loads of cash, which later enabled them to similarly open an outlet in Dubai when it became a major international air travel hub.

Unfortunately, long distance trust can be fraught with difficulty, and the partners had a falling out, which resulted in much bad feeling and litigation, although after a year or so, the courts partially found in Paul's favour and he retained the Dubai concession, now trading as 'Bishops'.

Although how he managed to survive there with the advertising catchphrase of 'You can't beat the Bishop!' was beyond many, with it obviously losing something in the Arabic or idiomatic translation.

Simon Crossley went into education, eventually becoming the Head Teacher at an American girls college, that position being a formal educational post, and *not*, as some cruelly or jokingly suggested, one where he taught 'head' to American college girls and refined the techniques of some advanced and very gifted pupils.

People can be *so* jealous!

But back in Hong Kong, Dogs was still totally enamoured with the lovely Lilly, so much so that he forgot to have his fortnightly haircut ready for the Monday morning inspection by the DMIs, which would be put forward to Saturday when they were allowed to take part in the proper parades. Never mind, and instead of hurrying up to the barber's shop at Wong Chuk Hang, as most of his mates had done, he decided to do it himself, using his cap as a template, hacking off everything that hung beneath it.

While he achieved some success with the front and top of his hair, the rest was a disaster, especially at the back, showing peaks and troughs which drew immediate laughter from fellow squad members, who attempted to minimise the calamity and set to with the scissors, making things worse by trying to even-out the hair, and resorting to shaving the nape of his neck, leaving a prominent six inch long, bright red shaving rash.

As was expected, the DMIs couldn't miss his butchered bonce, particularly as attention was brought to it by fits of laughter emanating from behind poor old Dogs, making most of the squad incapable of walking, let alone performing drill.

The result? 'Fall out, Mr Dinner!' while the remainder were subject to punishment drill for about fifteen minutes, breathlessly marking time on the spot, while Martin was in fits of laughter himself, watching them all being put through it.

That evening he was frog-marched up to the Wong Chuk Hang barber's shop and several people watched and admired the barber's skill at making some order out of the mess both Dogs and they had made of his hair.

The shaving rash, however, was with him for months after, a souvenir of his days at PTS.

And that, Ladies and Genitals, brings us up to date with matters as they stood when completing the Cantonese course, with everyone who'd taken the exam passing, three lads having departed and Martin 'Dogs' Dinner being now very neat and tidy, all spruced up for the start of the Law Course on a fine Monday morning.

See you all later.

We'll catch up with you shortly… don't go away.

Chapter Eleven

The Nitty Gritty

As mentioned previously, living in single Officers' quarters was palpably much more conducive to study than in the dormitory, with each room having a desk, sink, wardrobe, stand-alone electric fan and of course a bed. The shower rooms and toilets were at the end of the corridors, and they had to be up pretty early, at 06.45 hours, if they liked pampering themselves in front of the mirrors or liked to have a good spew in relative privacy if they'd had a heavy night.

There were however some evening interruptions apart from pissheads coming back from the Mess and knocking on doors, one of the most memorable being when a gang of lads manhandled Two Dicks' scrambler motorbike up the three flights of stairs to the top floor, and parked it outside his room door, in the corridor where Squad 102 were housed with some of the senior squads.

Being somewhat of a dab hand on the bike, and when he'd recovered from the shock of finding it where they'd put it, he fired it up and - well! - drove it back down very adroitly, to the parking space where they'd 'half-inched' it from, obviously filling the corridors with choking fumes and creating one hell of a racket.

(Yes, but while Two Dicks was undoubtedly very skilled on his motorbike, to some he later upset, he was thought more of as an Evil Conniver than an Evel Knievel.)

But it was indeed extremely fortunate that no one reported the incident to the guardhouse or to anyone on the Mess Committee, 'Squealer' Nairn being domiciled in a hotel with his family, and Mungo McMee, by now the PTS Mess Secretary - yes, hadn't he done well, so all that crawling and sycophancy had paid off, then! - away with the rugby crowd.

More on what shenanigans he got up to after those rugby matches, a little later. Just be patient because everything comes to those who wait.

Bob Y, luckily for Nev, AV, Lats and Two Dicks, but maybe unluckily for Yates himself, was also housed on the top floor, although the rest of his squad were housed beneath him, on the ground and first floors.

Their friendships blossomed, particularly now that he had the taste for gin and tonics, and for San Miguel beer, even (and *who* would have believed this just a few months earlier?) occasionally knocking on their doors to call them out for a beer or two.

Yes, under what must be said extremely fine tutelage, aligned with his own hidden depths, young Yates had gone from the rhetorical 'I haven't been this pissed since – well – last night!' and a rather plaintive, 'What are you boys turning me into?' to certainly and most deservedly become the fabled, 'Third of the Sons of Light' in the San Miguel Three's world, if one may be so bold as to quote Percy Shelley and the Bible.

But it wasn't only gin and tonic, actually, as one night Lats won a bottle of gin in an impromptu Mess raffle at closing time but, as they had no mixers in their rooms, some bright spark merely added Tabasco hot chilli sauce to the half-filled paper cups of Gordon's gin, then down the hatches it went without hardly touching the sides.

Spicy hot bum time the following morning, that's for sure.

One other noteworthy incident took place one night at about 22.00 hours, during a weekday, surprisingly, when Tenspeed and the Bucket had become a little emboldened by the ale and pulled two of George's girls from the Popeye into a taxi, with their consent one might add, and tried to take them back to Ging Chat Hok Tong (PTS).

One was a nice girl called Tina, but while Debbie (mentioned earlier) was supposedly accompanying AV, she hopped out at a convenient red traffic light, worried in case she'd be bumping into any of her other 'friends' back at PTS, at which she claimed she had many.

Good Old Nev, in for a penny, in for a pound, managed to get Tina up the stairs to his room and nearly remained unseen until a couple of the senior squad spied him as he opened his door. AV wouldn't have said anything, but once the word had leaked out, with half of the officers under training being jealous, presumably, they were a-banging and a-knocking on his door so the poor chap couldn't concentrate on the job in hand, let alone on the lovely Tina.

Nev however had a smile on his face the following morning, so enough said.

Unfortunately, Denny 'Mad Dog' Browning was also on the same floor, and caused a ruckus one night when well refreshed, trying to start a fight with two lads further down the corridor, Fulton Puller and Eddie Davidson, who were allegedly 'gay', although it wasn't termed like that back then.

The laws on homosexuality were still quite draconian in 1975's Hong Kong, and in fact the decriminalisation of consensual same-sex acts was only given in the early 1990s despite a 1967 Act doing so in the UK, following the earlier Wolfenden Report.

Had such decriminalisation taken place earlier then no doubt Jack Claymore may not have been drummed out so ignobly. (Yes, of course, more later on this.)

HK still awaits the passing of laws to protect the full rights of the

LGTBQ brigade, or whatever they call themselves, to bring it into line with most Western countries.

Times though do change as back then a BLT was nothing other than some fancy American sandwich, and faggots formed the basis of a splendidly hearty midweek family repast for common British folk, like what your scribes be.

But by the time the Cantonese results had been announced on that Monday morning, the two course instructors, Frick Jacobs and Frank Topley, were already laying out the formal groundwork they now had to cover, and it *was* a lot, the syllabus revolving around the following subjects:

Police General Orders, or PGOs, which outlined the police responsibilities cross-referenced to statutory legislation.

The General Duty Manual, or GDM, mainly all procedure.

Statutory and police powers and procedure concerning search, entry, seizure, arrest and detention, giving many practical examples and do's and don'ts.

The Hong Kong Court System of Magistrate's, District and High Courts and how they all work and interact.

Evidence and the law, and the Judges' Rules on confession statements, and police practice and procedure surrounding their application.

Criminal and Common law, and the main Ordinances such as the Police Force Ordinance, Dangerous Drugs Ordinance, the Theft Ordinance, the Crimes Ordinance, Protection of Women and Children, Gambling, Offences against the Person, Criminal Procedure and Amendment Ordinances, Interpretation and General Clauses Ordinance, Public Order Ordinance, Road Traffic and Construction and Use Ordinance and Regulations, Summary Offences Ordinance, Nuisances and Noise Offences, Cats and Dogs Ordinance and many others covering the whole spectrum of society, with laws often introduced, or amended or even rescinded to cover specific matters arising.

However, it irked some of the lads as, while Messrs Topley and Jacobs would cover the main points, then give out the page numbers from the PGOs or GDMs, for example, that needed private study, they were handed out in loose batches, with sometimes amendments having themselves been later amended, and thus it was never really clear if the versions they were reading and relying upon were correct or not. There were loads upon loads of these supplementary sheets.

Another difficulty while attempting to study inside their private rooms was desperately trying to use the fans to cool themselves, while loose pieces of paper were flying all over the place.

Add to that were the very annoying but prevalent mosquitoes, and those little bastards used to buzz around their ears at night, sounding like a propellor, and 'biting' their most tender bits and pieces, such as ear lobes, palms and soles of their feet, plus, of course, uncovered 'private parts', the most difficult to even talk about, as the advert went.

The ceiling fans in the dormitory and in the classrooms were much better than the stand-alone room fans, but everything was manageable, despite being somewhat rustic or 'bush' in some respects.

But yes, despite having to get up and prepare for drill in the morning first thing, often to the sound of the local Rock Jock Mickey Mok playing the Eagles' 'One of These Nights' and Kenji Sawada singing 'Fugitive Kind' on the radio most mornings between 07.30 hours and 07.45 hours, things were going quite well, and it's to their credit and to the instructors' that none of them ever failed a fortnightly exam, despite some paranoia setting in before the first couple.

Of course, the tomfoolery was a bit much on occasions, with a favourite trick being to wait until someone was fast asleep, then creep into their room, place a spare white sheet over the large fan, and switch the victim's stereo hi-fi system or radio to full blast then sneak out before the poor unfortunate was jolted back to reality to see a ghostly white apparition standing in his room, and his ears being pounded to pieces.

Then one day in daylight, they finally managed to take a Star Ferry, with its green and white livery. across the harbour to properly and, initially soberly, explore Tsimshatsui or Chimsy. Prior to that of course their only other trip there was at night when the Queen was on her state visit, and when she had paraded up Nathan Road so regally.

And what a lovely journey on those ferries, dumping people right near the Ocean Terminal shopping complex, with the rear entrance to the Hong Kong Hotel on the ferry terminal's left, then through the hotel's lobby itself to walk along Peking Road, beneath Chimsy police station, with the 'Squaddie Fountain' at the bottom, so nicknamed as a British soldier somehow contrived to electrocute and kill himself in it one night, not long after the lads had left PTS.

Alternatively, one could stroll to the right of the ferry terminal and take a longer and arguably more traditionally scenic route along the sea front walkway, admiring the glittering Hong Kong Island just a few hundred yards away across Victoria Harbour, then past the luxurious and colonial-looking Peninsula Hotel, with its fleet of Rolls Royces, and on into Chimsy that way.

And what a tourist and shopper's paradise Chimsy was, stuffed full of camera, hi-fi and watch shops, gold and jewellery emporiums, designer goods outlets and luxury hotel malls, with many types of international restaurants and bars at each and every turn.

They paid a visit to Palysound (as a thank you for helping 'Clicker' Cannon out with his lens) and each bought a radio cassette player, and had the company copy onto tape some of their favourite music for just a few Hong Kong dollars, AV purchasing the Beatles' *White Album*, Nev a Clapton tape, Yates an ELO long player and Dogs Dinner a Creedence Clearwater Revival recording, which he practically wore out by incessantly and annoyingly playing it loudly and at all hours back at PTS.

Yes, they visited the 'Red Lips' to say hello to Charlie and his elderly angels, then into a load of other bars, on both sides of Nathan Road.

The Waltzing Matilda, ('Wally Mats,' with steak egg and chips for just eleven HK dollars) Beefy's, Draggy's, Ned Kelly's, the Red Lion, the White Stag, the Stoned Crow, the Four Sisters, the Two Dragons, the Mariner's Club and the San Francisco to name but a few, the San Fran in Chimsy having nothing to do with the one where Lilly worked in Wanchai.

Better watch Steady Eddie, though, as he seemed to be getting nasty on the drink, telling a waiter named Alphonse to watch himself or he'd knock his bloody block off when Alphonse seemed to be getting a tad too friendly.

All good fun, though, until they met up at 'the Retreat' with Bill 'The Reverend' Robinson, who had 'Mad Dog' Denny in tow, but who was having a vociferous altercation with a bloke named Vic Arrowsmith, a balding, thirty-something chap who worked for the Public Works Department as an engineer somewhere, and who was invariably hanging around young police Inspectors as he seemed to otherwise be a 'Johnny-no-mates' type.

Something apparently untoward had happened, and quick as a flash Arrowsmith bashed Mad Dog over the head with a handy bottle of tomato sauce. Time to leave, chaps, and lucky that Dave Kensington wasn't there or it would be out with the blue card again, no doubt.

Arrowsmith was a consummate wind-up merchant and gossip-monger, the kerfuffle later learnt to be because he had been spreading the dirt about one of Denny's close friends, Arrowsmith unaware that they knew each other, just spouting out tales about whomever to whomever would listen and, unbeknown to the lads, immediately before they arrived at the Retreat, Denny had clipped Vic around the ear.

They visited the rabbit warren that was Chung King Mansions

across Nathan Road from Peking Road, where they ate cheaply at what seemed like an Indian's home on the 23rd floor of block D, or something like that, the whole place packed with such curry houses, cheap guest houses, residences and tailoring workshops, the smell of curry wafting out over everyone and everything.

The ground floor lifts were invariably packed, rattling up and down the building, hardly seeming safe. The ground floor itself was full of luggage stores, electrical outlets, general souvenir shops, drink stalls and a myriad of others, although there had to be overkill somewhere, as there were just so many of them.

To either side of Chung King Mansions were narrow side alleys, shortcuts to other roads and streets, in fact well spread all over Chimsy. These often hosted the ubiquitous and oh so colourful fruit-cum-grocery stalls, at which one could sit and order large bottles of beer which were much cheaper than in actual bars.

They were so casual that they had no public toilets, which didn't present much of a problem as a pee in the gutter was the accepted practice.

In winter, some sold '*da bin lo*' or large plated dishes of meat, offal and vegetables, to be either boiled or grilled at the table, set under charcoal fires.

Whilst down such a side lane and enjoying the food, drink and atmosphere late some evenings, post-PTS, Steady Eddie and AV several times encountered an old English tippler sat at another folding table, enjoying a few beers, and it turned out he was Arthur Glossop, a Labour Member of Parliament for some Northern constituency. He was engaged in regular fact-finding (or should that be 'fuck-finding?') missions to Hong Kong, hosted by an elderly expat missionary, and anti-police corruption and human rights campaigner, named Elsbeth Meddlemuch.

The two lads had to watch what they said, though, as Glossop had reported a gang of CID Kowloon expats who had spotted him in the Beefeater bistro and had burst into a raucous rendition of 'The

Red Flag', which he had deemed inappropriate and disrespectful, and several of the over-refreshed policemen lost their jobs over it, a couple who had actually thought themselves in the CID Kowloon Headquarters inner circle, and protected, as it were.

As for the latter point, being invited to a group, or attaching oneself to a group and dragging favoured officers, even rank and file, with you on transfer to another posting, particularly in CID, was called the '*ma jai*' system ('*ma jai*' meaning pony or young horse, i.e., a follower) thus encouraging a clique one could follow throughout one's career. This was based on many criteria, with some shielding of personalities within that clique, both up and down, a benefit, although often quite morally, and sometimes criminally wrong.

In some cases, 'plants' from one clique were inserted into another to see what 'rivals' were up to. Yes, as earlier mentioned, if you can't trust a policeman, then just *who* can you trust?

But maybe Glossop was ashamed to have been seen frequenting a more upmarket restaurant, rather than slinking down a side alley and imbibing amongst the rats and filth, although AV and Yates would never look upon themselves as either.

Well, maybe only once or twice then, when feeling, in the immortal words of Status Quo, 'Down, down, deeper and down!'

When trying to conduct anti-illegal gambling raids in Chung King Mansions, even when holding a valid permit or authorisation signed by a Superintendent allowing entry to specific premises to enforce the law, based on information received, it was often impossible to pinpoint where the gamblers were playing, until the Special Duty Squad (police unit conducting the raid) perhaps saw them from the 19th floor in an opposite Chung King Mansions' block, with the eighty or so gamblers also seeing *them*, and defiantly flicking or flipping the bird.

There was just no way to get across there before everyone fled.

We should mention that the Divisional Special Duty Squads (SDS) were drawn from Uniformed Branch (UB) Sergeants, PCs and WPCs working in various Sub Units within that Division, and were tasked with general anti-vice duties, in plain clothes, and for usually a three month attachment. The Squads were always headed by an Inspector as some statutes, such as in the Dangerous Drugs Ordinance, could only be enacted by an Officer of at least Inspectorate rank, with the OC/SDS reporting directly to the ADS or Assistant Divisional Superintendent.

More on specific SDS units a little further on.

But at the end of that wonderful first full evening, concluding in finding some great live music bars, they took a small boat from the Kowloon side back to the Hong Kong side of the harbour, just to experience it, and boy, was it worth the trip!

The sea level view of Central District, up to the Peak Tower on Hong Kong Island, was truly spectacular, with the biggest building on the waterfront itself being a round-windowed edifice called the Connaught Building, or, to locals, the building of a thousand assholes. These days it is dwarfed by the absolute explosion of buildings all around it.

A quick one in Popeye's, a brush and approach with and by May Ling and Ah Cheung, and then dropping Dogs in the San Fran to see his beloved, who was as pleased as punch to see him now that the Yanks and Ozzies had departed, then good night all.

Once they left PTS on passing out, Nev, Yates, Lats, Two Dicks and AV initially lived in Wanchai Mess but worked in Yaumatei Division, and all took the Hong Kong and Yaumatei ferries to and from work, and the sight of Hong Kong Island appearing out of the mist as they came back early morning from Kowloon after night shift, was really a sight to behold.

Unfortunately, a not-so-wholesome sight or sound, and a sickening, repulsive spectacle as a whole, were the many old Chinese men at that time of morning, coughing and hawking their guts up and gobbing the phlegm onto the bare wooden deck of the ferry.

The football was going well, with the Friday afternoon kick-arounds still much looked forward to, even on one occasion inviting a team in from the Customs Department where one of the local Recruit Inspectors, a Kim Chui, had formerly worked. An embarrassingly comfortable 5-0 win.

Another time they were invited to play at the Hong Kong Football Club in Happy Valley, along from the racecourse, by someone who'd formerly been in the police. Nev had the whole of PTS to choose from and under floodlights, a first for most of them, they did well in only losing 2-1. Back to the changing room and what was waiting for them? Oranges? Squash? Water? No, none of those, but even better, two very large jugs of draft San Mig beer!

AV, Nev and Yates were chosen to play for the full PTS Team in the Police Inter Division League and Cup matches, the games being held at the Police Club at Boundary Street in Mongkok in Kowloon. The problem with that was that the team would leave by PTS bus at 07.00 hours, then straight to a restaurant in upper Kowloon for '*yam cha*', or breakfast, which consisted of dim sum dishes.

Then to a game maybe starting at 11.00 hours, and by the time they'd changed back into their civvies, ostensibly to get back to PTS, it would be 13.00 hours and then to another restaurant for lunch, returning to the school at perhaps 15.00 hours or later.

It took up too much class time, frankly, and the lads couldn't justify that amount being wasted. Plus, the team consisted mainly of Sergeants on the staff who had a nice little number going, and quite a skive, the captain or team manager being able to reclaim the amounts spent on food and drink from a generous allowance provided by the Police Welfare Fund, as was the case with most police sports teams Force-wide.

How the few recruit PCs in the team managed to afford the time off, who knows? A free pass on a lesson or two, perhaps? AV would be in goal and antsy, as despite how much he shouted for the ball, either to 'take it' or for a back pass, his Chinese team mates darn near dribbled around him, or kicked it away from him, almost out of his hands.

Not worth going, actually, although later playing for their respective Kowloon Division was a far better experience, although the violence was often the same, as was the cussing.

Some of those games resulted in near full-on fights with kung fu kicks, and much verbal abuse, and the strange thing about it was that 'Fuck you!' or 'Fuck off!' given in English could result in a red card, but a Cantonese-spoken '*Dew lay la mo!*' meaning (can you remember?) 'Fuck your mother!' used so often by very practised vulgarians everywhere, resulted in no censure at all.

By the way, a vulgarian is not a pointy-eared, smart-arsed, mind-moulded scientific officer out of the original *Star Trek* series.

In some of those football matches, the lads, then with a few common Cantonese phrases under their belts, couldn't quite understand when some Police Constables from one team, mostly angrily, aggressively and challengingly asked others in the opposing team, after a bad foul or hard tackle, or whatever, '*High bin dough lay*?' or 'Where do you come from?' Surely whoever had demanded to know that must already have known which side they were playing against, and why the hell, 'in the heat of battle,' would anyone want to know where anyone else lived?

The question, as the SM3 later learnt, was actually a Triad identification challenge from one MOTS (Member of a Triad Society) to a suspected Triad member, to find out which, if any, Triad Society he belonged to, such answer determining in many cases whether they were friend or foe, and to lay down territorial or bragging rights, and demand 'face' and to acknowledge superiority or give deference, one to the other, according to respective rank within, and according to the relative importance of possibly rival societies.

The translation of '*High bin dough lay*?' as above is literally correct, but the street or gutter-level meaning is better phrased as, 'To whom do you belong?', which makes its aim a little clearer.

And *that* was amongst fellow police officers, supposedly enjoying a game of football, with such challenges all too common amongst young thugs in the real world outside of PTS, with the answers and possible escalation sometimes resulting in 'afters' often too dreadful and too bloody to recount in this section.

But Triad Societies didn't exist in Hong Kong, thought the SM3, because their PTS Instructor had told them so, hadn't they?

So, let's be charitable – shall we? – and just say that the players the SM3 heard and saw coming out with that stuff were merely winding each other up, because if they were truly claiming, professing or purporting to be MOTS (even allowing that Triad Societies no longer existed) then that would still be a criminal offence and surely the team coaches, usually Station Sergeants, but in some instances local Inspectors and Chief Inspectors, would have done something about that criminality, wouldn't they?

But back at PTS, the Mess had been closed for renovations, and temporarily relocated to an adapted room in a classroom block, which resulted in it being a pokey and claustrophobic little hole, and no thank you very much in the main for the SM3. In particular, the sight and sound of McMee working the rounds and toadying to senior squad members was anathema to AV, particularly after one previous incident when Nev had thought of throwing darts at the ceiling propellor fan in the old Mess, and it was then like Russian Roulette in trying to avoid wherever the dart pinged off to, particularly with the fan on high speed.

Fair enough, they'd caused three small holes in a wooden dividing panel, but McMee, with his upturned face and sneering demeanour, came across and told them that, being Mess Secretary, he couldn't ignore it, and would report them to their course instructors. Somewhat peeved, they thought that he was overreacting by 'grassing on them, early doors in their police careers', when they were merely exhibiting youthfully exuberance, and naïve high spirits.

But the next morning, Bob Y was bollocked by Frank Topley, who had the temerity to tell him that Nev and AV were not suitable companions for him, and Nev and AV standing tall 'before the man' in the form of Frick Jacobs, both also receiving a fierce roasting, and who warned woe betide them if they failed the next exam, which was the worst of the lot as it was mainly concerned with Road Traffic Legislation and Construction and Use Regulations.

It so happened that all three flew through the exam, with seventy four percent, the highest they would ever achieve.

Nev also involved them in a drinking game called 'Jacks' which they'd play when the bar was quiet or when they became more senior and had the run of the place.

Basically, four jacks in a set of cards. One lad would draw a jack and have to order a drink, or combination of drinks, such as a beer with a whisky in it, or a round-the-world cocktail. The second bloke to pick out a jack would pay for it. The third would sip it, and the fourth, and *this* was the challenge, would down it in one.

But now, some fifty years later, sad or glad to say, none of the surviving WCH5 could possibly down any alcoholic beverage in one, these days even struggling with cold Horlicks or cocoa.

They wouldn't want to, in any case. And it's a safe bet their relative spouses wouldn't allow them to, even if they should perchance wish to try and relive some exploits from their younger days.

Now please don't think it was all fun and games while training; the study was taken very seriously and they did have other outdoor pursuits, not totally involving drunkenness.

For example, Hong Kong was blessed with many fine cinemas, many of them, like the Lee Garden Theatre, also being multi-purpose venues, magnificently and lavishly decorated with balconies, orchestra pits, etc., showing the latest Hollywood movies in English, but with Chinese subtitles.

There was also a burgeoning HK film industry, particularly with

Shaw Brothers producing many films in Cantonese primarily for the local populace.

The gang liked a night out at both the theatres and the cinemas, especially the midnight shows on Saturday nights, with three specific occasions coming to mind.

The first was to watch *'The Eiger Sanction'* starring Clint Eastwood and George Kennedy at the New York Theatre in Causeway Bay, which was a large venue with a very curved, modernistic screen. Unfortunately, the five of them could only purchase tickets for the very front row and, with the curved screen, the film was almost unwatchable. During the mountain-climbing scene, it was a case of, 'He's over here!' and 'Now he's over here!'

Then they went to watch *'Jaws'* with the whole row of them a little tipsy, admittedly, leaping out of their seats when Ben Gardner's one-eyed, severed head popped out from under his shark-ravaged sunken boat.

A third time, Nev and AV took two girls from the San Fran, along with Dogs and Lilly, to watch a film called *'The Dove,'* starring Joseph Bottoms, or Joe Bum to his mates, but no hanky-panky in the dark, not even a grope or a kiss, and an awful film. Still, nice to have a bit of female company, and then it was egg curry time at Ming's Café just down the road, then a goodnight peck on the cheek as the girls left for who knows where, along with Dogs and Lilly.

Still, a pleasant enough evening, thought AV, until Nev turned to him and growled, 'Waste of fucking time, that was!' and wanted to then crawl up a few Wanchai staircases to see what was on offer.

They also went to see Helen Reddy in concert, she of 'I Am Woman' and 'Angie Baby' fame, and that was fine, and also Ray Charles, an icon of pop music. But I tell you one thing about him, he didn't like anyone joining in, especially on his ballads, and I swear that, despite his blindness, he was trying to stare Two Dicks down to get him to stop his raucous accompaniment.

Mind you, it was getting on the lads' tits too.

Now while they had started to think of Hong Kong as their new home, they hadn't of course forgotten their roots, especially as it seemed so hard to get one out there unless you paid for one, nor had they forgotten their families. But no email or satellite phones or overseas direct dialling, but rather the occasional trip on a Saturday night down to the Cable and Wireless offices in Central, to book a call back home to their kith and kin.

Generally, these calls were fine, *if* the intended recipient was at home because these ideas were usually spur-of-the-drunken moment affairs, and if there wasn't too bad an echo over those thousands of miles, otherwise the conversations were like the Two Ronnies' sketch of 'Answering the question before last,' where no one could make sense of what was going on. Better than nothing, though, even though it was difficult the next day, sometimes, to remember what had been said.

And Nev's posturing as 'rough, tough and hard to bluff' took a knock one night when he was close to tears after hearing his dog, Ginty, barking over the telephone, all the way back in Jersey.

One particular Saturday, while assembled on the drill square just before the parade commenced, Franny Fong approached AV and told him there was a telegram for him in the office and that he should immediately fall out and get it.

Oh Christ! Now what?

He had quite a few elderly relatives, and dreaded the worst, only to find it was from the almost forgotten Maggie Pigswill, delighting in telling him that she and 'The Perve' Purvis had married, that AV had had his chance and if he was jealous, well jolly well serve him right, at all of which he had a damned good laugh and drank their ill health down the China Fleet Club a little later.

So yes, there was also the telegram system, but one likely to instil fear and trepidation when initially received at either end.

AV incidentally briefly had it in mind to reply and wind-up the Perve by asking if his new missus was still shagging the driver from

Bond Worth's parent factory at Stourbridge, after he delivered bales of wool and acrylic fibre to Thrupp twice a week, and who was known to the Stroud girls as 'Tiny'?

He'd also ask him if she knew that 'Tiny's' nickname amongst the carpet factory workers in that Midlands town was 'Wart Dick', and that it wasn't only his thanks he'd passed on to some of his many conquests there, this information learnt by Mike Jones, the Stroud factory's Production Manager, from tit-bits he'd learnt at a Health and Safety Meeting at the parent branch, and which had filtered down to Gina, who in turn had taken great delight in including such a delicious piece of gossip in the letter or two before last.

However, with so much else now in his new life, the Bucket simply could not be bothered, and while Tom and Norman were really Petty, AV was trying very hard not to be. (Norman Petty? Buddy Holly's manager.)

Now Nev at this time, probably to help him pull the birds (which it didn't) bought himself a light-blue Ford Capri, his pride and joy for a good few months, almost as proud of it as he was of his imitation gold, almost-brick-sized Omega digital watch, one of the first on the market.

Yes, he *did* like nice things, such as Paco Rabanne after-shave, and dental floss, while AV and Yates were still quite content with the smell of their Lifebuoy toilet soap, and the occasional dig at their gnashers with a toothpick, should any be lying around and if and when they ever thought about it.

But after every pee he took, Tenspeed invariably washed his hands, though AV and Yates certainly had him there as they had been brought up not to pee on them in the first place.

He was very generous in taking the lads around in his car, though, the first trips being to Stanley where, when they entered a Park and Shop supermarket, there was a lovely girl displaying honey wine for sale and, finding out her schedule, they visited her for quite a few Saturday afternoons after that, enjoying sampling the wine, but never buying a single bottle.

And then to some of the beaches past Repulse Bay, very quiet compared to Deep Water Bay, and there they played footie, swam and messed around with a frisbee.

One time, though, an underwater swimmer suddenly poked his head up between Yates and Nev, who were frisbeeing, and the leading spinning edge of the frisbee caught him smack bang on the forehead.

One never thought that the pair could hold their breaths so long underwater, submerging themselves immediately until they thought the man would have left, which he had.

AV, meanwhile, didn't think it possible he could swim back to shore, having retrieved that errant piece of plastic, while laughing so much.

And while on a beach somewhere in North Kowloon, they decided to try water skiing, with a local fellow touting for business. But, as with many things, like marriage for instance, it's a damned sight harder than it seems. Nev and Yates could manage to stand up but not be pulled very far, while Bottomley quickly let go of the rope, causing the driver to fall out of his speed boat, which careered into the swimming area, the propellor cutting someone's foot very badly.

The bloke was prosecuted for not being licensed for hire, the SM3 having to give statements at the Marine Department to explain their part in all of it.

Another few times post PTS, the three of them sat high up on Radar Hill in North Kowloon, which afforded a spectacular view of the continual stream of aircraft landing at Kai Tak Airport which, instead of coming in over the sea, often flew at low level over the jam-packed areas of Mongkok and Kowloon City, depending on wind speed and direction of course.

When Gina and Geoff Bottomley flew into Hong Kong in 1979,

Gina was ashen on arrival as she'd been badly shaken by being able to look into peoples' homes and clearly see the features of Chinese folk sat at their dining tables, doing their ironing and going about their domestic chores, as their RAF aircraft flew what to her seemed dangerously low, on final approach into Kai Tak Airport, over those two districts which were some of the most densely crowded in the world.

No, Gina of course hadn't flown before, except on her broomstick, as some who had formerly felt the harsh, acerbic lash of her tongue and hair-trigger temper would jealously but stupidly whisper whilst she was abroad, but then immediately hoping to God that word didn't get back to her about it.

But coming back to Tenspeed and his Ford Capri, one particularly pleasant outing was to a restaurant in a boating area called Hebe Haven, near Sai Kung, but it caused the heebie-jeebies as AV reversed the car into a large stack of empty Coke crates on a pallet and sack truck, knocking the whole lot into the sea. Never mind, none broke, and ten quid for a young chap to retrieve them. Half-crown and sixpence time, that's for sure, but at least the rear bumper hadn't been damaged by the incident, although the same couldn't be said about their nerves.

They even took another Hong Kong and Yaumatei ferry back out to the then still rural Lantau Island, which they'd visited on their first week, where there were some lovely walks up Sunset Peak, or the five hours' hike from Tung Chung, on the west coast, over the island to Silver Mine Bay, on the east coast, from where the ferry back to Central, Hong Kong Island departed.

Wonderful times, sitting on the open back deck of the ferry, quaffing cans of Carlsberg (who had the concession) and watching the marine traffic and the approach to the main shipping harbour, and the comings and goings at the Kwai Chung Container Terminal, then slowly back to 'civilisation.'

They even once stayed overnight on Lantau Island and because there were no hotels, or guest houses, they very unwisely slept on the beach, with no towels underneath them, to awake to find they had been badly bitten by sand fleas.

It was one of those 'never again' moments! Yet again!

'Punjab Pete' Spicer had also bought himself a car, a rather underpowered white Triumph Spitfire sports model and to help him try it out one night after a few beveringtons, the SM3 and Peter, making four people in total, piled into it as best they could, as the King of the Khyber Rifles drove it up the busy Wong Nai Chong Gap Road, intending to take them to Wanchai, but the blessed thing kept breaking down.

Never mind, he had plenty of people to help push, and by hook or by crook, they managed to get it back to PTS, and onwards towards the car park at the back gatehouse end, past the drill square. However, as the car stalled again, two alighted and pushed and bump-started it again before jumping into the boot, out of exhaustion, for the final part of the ill-fated journey. Peter though, already well-oiled, must have been a trifle confused, as he turned right, down the slope and onto the drill square itself, performing ever-decreasing circles, much to the amusement and then horror of his passengers.

Horror? Yes, because centrifugal force being what it is, the passengers sat in the boot, clinging on with their legs hanging out almost touching the ground, were almost thrown out amidst the squeal of rubber, much smoke, and screeches from the tyres and brakes.

Then back up the slope to the car park, with some common sense and order restored, hoping to hell that the day's Duty Officer hadn't heard anything, nor the officers in the staff quarters almost overlooking the square.

Thankfully, all appeared quiet on the PTS front, but the next day there was a lot of concern as to whether the square had been messed up, with tell-tale rubber tyre marks left all over it.

But no! A miracle. Just a slight darkening in one place, which no one noticed except those who'd been responsible for putting it there, who had been very fortunate indeed.

Quite frankly, it wasn't so much the ships that pass in the night, but the nights that had passed in the ships, if you get the meaning.

You would have thought that by now the WCH5, and some of the others, would have learnt that alcohol, especially the abuse of it, didn't really go hand in hand with being a policeman, and supposedly an officer at that, albeit under training.

However, you must give the Young Turks some credit in so often 'going off the rails' because of it, in such an extremely masochistic manner, and then recovering so easily, but it did give them a 'buzz' and relieved pressure for a while, until its depressive affect, sometime later, and in some instances, began to take hold.

Yes, 'drink' does have a darker side, particularly when one may later reflect that life itself can have a sting in its tail, but at that stage there was absolutely no need to worry, with delirium tremens, gout, liver damage, renal failure, blackouts, hallucinations, and even death itself all joked about but not given a moment's serious concern. Not then anyway.

But more of that later. Let's have a beer for now, and forget it for a while, shall we?

I'll be back with a lot more serious stuff later, so for now let's concentrate on the lads as they could finally see the light at the end of the tunnel in respect of their training.

And I'll be advising you that peeing into a car engine's extremely hot radiator could either result in your nut cluster being scalded, or you not being able to direct the stream into the fill hole, and thus risk cracking the engine block!

But if your fruit and two veg are ever scolded by a woman, kick her out and say her tits are too small, and how dare she complain at what nature gave you and which are certainly too good for the likes of her!

You couldn't buy this advice, you know, just a result of my many bitter experiences that I'm now willing to share.

Take it or leave it, as you no doubt will, but in any case, I'll catch you in the next section.

Bye for now.

Chapter Twelve

Moving on Up!

Despite mildly and sometimes bitterly touching on the alcohol issue in the previous chapter, I will have to address the police drinking culture later. Sorry. But only if I sober up by then.

And now to explain my medical and mechanical concerns expressed at the conclusion of that last chapter entitled 'The Nitty Gritty', and it involves Nev and a car full of the usual suspects one Saturday afternoon in his Ford Capri, driving past Stanley on the south side of Hong Kong Island, towards a quiet beach.

'But goddang it, thar, boy,' just a half mile from the turn-off to the beach, steam came hissing out of the engine and, with a loud clunking from under the bonnet, the car came to a juddering halt. Managing to somehow 'pop the hood' and avoid the bubbling liquid frothing from the radiator, Nev prised its cap off with nothing further to do until it had completely vented its contents.

The car was on a very quiet stretch of road with no passing traffic, the mechanical knowledge and indeed aptitude amongst Nev's passengers being just as scanty as his; basically, you just put petrol in and drive. But obviously the engine had overheated; that was plain enough, and then Nev had a brainwave. 'Come on, lads!' he ordered. 'Let's take it in turns to stand on the front bumper and pee into the radiator!'

Obviously, all that leadership training at PTS had not gone to waste, so the five of them duly obliged, but it must be said it was a rather pathetic effort as AV couldn't manage to 'go', which was very unusual for him, as he had a terribly weak bladder, and the others were very hit and miss, sometimes finding the fill hole and other times peeing on the hot engine and getting a mini sauna of hot, steamy urine. No time for shyness, though; needs must prevail, but it's a great pity that it hadn't happened on the way back, as each bladder would surely have been fuller, and thus more able to make a meaningful contribution to the cause.

Maybe not, though, as their aims would definitely have been worse than they had been, probably drenching the engine and all those cables and bits and pieces on top with their beery widdle.

(But in hindsight, while there was nothing at all wrong with Nev's general idea, the actual method of implementing his intended plan could perhaps have been better served by just weeing into a bottle, or a Coke or beer can and *then* pouring the contents into the radiator. Oh well! We all learn!)

Eventually, a passing vehicle stopped, the occupants luckily having a large container of water with them, which was poured into the radiator, but sadly to no avail. The engine just would not start, and thus the very kind passers-by squeezed the lads into their van and drove them back to PTS, where Nev arranged for the car to be recovered and repaired.

Another lesson learnt; never commence any car journey of note without a full bladder and an emergency kit in the boot.

In fairness to Tenspeed, though, he wasn't all 'bluff and bullshit' and was very adept at thinking on his feet, a man of many interests, including golf and cricket, his heroes at the time being the golfer Johnny Miller and the footballer Chris Jones, who played professionally for Spurs, and with whom he had played at schoolboy level in Jersey.

Before joining the police, and while still at school, he obtained a scholarship to study for a private pilot's licence (PPL), which he duly attained, after which he had many adventurous jaunts with his two best mates from Jersey, flying across to France in a rented plane (somewhat briefly referred to in Chapter Nine.)

And *how* they enjoyed the change of scenery, experiencing the more laid-back culture, the magnificent cuisine, and, of course, throwing as much fine wine down their throats as they could, the limiting factor being whether Nev would collapse pissed - in which case they'd be stranded in St Malo for a night - or whether he would still be able to keep one eye open, handle the controls, obey the instructions of the French and British Air Traffic Controllers, and then be able to make a safe, although often bouncy landing, in St Helier at the end of it all.

That last section was obviously a parody, but Nev did admit to some wonderful tomfoolery, and magnificently carefree, high jinks with those friends. (As I've said before, there's no reason why this can't be fun!)

However, to keep his licence valid, he was required to fly a plane for a certified minimum number of hours per year, and so one Sunday he arranged for a refresher flight in a four seater, Cessna light aircraft, courtesy of the Hong Kong Aero Club at Kai Tak Airport, with Bottomley and Yates most willingly going along for a ride, if only to prove that Nev was not exaggerating about his aviation exploits.

Sure enough, accompanied by a flying instructor (who was also a Cathay Pacific Airways pilot), necessary because Kai Tak was a very busy international airport, all four poured into a Cessna 172 plane and took a fantastic one hour flight around the quieter and very rural parts of the New Territories, AV a little worried as he'd only flown once before, and that on the way out to Hong Kong of course.

Nev did all the flying under the watchful eye of the instructor and according to him, our hero did well.

It turned out to be a most memorable event for the trio, one of the highlights of their time in Hong Kong, and they followed it with a splendid Indian meal at the Gaylord Restaurant in Chimsy, the first time they had tried a dish called *aloo chat*, or spicy potatoes. Lovely stuff. The Gaylord's management incidentally substantially increased its business when it changed its name to the Bengali Tiger, the former name apparently putting off otherwise potential but 'straight' customers. How queer.

The Aero Club, coincidentally, was from where a notorious former senior police officer called Peter Godber gained access to a commercial aircraft out of HK, on his flight from ICAC on charges of large-scale corruption in the early 1970s, having a valid airport pass to further aid his ultimately futile and temporary escape.

It's a pity that Nev hadn't had contact with the Aero Club prior to a whole day PTS exercise involving their squads, or else they may have made use of it in similarly trying to gain access to a commercial aircraft, to test the level of security at Kai Tak Airport.

'May' is the operative word, but more than likely, the SM3 would still have done exactly what they did by walking straight to a fully manned security gate at the runway's fringe, and immediately allowing themselves to be 'arrested', the airport police already having become aware of the operation.

An Inspector John Hoyle picked them up in a Land Rover and very kindly deposited them at the entrance to the airport departure lounge where they plonked themselves at the bar and enjoyed the lively, cosmopolitan atmosphere of most airports in general, whilst pulling on half-pint mugs of draft San Mig. Well, pretending to be a terrorist was thirsty work.

To their amazement, they spotted Plod (Maurice Smiley) walking across the departure hall to Immigration Control, decked out as a pilot, epaulettes, cap and all, and carrying a flight case. He actually made it onto an aircraft that was readying for departure and thence the flight deck where the pilot was conducting final checks, and who was very surprised indeed to be told his aircraft had been 'hijacked'! Bravo to Plod.

Just imagine trying to do that in these present times. You'd be shot if you even strayed onto the runway, let alone a plane.

The WCH5 and three others subsequently attended the annual Aero Club Christmas Ball at the Sheraton Hotel in Chimsy that December, tickets arranged by Nev, of course, hiring dinner jackets for the occasion.

But presumably because of their short PTS haircuts, they were asked as they approached the entrance if they were members of the band, which proved to be a contingent of British Army bandsmen from the Stanley Battalion.

'You bloody what, mate?'

The ball's organiser then back-pedalled and asked if they'd like cocktails before the function commenced, receiving a reply from one of the aggrieved Probationary Inspectors of, 'Yes, mate. Eight pints of San Miguel please!'

Ah, class! You just can't buy it!

After the function, they all bundled off and some of them practically fell through the doors of a handily placed and highly respectable massage parlour and steam bath nearby, but where the management refused them service as they thought it was a police raid. Talk about ironic.

(They'd also incidentally worn rented dinner jackets when attending a Boxing Smoker at the Hilton Hotel, some months earlier. Them of all people! At a Boxing Smoker, puffing on Cuban cigars and supping fine brandy, after a slap-up feed, while mainly British Army pugilists were smacking the crap out of one another. Them – yes, hard to believe! It hardly seemed possible. If their mates back in the UK could have seen them, they no doubt would have laughed their socks off, probably thinking that their old chums were in fancy dress.)

Another fine day out though was when the SM3 went to an Air Display at Sek Kong airfield in the New Territories around that time, at which they had a short flight around Yuen Long for about 200 HK dollars each, which was great fun, and the highlight of that particular day was watching some amazing stunt aerobatics.

But blimey, wouldn't it take a lot of pee to fill the radiators in those engines!

Another sporting event they attended was the touring MCC cricket team playing the Hong Kong Cricket XI at the new Royal Hong Kong Cricket Club ground at Wong Nei Chong Gap where a very fresh-faced David Gower was making an early appearance, under the captaincy of Mike Denness.

And yet another was again at the Hilton Hotel, to watch the so-called 'David Hicks Test Match', where a bank of television screens had been set up, with as much beer as you could manage for a hundred Hong Kong dollars, until stocks ran out.

On a completely different topic, but as somewhat earlier mentioned, the RHKP were an armed body, with the standard issued weapon to beat Constables in uniform being a Colt 38mm revolver with six rounds of ammunition, carried in a waist holster and secured to their Sam Browne belts by a lanyard. WPCs did not carry firearms.

Plain-clothes CID officers were also armed with Colt revolvers, issued to them on a permanent basis, as long as they remained in the CID, and they were responsible for the maintenance, cleaning and security of their individual weapon.

This though was a heady responsibility, with rumours of some detectives lending or hiring their weapons to fellow Triad members or criminal associates (yes, it happens!)

One very young-looking local Recruit Inspector on a course after the SM3's, a fellow called Brendan 'Brenda' Cheung (so nicknamed as he appeared a trifle effeminate), after six months in the Uniformed Branch immediately after leaving PTS, was posted to the CID at North Point on Hong Kong Island. He was thus issued a personal revolver, which he took with him of course on being posted to other CID Formations as part of his career path. (Career path? Well, he went on leave and when he returned there was a hole to fill at another Formation and he was available, so he had to fit into it.)

However, somehow, somewhere, he lost it, had it stolen or lent it out but had not had it returned, but neglected to tell anyone, and thus didn't the proverbial barrage balloon go up when it was found in the possession of a notorious ex-police thug, during the execution of a search warrant some six years later.

Bye, Brenda. See you in two years. Have fun inside, dear.

But how could he have gotten away with it for so long when firearms should have been inspected by line supervisors at least once per month?

Thinking it through, though, he probably didn't tell his senior officers on transfer that he had been issued a revolver, as it was optional for male Inspectors, with a typewriter in fact of far more use to most of them than a weapon, the amount of administrative paperwork and crime and case reports they had to churn out.

An apocryphal tale had it that sometime before the lads on courses 101 and 102 joined the RHKP, a young Inspector, full of 'piss and vinegar' after being posted to the Criminal Investigation Department in some Division or other, 'tried it on' with a Woman Detective Sergeant on his investigation team, obviously desperate to impress and to be thought of as 'the big I am!'

He took her up to the empty Officers' Mess late on one evening shift, and there, for some goddam reason, but admittedly after a few beers, he simulated a game of Russian Roulette with his personal issue Colt 38 Detective special revolver, but badly miscalculated and blew his brains out!

What the hell? But the Woman Detective Sergeant's story could not be disproved, not with five unspent bullets in his pocket and one spent shell in the chamber, with gunshot residue on his right hand and clothing.

And apparently the story did seem about right, as many knew of the young officer's penchant for trying to push himself forward. But what a way to go about it!

It was a pity he hadn't been at PTS the same time as the SM3, so he could have learnt how to just throw darts at a high-speed ceiling fan if he wanted to push his derring-do to the fore?

Or would he have been more worried about making holes in the Mess fixtures and fittings, rather than a large one in his own head?

Anyway, 'Death by Misadventure' was the coroner's findings and quite right too. Done and dusted.

No, some people just could not be trusted with personal issued firearms, and, in fact, there were intermittent cases of police officers of various ranks committing suicide by shooting themselves throughout the time the WCH5 were in the police - and most certainly not only Mingus Muffet, whom you'll encounter later.

Anyway, back to the intended topic of firearms training.

The Police Tactical Unit and the Special Duty Unit within PTU Headquarters were the most heavily armed and had access to a wide range of weapons, such as tear gas, wooden and rubber projectiles, and Armalite AR15 semi-automatic rifles for long-range firing, all part of their crowd control, hostage, riot or serious emergency response situations.

New male recruits of all ranks at PTS were introduced to the Colt 38 and the AR15 rifle during their training, and thus in due course both squads began formal weaponry familiarisation, strictly supervised yet again by Tony Ho and Franny Fong, although really there wasn't much to take in.

Other than the strict range procedure and safety protocols that were drilled into them again and again, it was down to basics, just a question of pointing the revolver in the direction of paper targets mounted at suitable and varying distances away, taking aim, and then firing, either by single action (pulling the trigger once) or double action (cocking the hammer and then pulling the trigger, which did not require so much pressure).

With practice and guidance, the newcomers began to improve their accuracy and consistency on the Colt 38 with everyone soon up to the required standard, except, for some annoying reason, AV, Lats and the Scotsman, Sadler Wells. Lats and AV were standing next together on the range and were somehow hitting each other's targets and smashing the woodwork off the frames.

Bottomley initially, for a joke, then thought of an idea: he surreptitiously used a biro pen to poke a few holes in both his and the adjacent target to make it look as if he and Lats were doing fine.

Thus the legend of the Point 38 biro was born.

This continued for a while, and was thought of, by them, as a joke but both knew it had to stop, with the hope being that they'd naturally improve, which they could have done if Billy 'Whizzer' Nairn had not shopped them, and what a bollocking the CDMI Effin-Jones gave them.

He actually was flabbergasted at how they thought they could get away with it, as their maths were plain stupid. After the DMIs had been informed about them, they naturally paid particular attention to Lats and AV. Prior to that, though, they couldn't fathom how they sometimes found nine holes in their targets whereas the Colt 38 only fired six bullets? It looked as if they were hitting the target okay eventually, but had added a few holes for safety's sake, and in panic, just in case, before the targets had been officially checked by the DMIs.

However, with everyone else having passed their revolver course at the first attempt, Latimer, Bottomley and Wells had a carefully scrutinised and supervised reshoot and came through it with flying bullets.

In hindsight, the actions of AV and Lats were irresponsible, for if they had passed their final shoot by manufacturing a couple of extra holes, and then in the real world had shot a bystander in the course of their duty instead of, say, the deadly violent criminal they'd been aiming at, wouldn't the crap have hit the fan!

No one had any problems using the AR15, the Sterling machine gun or the Remington shotguns, though, which were great fun to use.

And besides, the targets for those were too far away to stick holes in!

But to raise an issue on irresponsibility, every trained officer was required to attend a qualifying firearms shoot once per year, with ranges at Mid-Levels in Central, Smuggler's Ridge in Kowloon, one in PHQ, plus the one at PTS.

PTU had their own up in the New Territories, which NT police officers also used.

It was the case though that many officers of all ranks, on range supervisory duty, would mark down their mates or senior officers on request as having attended, as a favour, as they couldn't be bothered making the trek out to the back of beyond. Thus, the range staff had six extra bullets a time, which they themselves could blast away to their heart's content.

This would obviously not go on in these more enlightened times. Would it?

Sour grapes? No thanks, I never drink English wine.

As for 'Whizzer' Nairn, what goes around, comes around, and he got the comeuppance he deserved, and was lucky to escape a few years in prison (more on this later), if only for missing that wide-open goal during that PTS football game if you remember (Chapter 8), and should have been hauled up for cheating in the final PTS exams. He was a smoker but despite no smoking being allowed in class, he had a fag packet beside him during the various papers and changed it three or four times for ones he had earlier prepared and kept in his briefcase.

No need to be a detective to realise he had crib notes written on those packets and the invigilator must have been as blind as a bat not to have seen it.

Some class members let him know he'd been tagged and thus he had to find a new way of cheating. I know! How about inside your cap?

Where oh where – as in so much to be brought up in further chapters – is the moral equivalency??

At this stage, AV had to visit the PTS doctor as he'd stuck toilet tissue in his ear to lessen the noise on the firing range but had stuck it in too far and couldn't get it out. Possibly a case of shit for brains. Then they'd gone swimming and thus the tissue had expanded inside, what with the ingress of sea water, and it hurt like billy-o.

The doctor fished it out with a large pair of tweezers, problem solved, with the advice to use proper ear defenders in future.

Steady Eddie's twenty first birthday on 16th August had come and gone, the exact same day and year that AV's sister Laura married, and two years later, the same day that Elvis Presley passed to glory, glory, hallelujah, but I bet Elvis really wished he was in Dixie, or in the land of cotton instead, although his soul certainly continues to go marching on. (Just listen to 'American Trilogy' by the King if you don't believe me.)

They had spent a pleasant, relaxed yet celebratory afternoon in the China Fleet Club on gin and tonics, sat in very comfy armchairs, ceiling fans gently circulating the air, with a table of American Marine Officers seated behind them. Tommy arrived late and, on asking how many drinks he needed to catch up, ordered nine gins in a large glass, topped up with tonic, from the dickie-bowed waiter they'd kept busy all afternoon, and walloped the whole lot down in one. But it doesn't work like that – does it? – and he was immediately well on the way to being totally and royally off his head.

Nine gin and tonics is actually a lot for most people, and it was amazing how Steady Eddie was managing, although his Mr Kool act was tarnished somewhat when he threw a handful of ice over his shoulder, landing it right in the middle of the American marines.

Whoops! Apologies! 'He's twenty one today, gentlemen!' and they showed they *were* gentlemen by smiling and shrugging the whole thing off, and even with some congratulations being thrown around.

Then a wobbly walk along Hennessy Road to the Furama Hotel with its revolving top-floor restaurant, and into the Go Down Bar in the basement, the front entrance always manned from early evening by a large, portly Chinese chap who invariably wore an evening suit.

Then Jesus H Christ, they could hear him before they saw him, and there was 'Mouthy' Mungo McMee sitting amongst a table of sixteen or seventeen year old International School students, all Caucasians, mouthing off about how the proper way to hold a weapon in a knife fight was to keep it low and move it up quickly, and how he had such big biceps that no one could ever beat him at arm-wrestling, but challenging them to have a go anyway.

The kids were looking at one another, embarrassed it seemed, but what was the score there? Was he helping them buy drinks as they were underage, or something like that?

Was he lonely and they happened to be the only ones he could inflict his ego upon?

On spotting the new arrivals, no, he didn't dip his hand in his sporran, but asked Two Dicks to arm-wrestle, as he pumped himself up, which Two Dicks, red rag to a bullshitter, declined, chiding McMee that while he was a strong enough bloke, he should be a lot more muscular than he was, bearing in mind the frame he had.

Mungo was taken aback by the public affront but couldn't find a suitable reply that wouldn't have further embarrassed him in front of the kids, so clammed up, discretion being the better part of valour.

AV thoroughly enjoyed the put-down! Yes, Tommy generally spoke his mind, especially with a bellyful of drink inside him.

But Mungo presumably never told those youngsters about what he did after rugby with some of his mates, how they liked to take a Canadian team member, a Clint 'Chopper' Woodman, who apparently had a huge dong, to a brothel, and try and find a harlot who would take him on, and then watch him 'at it' as the poor girl writhed and screamed (which was probably simulation, in fact). Not only once, but this appeared to be a regular occurrence.

Something not quite 'right' there, one feels. Some people live their lives vicariously, but do some also have sex through the same concept, or was it mere voyeurism?

Mind you, there was a forty-something Senior Inspector named Roger Benton in the Commercial Crime Bureau at PHQ whose former PTS mates back in the sixties, apparently, used to think it fun to watch *him* shagging after a night on the razz, they all rising up the ranks while he remained more or less as he was back then, forever labelled as 'immature'. Of course, his erstwhile mates later decried all knowledge about what they'd been up to.

Something else to remember about the Officer Corps in the RHKP; there's nothing so self-righteous as a reformed whore.

So, another way of 'getting on' in the RHKP was not to do anything untoward with and around equals that you could regret when they could be your senior officers in years to come and who could decide or influence your future.

But Mungo had been bragging about this in the reopened Mess after he'd bought Nev a yard of ale and insisted he try and drink it, probably as compensation for turning them in over the darts affair.

Nev accepted, at which AV had thought he was selling out, while Stroudies never forget, which you may remember from earlier chapters.

With almost two months under their belts at PTS, it was time for them to plan and execute the wind-up of the next batch of Recruit Inspectors to arrive from the UK as freshers, but it became evident that McMee already had matters well in hand, with him taking the same leading role of Chief Inquisitor as Piggard had done, but so full of his own ego that there was very little humour in his banter, and him not being quick-minded enough to change tack or issue witty rejoinders to answers given him.

The whole affair, a damp squib in fact, was conducted exclusively by course members from 101, with 102 only needed as spectators and to buy a few beers in the Mess for the new lads once it was over, then to take them down 'The Wanch'. (Well, McMee surely wasn't going to pay for anything himself, was he?)

So, one beer only it was and back down Hennessy Road, having a potato fight with a few pounds of spuds bought from the Go Down's kitchen, and then to 'The Wanch', once again laughingly refusing the solicitations of May Ling and Ah Cheung, to Oriental Bob's, the Popeye's Bar, and, after that, no one could remember What? Where? Who? How? or Why?

But now that the theory and practical training were at times becoming more intensive, it remained rather routine in other ways for the SM3, although the very professional and structured nature of their training resulted in them developing more confidence and become more rounded individuals.

Hong Kong was most definitely now their home and they were gradually becoming more committed and accustomed to the idea of being real policemen, maybe even beyond the initial three years they had signed on for.

Not only did they progress up the pecking order at PTS, by now wearing yellow flashes on their wristbands, but they had to accept more responsibility.

One example was that perhaps once every two months they were expected to do an overnight guard duty shift at the main gatehouse, supervising all pedestrian and vehicle traffic in and out of the main entrance.

In practice, though, they usually hung around until midnight, then delegating the responsibility to rank and file trainees, who'd be told to call them if anything untoward should happen, like juvenile expats driving a car around the drill square, an Inspector bringing an unauthorised lady back to his quarters, or to help a Superintendent in an apparently broken-down car.

Yes, the art of delegation was being quickly learnt and put to use.

However, the Duty Officer had to conduct the PTS roll call alone the following morning, which was easy enough, with no one ever reported missing.

And then there were the Dining In and Dining Out nights (Mess Nights), formal functions where the gentlemen wore their 'penguin suits' or Mess Kits, with striped trousers, cummerbunds, white shirts, dickie bows, pips worn on cutaway jackets, with the ladies in black gowns, and very elegant they looked too.

Speeches from the Baton of Honour winners, the Commandant and any guest speakers whom it was thought had something of worth to tell the Dining Out squads, those Recruit Inspectors who'd satisfactorily completed their eight month course and who would be posted to various Police Formations within a matter of days, after the following Saturday's formal Passing Out Parade, which replaced the normal Commandant's Parade and was much grander. Picture the scene with the departing Inspectors and the senior rank and file squads, all spit and polish, proudly marching past the dais in full uniform and saluting the guest of honour, invited dignitaries and selected guests, with the remainder of the squads on parade almost giving homage to their success and wishing them farewell as they passed out of the PTS.

On Dining In and Dining Out nights, the Mess Steward, the cooks, and the bar and waiting staff had to be at their best, laying out the finest Mess silver and serving up a fine three-course meal, and keep the wine flowing, while the Mess members were required to observe tradition such as formally passing the port to the left and not being allowed to leave the tables until the meal was over, which was one hell of a trial for some with weak bladders.

But after all that ritual, it was down to Mess games such as tug of war and King of the Ring (piggy-backed pairs trying to knock other pairs over) a quasi-military version of 'Off Ground Galloping Knob Rot', and everyone was at it, from the new recruits, to the Deputy Commandant, to the CDMI, to a Fire Services Department's Superintendent who was someone's guest.

A section of the police band would be playing music all the while in the background but cleared out of the way at the first sign that someone could take a tumble and scatter their instruments.

On one occasion, Tommy Two Dicks tried to use Tenspeed as a 'piggy' and then Bottomley, but they refused, although he needn't have worried; he'd certainly be piggy-backing off of them, starting some three years later, having stolen a non-police business venture idea from them, and for infinitely longer than merely ten minutes on a Mess Night too.

It was probably fortunate for Two Dicks that Nev Tenspeed had by then left the Force, by the time Tommy had prevailed on his in-laws to act on the stolen business idea, with more on this in the final pages of 'End Games' (Chapter 15).

AV 'The Bucket' Bottomley, while still in the RHKP when Two Dicks 'did the dirty' just cynically, resignedly and disappointedly put it down to yet more betrayal, and another example of the dangers of trusting anyone. However, he did revert back to his Stroudie roots and sneakily and slyly duly obtained some measure of revenge and payback in due course… read on, dear readers, read on.

But back to Mess Night, the WCH5 bucked up considerably when it was time for the Boat Race; a team of four with a half pint of beer before each man, and at the whistle the first had to down his drink, then the second could start and so it followed to the last man who was usually the biggest glutton, or swilly, or pisshead, if you like.

Well, with the Bucket, Tommy, the much-improved Yates and Tenspeed, by crikey, what a team, and they won it on two or three Mess Nights in a row.

Then, as the throng thinned out, it was either a few final beers in the Mess, or down to 'The Wanch' in their Mess Kits, and a matter of honour to still be wearing them when fronting up for roll call the following morning, taken particularly seriously by Nev.

Once, whilst the PTS Mess was being renovated, the function was held at the Superintendents' Mess at Police Headquarters, and thus everyone it seemed sloped off afterwards to 'The Wanch' just a stone's throw away, particularly as in those hallowed halls no Mess games were allowed, not even the Boat Race! That *was* a disappointment to the SM3 and friends, as you'd probably imagine, not least because the beer for the competition was free for contestants, the cost coming out of Mess Funds.

On another infamous occasion, back at PTS, during the lull before the speeches, and the port being of a particularly strong vintage, some banter took place between Nev on one table, and Norrie Pinkney on another, and then a few bread rolls were thrown both ways, and before they knew it the place was in an absolute uproar, bread rolls flying all over the place, all in good humour it must be said, but most upsetting to the Brass and invited guests at the top table. It took a while before order was restored and for the formal side of the evening to continue.

The following day, however, everyone was called to a meeting where the previous evening's shenanigans were decried by the Commandant, reminding them all that they were officers and gentlemen and not to show themselves up like that.

Well, presumably not until the speeches were over, anyway.

After another Mess Night, the Red Cross arrived the following morning, seeking blood donors, no one twigging they'd be coming on a day when most of the young men would still be half pissed, and their blood full of booze. But never mind! Everyone was still expected to 'volunteer' or explain why not.

It wasn't all bad, though, as after blood was given, the donor was rewarded with a bottle of beer, yes, a free hair of the dog. Only in Hong Kong.

Their own Dining Out dinner later in December was a real doozy, as will be revealed later, and, as has been hinted at earlier, it left one of their classmates literally in stitches.

There were other Mess functions, not nearly so formal, such as the barbecue where Piggard had tried to stick AV with a two-pronged barbecue fork, and another where a buffet meal was the highlight, but where eighty percent of those attending went down with food poisoning the following day, the outbreak attributed to the dodgy roast beef.

Only three or four Inspectors were fit enough to attend morning parade.

Unfortunately, at one of the less formal Mess functions, after the crowds had thinned out, a blond-haired bloke, who someone said was a Chief Inspector, but who was not in uniform, was leant against the bar, smiling to himself as if he had the biggest joke in the world in his head, or had been tipped the Secret of Life but was unwilling to share it with anyone else. There he stood, still smiling, and blimey, wasn't he staring and smiling at AV? Was AV the cause of some amusement?

One thing about the Bucket, he certainly knew his own faults. He couldn't or wouldn't do much to remedy them, mind you, but he knew them all right, and so he asked Nev and Two Dicks if he was wrong. Had he imagined it?

They looked and confirmed he hadn't.

After a while this began to annoy him, to the point whereupon the red mist began to form, and instead of going over and saying a polite 'Good evening, sir, can I help you?' (to someone who after all was a senior officer), he merely came out with a challenging 'What the fuck are *you* looking at??'

But then only to learn that the fellow was a Jerry Benfield CIP, who laughed and apologised for staring, and who had only crashed the function to meet AV and invite him to play for a social football team he ran called the Galloping Gwailos, and who'd been waiting for a chance to speak to him, but in all honesty hadn't been able to equate AV's reputation as a goalkeeper with his size and stature. (Not many ever could, in truth. Not even himself.)

Bloody hell, labelled with the stigmata of irascibility again, but nonetheless the invite stood, although once more having to fight the prejudice he'd invited against himself.

Apologies, handshakes, drinks swapped, and playing the following Sunday against an Army Sergeants team from a Mechanical and Transport Unit near Kam Tin.

(Does Kam Tin ring a bell? Of course it does… the Walled Village in the New Territories.)

Then Jerry left and Faidee Aidi came across and introduced the lads to his European lady guest, who was none other than Linda Bailey, who worked for the ICAC, and whose telephone number had been given to AV by her sister Teresa, or 'Terry', who had worked with him at the Nat West bank back in Stroud.

But since arriving in HK he hadn't called her, and never would have done, but that was probably quite wise as her opening line was, 'I thought you'd be bigger!' ('Well, *you* can get stuffed, madam!') although the ice was thawed a little when she bought a round of drinks, and they agreed to meet later that week, on her request, on Friday – oh God no! – in the Bull and Bear of all places.

Incidentally, the kilt-wearing Inspector Bullingham, who'd apparently once been on a British Rail Weekend Break to Edinburgh when he was fourteen, not only showed he had some *cojones* (that's 'balls' to you none Spanish scholars) in wearing his full Scottish gear to the Mess function, but also in inviting an ICAC Investigating Officer along as his guest, which would not have gone down at all well had her occupation been revealed to any other than the WCH5, such was the obvious detestation felt toward that organisation by many worried, indeed fearful, police officers.

But *that*, my pedigree chums, is where I'll leave you, with the subsequent meeting with Miss Linda Bailey leaving AV very confused about corruption within the Force and whether it was truly a thing of the past.

The *South China Morning Post* was full of news about continuing police arrests, as were the television channels and so, basically, what *was* going on?

Stay tuned, won't you? All will be revealed in due course.

Chapter Thirteen

Fun and Games

Now despite what you may think from the narrative so far, the girlie bars, massage parlours and brothels in Hong Kong were *not* exclusively for tourists, servicemen, expatriate policemen (under training or not), government lawyers, and the high-flying business set. Not by any manner or means, with a huge sex industry outside of *that* small part of it, catering almost exclusively for the Chinese, and from which expats were almost totally excluded, apart from, as will be shown later, the underground and then still illegal homosexual side of the trade.

Even so, for many expats, being let loose in Hong Kong was like taking the Love Boat to Fantasy Island ('The plane! The plane!'), with excesses available that some only ever dreamt about back in Blighty or wherever.

But go up Nathan Road in Chimsy scarcely a quarter of a mile or so to the start of Yaumatei, or exit 'The Wanch' towards Eastern District, and you'd hardly see a 'round-eye', or expat, apart from a policeman or two, let alone a bona fide tourist beyond that. You would however be absolutely amazed and almost mesmerised at the absolute plethora of bright neon signs hanging from tall buildings, and at their entrances, with the hundreds of yellow ones synonymously advertising all manner of 'adult services' but written only in Chinese characters.

Most popular were the small or single-woman brothels, and the charmingly phrased 'fish ball stalls' or *yue dan dong* in Cantonese, which were, basically, dimly lit wankatoriums. (I claim worldwide rights on that word, by the way.)

Massage parlours and sauna houses were generally brothels too; the low-end night clubs had sex as their main bill of fare, while even the more supposedly high-class Chinese and Japanese nightclubs had sex for offer with much more beautiful girls, at a much higher price as a corollary.

Then there were the Chinese-only bars, escort agencies, streetwalkers, touts, blue-movie shows, strip joints and what have you, many thousand times more of each than what was offered to the tourist and expatriate resident in Chimsy and Wanchai, and even though it may be going on all around them, few of them would even realise it.

Never mind all those temptations on offer in the many ad-driven Chinese-language daily newspapers and sleazy magazines.

But *who* controlled the sex industry and operated it, profited from it and, very importantly, who protected it? More later, but I'll give you three guesses, and three clues.

Well, it wasn't UNESCO, the British Council or Jeffrey Epstein, so guess away.

Certainly, the very naive WCH5 never gave a second thought to matters like that as they busied themselves with their studies and ran around at weekends like headless chickens.

However, you'll have gathered from that episode with the lovely Tina from Popeye's Bar that Nev Tenspeed had again become sexually active, but in fact he and AV had broken their ducks, as it were, a while before that in Causeway Bay, almost accidentally, while stomping and puffing up the stairs of a very multi-floored building, wherein the lift was out of order. Ostensibly it was to register at a martial arts gymnasium to learn kung fu or taekwondo, just trawling upstairs following a bilingual advertising board they'd seen hanging from out of a window on the tenth floor or something.

Poor lambs. They had no idea that such martial arts clubs, gyms and associations were largely affiliated to various Triad societies, which did exist, despite such existence being officially denied.

More on this later, but as a taster, the predominant Triad society in Wanchai was the Wor Lee Kwan, but most police officers wouldn't have known the Wor Lee Kwan from the War on Want charity or even the *World at War* TV series, so much were they kept in the dark about the real underbelly of Hong Kong.

Never mind, but call it fate or destiny, there they were, on a landing, Saturday mid-afternoon, trying to get their bearings, when a door opened at what was learnt to be 'Paris Apartments', as two lovely young Chinese girls were exiting, and it was lust at first sight. And yes, they'd stumbled upon a house of disrepute, were invited in, and that was that.

Goodnight, Vienna!

You don't want to know the graphic details, but Maggie Pigswill... eat your heart out! Nev had that broad, cheeky grin he always had when he felt particularly chuffed with himself, at the end of it, although they had been in separate rooms of course.

Good God, they weren't exhibitionists, you know!

It's not as if they were members of the RHKP rugby, golf or cricket teams, or HK delegates of the International Police Officers Association visiting Manila, where mass orgies or communal oral sex in the flesh spots were, to some, more important than the sporting or cultural event they'd told their wives and girlfriends they were going there for.

If only those poor ladies knew, and they might well have found out if there hadn't invariably always been a frantic scrambling by gazetted and inspectorate officers to destroy photos the participants had taken so ill-advisedly during their drunken escapades, in the infamous red-light district of Ermita in Manila, or at wild sex and drink parties often hosted by the local opposition team, such as the Manila Nomads Rugby lads. Or indeed, by some of the Philippine Constabulary, who found it most amusing to watch initially prim and proper Royal Hong Kong Policemen turn to sex-crazed beasts once the wonderfully smooth local San Miguel beer, and the presence and availability of 'swish and tit' took hold.

Those photographs however were never developed or printed outside of Police Headquarters, being processed 'in house' by friendly officers within the Identification Bureau (IB) and then handed to a rugby, cricket, and golf-playing Senior Inspector at the Commercial Crime Bureau, who duly passed them on to a conveyor belt of sheepish, yet very grateful and relieved, Superintendents and various grades of Inspectors.

(The Identification Bureau were responsible for all photographic, fingerprinting and comparison needs of the Force, including sending photographers and fingerprint officers to most scenes of crime upon requests from the relevant CID Units.)

Now before anyone of you out there in front of the Fourth Wall, which hasn't so much been breached in this saga as having been completely obliterated, has the impulse to check the internet or call your travel agent to find out the price of a return ticket to Manila in view of the excesses you've just heard about, then you're too late, I'm afraid. The Ermita District has been completely sanitised, and the sex industry there closed as the Philippine Government was mindful of the negative image it projected to the rest of the world. Hard luck!

But back to Paris Apartments, and having disposed of some dirty water, Tenspeed and Bottomley could shuffle out and get down to the China Fleet Club, and rejoin their mates and obviously brag a bit. Ha! It was great to be fresh and so naïve in those halcyon days of youth.

Months later, despite a few 'regulars' having been sorted out and put on retainer, as it were, Tenspeed and Bottomley surprisingly found themselves late on a Saturday night almost alone in the PTS Mess, and Nev suddenly burst out with a glazed-eyed, very strident, 'I feel like a woman!'

The Bucket shot back, 'Well go and put a dress on, then. I shan't tell anyone!'

The upshot? Taxi to Central, Star Ferry to Chimsy, and a short yet very brisk, purposeful walk to another 'knocking shop' in the very aptly named Pratt Avenue.

Oh, so simple, but hardly pure, yet even those two sometimes wrestled with the emptiness that sin or errant behaviour can bring or leave one with.

Only sometimes, though.

Such negativity and self-reflection, or recrimination, however, never troubled Tommy Two Dicks in the slightest and he remained a rampant misogynist until he married, and thereafter he changed somewhat to only stray occasionally, a fact he never bothered to hide from anyone except his wife and her family.

Obviously, he was very thick-skinned, which was probably just as well.

Lats and Yates were paragons of virtue compared to AV, Nev and Tommy, being men of high principles and stricter moral compasses, despite how much the other three may have tried to involve them in their sordid machinations.

Oh well, it takes all sorts, and no one is perfect.

However, Nev had some classy ladies in his retinue; one was a Mona, although admittedly she tried to keep as quiet as she could, while AV liked to frequent the Two Dragons, becoming very pally with both Anna Lee and the unfortunately, but very aptly named, Fanny Chew, the two dragons themselves.

Well, that was one primal urge somewhat temporarily sated in rather roughshod fashion, so now onto the other. Food!

By then they'd discovered the wonderful all-you-can-eat buffets and brunches laid on by the major hotels, with the Hong Kong, Hyatt and Park Hotels being their particular favourites. They had however from experience learnt to forgo the prawns, crab and oysters when they arrived at the buffet table, as there was always an almighty rush from the locals to get as many on their plates as possible, in a veritable feeding frenzy, invariably combining seafood, meats, salads, cake, custard and ice cream all on the same plate so as not to waddle up to the table more than three or four times.

Sunday morning buffet brunch was great fun, too, just the job to blow away the cobwebs.

The set roast lunch in the Hyatt was just a tad problematic, though, as both AV and Lats liked the end portion of the roast joint of beef. Toss you for it? Christ, no need to go that far! Have it!

In the fullness of time, they'd experience a fine range of the wonderful gastronomic fare that Hong Kong had to offer and often seasonal delights such as the yearly 'hairy' crabs, and the diversity of food from various regions in China.

This would include *wor tip* and *siu lung bau* dumplings, along with thick noodles from Shanghai, stuffed breads from Shantung Province, spicy dishes from the Sichuan area and the fine fresh seafood caught from within the South China Sea, and which formed such a large part of Cantonese food.

Lats and his later wife Connie (more later) were particularly fond of food from the Chiu Chow region of China, famous for its small cups of strong tea, although the SM3 generally made an excuse not to join them for a Chiu Chow meal after the first few times as they had a particular liking for crispy green leaves from some plant or other, followed by ducks' tongues, and fried goose intestines, which Connie delightfully referred to as 'goose guts'. Two Dicks however had no qualms about joining the pair for such food (or any food) whenever the chance arose, and obviously poultry (web feet anyone?) as well as sheep (apocryphally), had to be extremely wary around that particular Welshman.

But the convenience of being able to obtain a meal at virtually all hours of the day and night was something very easy to become accustomed to and to rely upon, and even when the host of nightclubs kicked out early in the morning, very many of their customers and workers would continue on for *see-ooh yeh*, a final snack at restaurants which had remained opened just to cater for such trade. However, a 'snack', to well-oiled or tired tables of Chinese people at that time of the morning, would generally constitute a full meal to most Westerners.

The variety of food on offer all over Hong Kong was such that the locals claimed that the Hong Kong Chinese would eat anything and everything with four legs, apart from a table, and even then, if it was hewn out of bamboo which could be soaked until it was tender…

AV had been forced to see the PTS doctor again as he had very sunburnt knees, having been with Nev and Bob Y when instead of trying to find somewhere to park in Deep Water Bay, they decided to walk there but, halfway, climbed over a wall and sat on some rocks, with pleasant views across to the bay itself. And there they slept, Nev and Bob Y under towels but AV without even a thought about covering himself as protection against the fierce sun. (Well, he'd been fine sunbathing like that over a year earlier on the expansive beach at Weston-super-Mare in Somerset.)

Come Monday morning, the only way he could walk, never mind march, was to lift up the bottom of his shorts so they wouldn't rub on his red-raw and blistered knees. If everyone else had done the same, so presenting an orderly and uniformed squad, then he would have been allowed on the square, but instead he was granted a pass for three days.

But to this very day in the Summer of 2023, he still has not one single hair on or around either knee because of those burns, not that he misses them, you'll understand.

Loads on his palms, in truth, but none on his knees.

Outside the entrance to each corridor in their accommodation block was a small seating area, and while AV was having a chat with Norrie Pinkney, who was as amused as hell about AV's blisters, Mungo obviously thought he was missing something, so out he came, but this time with an acoustic guitar and burst into what came out like a guttural call to the Highlanders to take up arms for the Young Pretender and the Jacobite cause.

What an awful noise, and he could hardly get a chord right, either!

Norrie loved riling him and merely looked at AV and pointedly quipped, 'Cat Stevens!' to which AV added 'Robin Hall or Jimmy McGregor?' but Mungo finished the song anyway, very pleased with himself indeed. God knows why.

(Robin Hall and Jimmy McGregor, by the way, both individual Scottish musicians in their own right, formed a very popular folk duo in the 1960s and well beyond, with much British TV coverage, their biggest commercial hit being 'Football Crazy', which is known to - shall we say? - we elder British soccer fans the world over.)

Now the trouble with showing off one's guitar skills is that unless you know who you are playing to, then you could be making a real fool of yourself. Not in this case, though McMee was not to know it, but AV very nearly did in a Dublin bar, some two decades later, when chatting to a bloke about the pub's live band, having taken up the plectrum himself.

While just about to talk about his new guitar skills, of which he was equally as proud as McMee obviously was of his, the chap went to the bar and while he was there, a waiter (not Alphonse from Chapter 12) came across and asked if AV knew who he'd been talking to?

Actually, he had no idea, as he'd talk to, and buy a drink for anyone (but only when pissed), so he shrugged a 'No', only to find out it had been Eric Bell, the founder and original lead guitarist of

Thin Lizzy, and the chap who played the iconic lead on 'Whisky in the Jar-O.'

Lucky escape and a lesson for us all. I digressed. My apologies. Now back to the main story.

And I just bet you are bursting to know how Bottomley's debut for the Galloping Gwailos football team went, and if you're not, then hard luck.

Fortunately for him, he didn't go alone as Bob Yates was co-opted in on the day of the match, one midfielder backing out as he was required to attend to some urgent unspecified Police business back at his parent formation.

Unfortunately, Nev was playing cricket for the Police 1st Eleven team that same day and was thus unavailable to fill another late vacancy up front.

The football was fine, played at the extremely well-appointed Yuen Long Stadium, and the Gwais won 2–0, AV making a couple of reasonable saves from shots pushed across him, low to his right, but other than those he hadn't been troubled much, especially with the reliable Steady Eddie forming a solid barrier between him and the opposing forwards.

The opposing Army Sergeants team were mostly a bunch of tryers. AV and Yates, though, were surprised at the high standard shown by most of their own teammates, with Benfield himself being a fine midfielder, and a couple of other obviously really good lads, especially a forward named Nick Scrimshaw, who although built like a rugby front rower, had a deft touch and a kick like a mule.

The after-match piss-up was a bit too frenetic for their liking, though, the two lads being the only ones still at PTS and not knowing who was who, or if they'd be asked again, so when a Brian Wilkins said he'd be leaving the Sergeants' Mess early to return to Hong Kong Island, offering lifts to all and sundry, they jumped at the chance to be off before they made bigger fools of themselves than they thought they already had.

They'd been brought to the game by a Chief Inspector Bob Hewlett in the spectacular red Jaguar he'd apparently imported from the UK, but he seemed more of a throwback than a full back, judging by the way he was really hitting the drink, and singing his head off, and who showed no signs of wanting to leave for a good while yet, such was the heavy-handed hospitality from the Sergeants.

Mind you, Mr Hewlett was apparently due to commence four months' long-leave the following week, so one can perhaps appreciate his high spirits.

So off they set at dusk and in his Volkswagen Beetle, this garrulous Londoner, Brian Wilkins, who apparently worked in Special Branch, gabbling on and on, and was obviously so much engrossed with trying to impress two 'sprogs' that he didn't spot the well-lit roadworks on his left until after he'd driven into and through them, ending up in a perhaps one foot deep section of torn-up road.

No one was hurt and the car wasn't damaged, but just stuck there.

Despite the Yuen Long-to-Kowloon road being fairly isolated, it was just bad luck that Brian had crashed where there were a few houses either side of the roadworks, and it was obvious that the police would be called.

Quick as a flash, he alighted and unscrewed the cabled red lights from the front section he'd driven through, so that they were no longer on, and then stood by the vehicle until the inevitable police Land Rover turned up, with uniformed officers only too keen to attach a rope to pull Brian's car out, which was done with ease, Senior Inspector Wilkins having flashed his warrant card, of course.

To the Police Sergeant in charge, it was obvious what had happened and what needed to be done; the roadworks contractors had failed to display lighting sufficient enough to warn motorists of the hazard the roadworks posed to drivers and, in view of Brian not wishing to press charges, he'd merely warn them the following day when the roadworks were due to recommence.

A salute, and on their way. As simple as that!

Well, that had shut Brian up all right but Bottomley and Yates were a tad confused by it all. Wasn't that perverting the course of justice? Were they in a conspiracy to pervert the course of justice? Was Brian's warning for them to keep their mouths shut criminal intimidation?

Or was that an example of the ways and means that justice was arbitrarily dispensed in Hong Kong, and to make a fuss of it (as after all, no one had been harmed by it, the contractor not to be prosecuted) would put them in invidious positions as boy scouts at best, and informers at worst?

Well, discretion was the better part of valour – now where have you heard that before? – and after a chat with the rest of the boy scouts in the WCH5, the matter was not forgotten but just kept in mind for future reference.

They did wonder though whether they would ever be asked to turn out for the Gwais again.

Now back to the main story.

They bumped into Jack 'Fingers' Claymore many times and though he seemed a trifle cynical, if not world-weary, probably leave-happy, he did occasionally cut loose and come out with information he thought could help them along, his homosexuality not being openly known until several years later.

But looking back on it, no wonder he usually kept very much to himself, probably not knowing who to trust, similar to those senior officers who were scared of being lifted by ICAC that he'd previously told them about.

He had a PTS course mate, apparently, named Julian Weaving, who was currently serving a two year prison sentence for some corruption offence, namely receiving fifty thousand dollars over a nine month period for doing something illegal or not doing something he should have done to stop illegal activity – he wouldn't expand – caught because he had tried to send the cash back to the

UK via the Post Office, the package splitting and thus the Post Office notified the police when the contents became apparent.

'Fingers' was totally outraged as Peter Godber, a very senior police officer (yes, him again), was the head of a totally and openly corrupt operation and had squirrelled away millions over many years, but who was sentenced to only four years' imprisonment, while Weaving was a mere two pip confirmed Inspector who had taken a miniscule sum, in comparison, just the once, but had received two years.

What did I say about moral equivalency?

Even the inexperienced WCH5 could see the apparent disparity, with Fingers reckoning Godber had done a deal and shopped everyone that he'd ever had corrupt dealings with, knowing his sentence even before he went to trial.

He'd done what another convicted corrupt senior officer, an Ernie Hunt, apparently had done, to minimise his own punishment, and squealed, with Weaving having no information to give as a bargaining chip.

(And no, it wasn't the Ernie Hunt who AV 'followed' in the sixties when he played football for Swindon, and then Coventry, being particularly remembered for that spectacular volley, and the way the ball had been two-footedly teed up for him.)

Still, he was being treated quite well in prison, and Claymore had visited him a few times to find him keeping his pecker up.

But what about being told that large-scale corruption was a thing of the past?

'Don't be taken in,' was his mumbled and beery advice, 'and keep your eyes open and your wits about you on what's happening around you because no one will come out and directly tell you what the "score" is, when you are posted to Divisions.'

The irony about it was that Claymore was the first Assistant Sub Divisional Inspector (ASDI) the WCH5 would work under, at Yaumatei Division, from January 1976.

And with that, Fingers fell off his barstool, then staggered away home.

After passing another fortnightly exam early on the following Friday afternoon, and thus incurring Nev's indignant ire and a belligerent 'Fuck that!' and forsaking the customary end-of-week football, AV and Bob Y sloped off and duly met with Linda Bailey of the ICAC at the Bull and Bear pub in Central. This was a good half hour before the 'Friday Night Swill' mob arrived, and thus the three of them had a cautious, sparring chinwag about her sister Teresa, or 'Terry', back in the UK, Linda's life in Hong Kong and how they were settling in, briefly mentioning Faidee Aidi, who hadn't come, as he thought he'd be intruding.

That was strange; he usually didn't like to miss anything and surely wouldn't ordinarily have failed to be jealous of AV going for a 'date' with the blonde-haired, blue-eyed, well-breasted, trim and professional young lady of twenty five he'd been 'squiring around' for the previous month or so. Still, Bob Y was with him and surely AV wouldn't try anything on in decent company, especially as it was early-to-mid-afternoon, and if running true to form AV wouldn't be pissed until at least 6pm by which time Linda would ordinarily be back home, and safe in her Mid-Levels flat within 'The Hermitage' complex of serviced apartments in Central District. She was of course as safe as houses with Inspector Yates.

(All right, you win, and so to illuminate the coarser elements amongst you, 'squiring around' was a polite way of intimating that he'd been having sex with her for most of that period. Satisfied? Good. So was he, apparently. I'll continue to move on with the narrative then, if I may.)

Be that as it may, the question about her work arose, and Yates queried if police corruption, according to the ICAC, was a thing of the past, and if so, was the spate of recent arrests just old matters being tidied up?

But before they could get into it, her boss, a huge sandy-haired chap in his early thirties and named Toby Robling, conveniently arrived, and confidently introduced himself, forthrightly stating he was a former RHKP officer, but because he now worked for the ICAC it had meant he was unfortunately shunned by his former police mates, and was mercilessly targeted when he played rugby for the Happy Valley team against the RHKP 1st XV, although laughingly claimed to give as good as he got in those games.

When he popped into the Police team's dressing room at the end of those matches, as captain of the Happy Valley side, to mostly congratulate the opposition as the Police XV invariably won, it was always crystal clear that he was just about as welcome as a sewer rat in a penthouse!

But after a couple of increasingly social beers together, and some more idle chit-chat, during which he merrily let it be known his nickname was 'Jugs', as in Toby Jugs, and because of his rather unfortunate 'man tits', he then switched in an instant to answer the question Yates had earlier asked of Linda about corruption. Soberly and candidly, he said that corruption was still continuing, but not quite so openly as before, telling Yates that he and his mates could jump on the bus, run alongside it, or stand in front of it and try and stop it, but then with the risk of it knocking them over and 'killing' them.

Bottomley queried him on what exactly *was* corruption according to the Law, with Toby explaining it very plainly as accepting gifts above a few hundred dollars without official permission ('No, don't worry, a few beers down Oriental Bob's doesn't count!') or soliciting for, or accepting an advantage, be it cash or other 'considerations' such as sex, holidays or goods, for 'favours', such as turning a blind eye to criminal activity or dropping charges on the request of underworld figures or ceasing an investigation to aid the continuance of illegal enterprises.

There were obviously conspiracy charges relating to those offences as well, particularly when so many people were involved in common nefarious aims and perverting the course of justice in myriad instances.

Then there was the charge of possessing cash or assets disproportionate to official earnings, or 'emoluments' as the law termed it, where the accused had to prove they had obtained their suspicious or challenged investments, property or whatever by lawful means.

Those were just very simple and by no means complete examples, but Toby also informed them that during some investigations, offences under the Theft and other Ordinances also came into play, such as Aiding and Abetting a substantive crime or crimes, Handling Stolen Goods, Obtaining Property by Deception, Blackmail, Criminal Intimidation and actual Theft itself.

Bottomley and Yates were 'all ears', which made a refreshing change from them usually being 'all gas and gaiters'.

Toby Jugs then said large-scale corruption formerly involved just gambling and sex, but involvement with drugs was now included and was increasing, the syndicates mostly run by Detective and Uniformed Station Sergeants, with many of the big boys having fled to Taiwan or Canada, taking their stash with them.

The biggest of them were known as the Five Dragons, the kingpin being a Lui Lok, he and his cronies being known as 'Majors' when still in the police.

There were close to fifty of them in Taiwan alone, making new lives for themselves there, with the expats and senior local officers here in Hong Kong not setting up corrupt enterprises themselves, but just placidly fitting in to a well-organised, almost mechanised machine and taking their rake off to turn a blind eye, not even considering the illegality of it all, or their accountability, either.

Others had taken the place of all those who had fled, and no doubt they and their mates would hear of some of them on TV, and in the newspapers in times to come, and may even be surprised when they get to know some officers in Divisions who could perhaps later be brought to book for corrupt criminal acts or omissions.

He then warned them, as Claymore had, to be very careful, as money could be collected in their names without them knowing it, but with it in the main no longer being passed to post-1974-joined expat or local Inspectors as in previous times, 1974 of course being the date that the ICAC was formed.

Linda and Toby claimed only to be telling them this as Linda's sister Teresa had thought a lot of AV, and if they had any problems in thinking they were being pressurised to accept money or gifts, or if mysterious brown envelopes of cash appeared in their desks or in-trays, or if ordered to do things their conscience rebelled at, they could always contact them.

And with that, a shake of the hands and away Toby went, after having given them his name cards, with Linda staying for as long as she felt politely appropriate, then she slinked away as well, giving them both a peck on the cheek before she did so.

Of course, they'd left the lads with a lot to think about, but they weren't going to do that in the accursed Bull and Bear, oh no siree, and before they got 'the taste', and as they were on the parade square for the Commandant's Parade next morning, they scurried along to the Central Bus Terminal, next to the Star Ferry, and caught the crowded 14B bus from Central to Aberdeen, then walked, yes walked, along the main road back to PTS.

Was it a genuine, friendly warning? How strange Toby Robling turning up like that. And just how had 'Jugs' known what Yates had asked Linda before his arrival?

Christ, did Linda have a transmitter of sorts in her handbag, or whatever?

Were they trying to 'groom' them? (But admittedly, they did need haircuts.)

Should they report the meeting (but to whom?) and risk making a name for themselves – yet more – as paranoid prats, or should they let that happen by itself?

What was Faidee Aidi's part in all this, if at all? Best not to mention anything to him beyond saying they'd had a pleasant meeting with Terry's sister and leave it at that.

If Faidee had anything to pass to them, all well and good, but best not to make any overtures to him about it. A few ditties, maybe, but not a song and dance.

Still, forewarned is forearmed, as it were, and so after making their uniforms ready, they had a chat about it with Nev (who had by then forgiven them for leaving PTS), Lats and Tommy Two Dicks, taking care that no one was earwigging.

All agreed it was useful information to have, and that wherever they'd be posted, to keep in touch with each other and compare notes and experiences and write down anything they thought not quite right.

They obviously realised that, unless they were careful, if Robling was to be believed, they could unknowingly and easily be metaphorically up to their necks in crocodiles, when all they'd come for was to help drain the swamp.

And so to the Saturday Parade, but instead of now being drilled in a squad consisting of combined members of squads 101 and 102, they had been allocated rank and file squads to drill themselves, four or five Recruit Inspectors to each unit.

AV was with two local men and Bandy Yat-ding Lam, all short asses like him, and the squad they'd be with every Saturday and morning until the very moment they'd end their Passing Out Parade, consisted of thirty recruit WPCs, who were very much up to scratch and who probably hoped and prayed that the Inspectors would also be.

Despite that one incident when Bandy 'froze', things went very well, with the two Chinese guys, David Hon and Phillip Yip, having risen from the ranks and thus had seen and done it all before.

AV had driven the cattle around quite competently when it was his turn, although, along with Nev and Yates, was glad that they never had to be in charge of the whole parade of maybe twenty five squads at any stage, smugly thinking that they obviously were good enough not to be exposed to that challenge.

Things became even better for Steady Eddie and Bottomley when they weren't chosen to be in charge of their respective squads for the final bash in December, on the grounds that let someone else mess up the Passing Out Parade, not them.

It also meant that most mornings and every Saturday parade henceforth, Phillip Yip would be in charge of the WPC squad, AV standing at his right as first reserve, as he would need to practise being in command just so he'd be fully prepared.

Steady Eddie was part of a five officer contingent responsible for drilling a squad of thirty male Police Constables, with another ex-rank and file Sergeant, Frankie Chan, chosen to lead them around on D-Day, which everyone hoped wouldn't be 'D for Disaster-day.' Similarly to AV, Yates was the first reserve in case anything untoward happened to Frankie Chan before then, which in fact it didn't.

The now senior WPCs and PCs, from those daily and Saturday parades, knew that the Recruit Inspectors 'fronting' their squads were really 'on the ball' by then, especially important to them as a matter of 'face' as their friends and relatives would obviously be coming to see them strutting their stuff, all discipline and regimentation, at the Passing Out Parade, with all the ensuing pomp and ceremony that function entailed.

And the families would certainly be delighted that their offspring, having been confirmed as PCs or WPCs, henceforth had a '*gam faan woon*' or a 'golden rice bowl', with a good income and a job for life, or for as long as they wanted, or unless extraneous factors intervened.

Nev, to his surprise, was chosen as 'The Man' to lead his squad of PCs around, but which was great for him as his parents were coming out in December for the ceremony.

The lads had also developed in many other ways as well, especially in deflecting bullshit and identifying the many blatant posers and ponces they'd so far come across in the RHKP, and even Tommy, as far as possible, was being somewhat more circumspect in his views and opinions, not wanting to share unguarded information or experiences that could be used as ammunition by anyone.

Yes, one had to be so careful, even more so when working amongst 'real policemen' in Divisions, many of whom seemed totally paranoid about newcomers in case not all of them were as wide-eyed and innocent as they seemed.

In addition to continuing their studies to enable them to pass their finals, and also practising their drill and musketry, the recruits were now also introduced to a wide range of practical scenarios.

The first was a mock trial as if in a Magistrate's Court, with a government lawyer, a Senior Crown Counsel, acting as magistrate for the day, with two junior Crown Counsels as prosecutor and defence counsel, with a course instructor, Chief Inspector Guy Shaver, as the defendant. This was quite ironic seeing as how about eighteen months later he was in the dock for real, on corruption charges relating to his two years as Assistant Sub Divisional Inspector (ASDI) at Mongkok Division, being convicted following a Not Guilty plea, and sentenced to eighteen months' incarceration.

This allegedly would have been substantially more if he hadn't done a deal and 'grassed up' others who would be arrested in due course, including a CID Chief Inspector (CIP) known as 'The Big Drain'.

That nickname had apparently been given him by the Chinese rank and file, because of the amount of cash poured into him, and him always wanting more to pad out his pension on imminent retirement.

But if that CIP was known as 'The Big Drain', was there any connection with Kevin 'Tits' Monkman allegedly being nicknamed

'The Little Drain' you should be asking yourselves, *if* you've been paying attention.

However, the mock trial at PTS was a very interesting exercise, highlighting the presentation of written, physical and spoken evidence, admissibility or otherwise of statements taken under caution, how the chain of evidence in relation to the collection and handling of exhibits is crucial, how some defendants will lie their heads off, and what to do when a witness turns hostile, that is, changes their expected version of events as already told to police.

It was nothing like *Perry Mason*, that's for sure.

A visit to the public mortuary in Western District to watch a post-mortem conducted by the HK Government's Head Forensic Pathologist was a little more sobering, though, even for those who'd come from a police or military background, but once the initial shock, horror and revulsion could be controlled, it was a very interesting morning, again from an evidential and procedural point of view.

But while Dr Ignatius Ong was a pleasant enough chap, and with whom AV would have many future professional dealings, with the best will in the world he was in no way as gregarious or amusing as 'Quincy' from the American TV series.

Then there was an afternoon spent outdoors being lectured by an Army Bomb Disposal Officer, who actually set off some charges and showed how explosions could be tailored to exact specifications in the right hands, a really fascinating insight indeed.

Next came an introduction to crowd control techniques, culminating in the whole squad entering, and very quickly exiting, a room full of tear gas. (Some advice to you all: if any is coming your way, then *run!*)

And as an example of leadership technique, they were shown the Gregory Peck film *Twelve O'Clock High*, demonstrating that the main goal in any professional organisation must be based around discipline and teamwork to achieve a set aim and standard, and not around the individual.

This film was apparently also used in the US military to the same aim, but what about poor old Gregory having a total nervous breakdown for his efforts at the end of the flick?

Frank Topley, and Frick Jacobs were very non-committal on that one, when questioned about it, just giving a 'needs must' wishy-washy reply.

Anything not adhering to the official line was invariably smudged over, time and time again.

The SM3 were a little worried in case they were expected to go around all the time making incisive leadership comments, observations and directions, pointing out this and that, and bollocking everyone, like a military version of Oscar Wilde, but instead of coming out with a continual stream of witty, pithy one-liners, they had to spout out commands with every breath.

Still, the point of the film *was* taken, and while it has already been noted, after their initial excursions to 'The Wanch', that none of the squad intake were William Holdens (as mentioned in Chapter Nine, 'Up and Running'), it was also clear that none of them were Gregory Pecks either.

Good film, though, but a pity there were no choc ices, Kia-Ora squashes or popcorn given out during it, but one can't have everything, can one?

And then there was the *pièce de resistance*, though not many resisted except for the four ladies on the intake who were excused anyway, referring to an early afternoon session watching hard-on, hardcore pornography, so as to be prepared for what they could possibly come across, either being sold, made or shown to the public in makeshift, ad hoc and temporary blue-movie venues, or, so they'd heard, at some 'all lads together' stag-do evenings at certain Police Messes.

Such perversions as sodomy or having it off with a dog or donkey showed no punches being pulled, with one particular period piece being entitled *The Red Coats are Coming*, a peculiar way of portraying the activities of some British soldiers during the American War of Independence, one must say.

Yankee Continental Army propaganda, obviously.

And yes, a load of juvenile jokes were being bandied around, like something out of the *Benny Hill Show*, but by golly the whole squad must have been totally exhausted because after the session was over, no one could hear a pin drop in the accommodation block corridors for the rest of the afternoon.

But that evening, after a few more beers than usual in the Mess, very early doors, and while it was still light, oh what a tangled web would be woven, and very unexpectedly, as it seemed Morgan Effin-Jones, the CDMI, may have 'had a few' himself somewhere, and had reverted back to his Army Mess days, wanting to involve as many as he could in helping to relive them.

A gang of lads were sat outside and over he came, telling them to clear a couple of trestle tables of crockery from inside the Mess, but they were apparently doing it too slowly for his liking, so he whipped the tablecloth out from under it, in the manner of a Vaudeville act, except that every blasted cup, plate, glass, knife, fork, spoon and floral display went crashing onto the carpet, flying in all directions.

And where was the Mess Secretary while all this was going on, and what was he going to do about it? The answers? Hiding, and bugger all.

Or maybe he was busy looking for dart holes in wooden panels.

The CDMI then ordered them to carry the heavy tables out of the Mess, to the grassy area immediately outside the accommodation block, which led to a steep slope about fifteen yards from it, and that's where he set the tables up, against each other.

'Time for Table Riding!' he shouted, and like a rampant, rampaging elephant he rushed around, gathering as many recruits as he could, to come and play.

Table Riding? It might as well have been another Yorkshire Riding for all anyone else knew, apart from him.

He then loudly explained the basics of the game, where quite simply one 'contestant' or victim, would jump on the table and then people manning the sides and corners would shake and lift it so the bloke atop would have to see how long he could stay on without coming a cropper.

So you see, yet another kind of 'Off Ground Galloping Knob Rot', with obviously different versions all over the world.

It sounded as if it could be great fun, if it had been held in the Mess, with only a soft carpet to land on, but blow me down, that slope didn't look at all inviting, but never mind, it was certainly more politic to have a go rather than risk the beer-fuelled wrath of the CDMI.

But, fair enough, he was the first one to try and was hoisted off very easily, tumbling on the grass with no apparent injury.

Oh well, one by one, the initially cagey and somewhat drunken recruits mounted the tables and, one by one, were duly sent flying, but what with the relaxing effect of the beer and being as fit as butchers' dogs, rolled on the grass when they landed, feeling no pain whatsoever, glad they'd 'manned' up.

Now to get some other bastard!

Somehow, after about twelve lads had been tumbled off, they managed to persuade that particularly unpleasant instructor, 'Tits' Monkman ('The Little Drain'), as referred to a little earlier, to have a bash, probably shamed into it by the CDMI, the recruits remembering not to salute him with their caps off, because he just didn't like it.

Unfortunately, it was apparent that Two Dicks had imbibed a little more than the rest, or maybe he was feeling particularly mischievous that night, but as 'Tits' was balanced on the tables, as relaxed as he could be, while the point of the game was explained to him, and before the command of 'Go!' to start shaking them was given, Tommy had upended one of them from the accommodation block side, sending the unprepared Monkman flying over backwards, straight down the slope which everyone had been so careful to hitherto avoid.

Well of course, it was absolutely bloody hilarious, people actually crying with laughter, but realising that the game was well and truly over at that stage, without a thought for the well-being of Mr Monkman, who dragged himself slowly up from the incline, dazed and confused, grazed and abused, and crazed as a rabid dog.

He couldn't do much about the laughter, which increased in volume when the lads caught sight of the state of him, but he could certainly pinpoint who had sent him over the edge, as it were. Tommy 'Two Dicks' Allcock.

'I won't forget this, Mr Allcock!' he angrily and petulantly shouted, as off he staggered, having picked up his swagger stick and briefcase from outside the Mess, limping away with what dignity he could muster, his threat proving to be an empty one, thank goodness. Well, as far as they knew it proved to be an empty one but there were surreptitious ways and means of recording any untoward incident in individual Records of Service without the individual ever knowing (more later).

But not surprisingly, Table Riding never again featured as a suitable Mess game for the officers and gentlemen of the RHKP.

The only injury that night was to AV, not from Table Riding but from being pushed by Faidee Aidi, with Punjab Pete Spicer, the King of the Khyber Rifles, kneeling immediately behind him to make an obstruction over which he tumbled, and landed hard on the grass, cricking his back.

AV slowly pulled himself up, mightily miffed, having dropped his beer, but he kept his cool when he thought, *Fair enough!* and he'd take that as their combined revenge for messing Pete about at Nat West bank previously in Stroud, for meeting Faidee's girlfriend alone, and for keeping quiet about the conversation with her boss.

Moral equivalency at its very best.

'Have you ever been mellow?' asked Olivia Neutron Bomb.

Just one or two times, would be the reply, only one or two.

And so now, with squads 101 and 102 being top of the pile, with white flashes on their wristbands, it was time for an orienteering race, a three day camp in the New Territories, attachments to Police Divisional Formations and preparations for their final examinations with all the pomp and ceremony surrounding eventual success.

Oh, yes. And Dogs Dinner's marriage to Lilly! I nearly forgot that one.

I bet you won't go away now, will you??

Chapter Fourteen

The Final Stretch

Despite still having loads of formal study to complete, drill to practise and not only shooting skills to be continually honed but various weapons to be learnt about and set to memory as part of the December examinations, there was still much emphasis put upon physical activity, culminating in a large-scale Orienteering Competition, and a three day combined 'officer and rank and file camp' in the New Territories.

The orienteering took place among the hills, heavy foliage, rugged trails and water catchment areas towards the top and south of Hong Kong Island, and all Recruit Inspector squads still under training were required to participate.

The two-man teams were paired off by lots drawn, but as far as AV was concerned it was in no way a 'Lucky Draw' as he had been teamed with Faidi (or Faidee) Aidi, although the portents seemed very good initially as Faidi claimed to have done a lot of orienteering in Scotland and could use his self-proclaimed expertise to suss out the best route between checkpoints on any map.

The couple thus agreed that Faidi would plot the best way

round the course, while AV would set the pace for him to keep up with.

Bob Y had been very fortunate, or so it seemed, having been teamed with an ex-New Zealand Army chap called Kieran 'Kiwi' Meads, who seemed a very canny, fit young man, possessing the best pair of Ray-Ban sunglasses anyone had ever seen, ex-Army issue, no doubt.

But what a laugh when it turned out Two Dicks had been hooked up with Tenspeed, and even they had a quiet chuckle about it, both by then having been recognised as, shall we say, 'characters'.

And so, armed with sections of an Ordnance Survey map upon which the start and end points and interim checkpoints were marked, and with a compass each, off the teams trotted at five minute intervals.

It seemed to AV that it would be prudent to check the contours on the map and select which checkpoints, if any, were on the same level, so as not to be up and down like a 'Nodding Donkey' in an oilfield, but Faidi said he had it all in hand.

Well, he may have had something in his hand, and that was what probably distracted him, and that's why he 'took the low road, not the high road', missing the first checkpoint, and thence every subsequent one, with virtually every team finishing in front of them.

Indeed, they only found their way to the finishing point by tagging onto Rita Ho and Irene Chu, Recruit Woman Inspectors (WIPs) three courses beneath their own at PTS (the shame of it!) whom they'd found, quite by accident, coming down off a hill onto a wide, clearly marked path only about three-quarters of a mile from where the judges, observers and monitors had assembled to await the last teams to have set off, and the stragglers.

Maybe it would have helped Faidi if the map had been in Gaelic, or even braille, but it was a monumental balls-up, one of many he would later be found out about, but thinking on his feet, he could always come up with an excuse, and find a reason or, in truth, a cock-and-bull story.

But when the finishing gate, according to Rita Ho's reckoning, was less than 200 yards away, apparently hidden by a sharp curve in the track and the scrub on both hillsides through which it ran, Faidi Aidee put on a spurt and broke away from the ladies so as to finish in front of them, which was awfully bad mannered as the girls had, after all, 'rescued' his team.

However, the sprint and blatant attempt at chauvinistic one-upmanship proved ultimately futile as AV walked across the line behind the WIPs, the time for the run being clocked when the second member in each team reported to the timekeeper. Faici Aidi didn't know whether to laugh or cry with embarrassment, especially when he was informed that Irene and Rita had started off twenty five minutes after them, but blustered some excuse and then rather bashfully clambered on board one of the lorries to take them back to PTS.

Yes, Bullingham by name, and 'bulling them' by nature.

As for Steady Eddie and Kiwi, well Bob hadn't realised quite how canny Meads was, because as soon as they were out of sight of the starting gate, and out of view of those in front, Kiwi studied the map and then shuffled them down a long, steep embankment to the nearest semi-tarmacked minor road, and after a few minutes hailed a taxi which had fortunately just delivered an engineer to a remote water-pumping station, and which then dropped them within about three-quarters of a mile from the hidden finishing line.

Kiwi had also spotted a few parks on the map, and in one of them the pair seated themselves, enjoying an ice cream and a soda pop (yes, in 'good' company Bob Y could regress; he'd have to watch that!) re-emerging onto the track after having done some exercises to make it look as if they were knackered, all hot and sweaty, and triumphantly presented themselves at the finishing gate as the first team to complete the course.

The deception worked initially, until they were asked to point out the route they had taken, and what major landmarks had been seen.

Well, the game was up. 'It's a fair cop, Guv'nor.'

But their disqualification handily meant that AV and Faidi weren't the bottom pair after all, then!

Indeed, they even moved up one notch more after it was found that Two Dicks and Tenspeed had not reported to the finishing post, where the second lorryload of tired orienteers were impatiently waiting for them.

Just as the instructors were becoming concerned, they saw them alighting from the 'bush' onto the road, with Two Dicks limping, using a snapped-off branch as a crutch, having twisted his ankle and fallen down a gulley way up yonder, and had one hell of a job to hobble down, having to be supported by Nev.

Allegedly! And yes, he had been supported by Nev, in their excuse anyway, and the instructors had no choice but to accept that explanation, although the truth was a little more prosaic.

They'd joyously found a well-stocked refreshment kiosk in another small park and had sat at a table, hidden from the trail, and had watched all the teams pass by, drinking a toast to each and every one as they did so, until it was obvious to them that they weren't in any fit state to participate.

But they did use the map to find their way back, which was an achievement of sorts.

What a pity that Bottomley and Faidi hadn't been able to find that park, or no doubt there would have been four of them for early- and then late-afternoon drinkies.

Oh well, back to PTS.

There was still time for diversions, however, as on Sunday 2nd November, the Bucket's twenty third birthday, the SM3 tried their hands at canoeing.

Obviously, they were feeling a trifle under the weather from the after-effects of the birthday bash, but were still game for anything, being joined by Lats Latimer, Mungo McMee and Richard 'Dick' Short, mentioned much earlier.

The canoes belonged to PTS and were stored at the Aberdeen Marine Police Base, from where they were retrieved, and wobblily launched into the harbour, a typhoon shelter, at about 10.00 hours, on a sunny, though slightly windy day. Bottomley was in the same canoe as Nev, while Steady Eddie had McMee in his, and Lats was with Short, just gently paddling away, but none of them wearing life vests, a few bottles of soft drinks being the only items carried with them.

So much for Hazard and Safety Awareness!

Bottomley and Nev's canoe had launched last and thus the other two were ahead, and seemed to be getting away from them, but no problem as it wasn't a race, just a gentle paddle, supposedly, across to the island of Aplichau, just out of the typhoon shelter and turn right, or, in nautical terms, 'A starboard heading, Mr Christian, if you please!' across the East Lamma Channel to Lamma Island.

Well, it was all very pleasant, looking at the yachts and other various pleasure craft at their moorings, with fishing vessels coming and going, until they left the safety of the extended stone breakwater at the Aberdeen exit, but twenty or thirty yards into the Channel itself, things were a bit different and dangerously so.

The others by now were well ahead, in the middle of the crossing to Aplichau, but bobbing up and down, with AV and Nev's canoe not doing so well, seawater coming into it alarmingly, with it being necessary to bail the water out as best they could. With some difficulty, they turned the canoe around and with all the strength they could muster, managed to work it back inside the typhoon shelter, which itself was much choppier than they'd experienced when leaving it just thirty or so minutes earlier.

Both vomited – bloody landlubbers – and they were forced to try and wave down a passing fishing smack, the crew of which obviously didn't know them, and thought they were trying to be friendly – as if – and waved back, continuing on their way.

Finally, though, another fishing boat stopped and picked them up, and kindly dropped them off at the Marine Police Base, where they reported to the Duty Officer that two canoes in the Channel may be in trouble.

A police launch was immediately directed to investigate and indeed both remaining crews were in difficulty and were plucked out of the sea along with the canoes.

Bob Y, though, saw his brown leather shoes fall out of his canoe as it was being lifted onboard, and worryingly plop into the sea and so, despite having been sort of rescued once, he immediately plunged in to retrieve them (well why not, as he'd brought them all the way from Africa and they were of great sentimental value to him). He had to be fished out once again by some very bemused Marine policemen, Yates all the while clutching his footwear, and with a triumphant grin as soon as his unclad feet once again hit the vessel's deck. 'Yes!'

But thus, along with Table Riding, canoeing was obviously another activity consigned to the metaphorical 'Do not do!' filing cabinet.

One of the very last leadership exercises to take place was a three day camp in the New Territories, for which the intake was split into two, but not according to squad numbers, and thus there was much mixing and matching.

The second batch of campers were the luckiest as they only had to take the tents down, erecting the flapping canvas in the blustery wind seeming to take an age, and beyond the capability of some.

Once again, AV was in the first group with Bob Y, with Tenspeed and Two Dicks being in the second, with Lats not attending as he'd commenced his rugby tour with the police team and had jetted off to the UK.

The senior rank and file squads were also attending, along with their respective Senior Inspector Instructors, and of course Frank Topley and Frick Jacobs.

It was held in a wild, rural and totally unspoiled part of the New Territories, but it came as a shock to the expats to experience how cold it became up there at night. It wasn't as if they had to rough it, though, because the camp beds, four to a tent, were comfortable enough with double blankets provided, and a gaggle of WPCs had been designated as cooks, doing a fine job of preparing eggs and rice in the morning, fried noodles at noon, and getting large pots of steaming chicken curry ready for the evening meal.

No one however had warned them that no beer would be available, but never mind, and being so remote they couldn't even give a 'heads up' to those following in three days to pack a few cans.

Other than exercises such as coordinating tasks with British Army and RAF personnel, the main purpose was team building, and to learn bush skills like tent erecting (!), map reading, managing medevacs, how to bury your crap in the country and go without a drink for three days.

'Thinking on your feet,' the instructors called it, which as clearly has been demonstrated through this whole narrative, most of them had become pretty good at, although to be honest it was like a works outing and jolly good fun, and a wonderful break from the crowded, sometimes oppressive atmosphere back in the urban sprawl of the city.

It seemed that despite the unofficial 'No fraternisation!' policy between the rank and file and the Inspectors and the instructors, one local Senior Inspector instructor at least had broken that agreement, being spotted getting a blow job in his tent from a disarmingly beautiful recruit WPC, forever after known as Gobbler Wong.

(But if it was the case that the WPC had carelessly forgotten her toothbrush, and the Senior Inspector was merely helping out by cleaning her teeth other than by the normal, accepted method, then Steady Eddie had brought a couple of spares along with him. All she had had to do was ask!)

Another time, she even held a ghetto blaster on her knee and squatted nearby so that the said-instructor, could hear the music while he was sat on the tented-outside crapper. Talk about obvious!

And the stick (!) she must have taken from her course mates, particularly *if*, as one imagines, she gained favour by it, would have been horrendous, if fully justified.

The SIP surely should have been kicked back to Divisions, although this would probably have caused Gobbler Wong to be posted wherever he was.

They'd later find that that sort of thing was not too uncommon and not confined to just some loose WPCs, but also involved certain unscrupulous Women Inspectors, and even – and this may shock you – aspiring and highly motivated male Police Constables, with some determined junior police officers often having several senior people to call on and 'help them up the ladder' at the same time, which can be termed either – whichever way you choose to look at it – as naked ambition on one side, or grooming, exploitation or abuse of power on the other.

This could often, sadly but inevitably, lead to fingers burnt, minges singed, heartbreak, separations, divorces and, yes, suicides.

One such example was in the case of a virginal and extremely naïve, twenty one year old Scot, an Inspector Mingus Muffet, with eighteen months' service, who took up with a very 'forward' and extremely ambitious twenty two year old English speaking WPC from Kwun Tong Division, and fell 'head over heels' in what he thought was love, with the worldly and streetwise WPC being already marked as a Potential Officer, and thus continually being kept an eye on as possible Inspector material.

Mr Muffet gave her such glowing reports, being her Sub Unit Commander (SUC) in Kwun Tong (as well as thinking he was her 'boyfriend' as, after all, she was affording him a previously unimagined yet wonderful variety of sexual favours at every possible opportunity). This really put the 'icing' on her many previous positive reports, that she was duly selected for a formal three day Inspectorate Recruit Assessment at PTS, which she shot through with flying colours. (The same kind of selection process that Tommy Two Dicks had gone through, as he of course had joined locally.)

She was obviously full of beans, and a lot more besides, but the very weekend before joining her Recruit Inspector course, she callously let it be known, in a telephone call to poor Mingus, that she had gotten what she had wanted from him, and was grateful, but frankly, what could he do for her now, when he was stuck in Kwun Tong, and she now needed help from 'someone' (anyone or everyone) at the Training School?

And that was *it* as far as broken-hearted Muffet was concerned; Recruit Woman Inspector Stella Lai, as she had become, had moved on to bigger and better things, and shortly thereafter became the 'mistress', in old currency, of one of the married British Chief Inspector Instructors at PTS, and coincidentally one of the panel who'd earlier interviewed and 'put her through her paces' during that three day selection process.

On graduating from PTS, the general scuttlebutt had it that she was soon under the wing - and bedsheets - of yet another married expat Chief Inspector, her immediate senior line supervisor.

And the next one please!

So it goes!

More happened to Mingus Muffet much later... his unfortunate and messy suicide in 1980, and the subsequent 'Muffet Judicial Inquiry' partially opened the floodgates and broke some of the secret barriers on the extent of homosexual activity at all levels of society in HK. Allegations were even being levelled that the then Commissioner of Police (allegedly), and many other prominent personages, had themselves been Wildesquely 'feasting with panthers'. And just look at what happened to Oscar!

The paranoia over investigations into homosexuality within the Royal Hong Kong Police *will* be briefly mentioned in the following chapter, although the prelude to, and the actual suicide of Muffet, along with its ramifications are not really within the remit of what are supposedly 'Training Day Tales'.

However, the temporary, very one-sided and cruelly mercenary tryst between Stella Lai and Mingus 'the Dingus' Muffet was by no means an isolated incident, and proves that in many instances, no indeed, they'll *never* forget you until somebody new and of more use comes along.

And, to further shock you, this was allegedly one of the reasons that Jack 'Fingers' Claymore was 'moved on', for 'grooming' Police Constables, while nobody was ever disciplined for 'helping' a Woman Police Constable or Woman Inspector to achieve her potential, by whatever means.

Claymore vehemently denied those allegations, and the WCH5 never saw anything in the slightest to substantiate them, either while working with him, or as a good friend. Indeed, when he came 'out' he seemed to be in a steady, discreet relationship with a local chap who had no connections with the RHKP whatsoever.

Nonetheless, Jack Claymore was 'retired in the public interest' in about 1983 and remained a broken man until his early death at the turn of the century, all but the surviving Wong Chuk Hang Five amongst his so-called police friends having disgustingly dropped him like a hot brick, and treating him as persona non-grata thereafter, for fear of guilt by association, and worry over the secrets and dangerous information he carried in his head.

As Frank Sinatra sang, 'That's life!' Yes, once again, moral equivalency raises its ugly head.

But by now the first batch of campers were back at PTS, where there was not much to do, what with the other half of the combined intake away, except a bit of drill, some shooting, revising, and catching up with mail from folks in the UK.

Gina (AV's mother, if you remember) was a regular old gossip in her letters, so her son and heir was very surprised at her veiled and ambiguous, 'There'll be a surprise for you in December, just you wait and see!'

Why couldn't she just tell him if sister Lena was getting married, or if he would soon be an uncle, or if either or maybe both of Geoff's brothers were having sex-change operations?

Maybe another jar of Lil's pickled onions and beetroot would be winging their way to him, but if so, he hoped she'd made sure the vinegar didn't leak this time. Christ, what a pong!

Never mind, all will come out in the wash.

Steady Eddie's brother Kevin was intending to visit early in the New Year, which he'd be looking forward to; Nev's parents were due out in mid-December and he had been spotted as a cricketing talent, soon becoming the star opening batsman for the Police First XI, and so, all considered, things were not looking too bad for any of them.

(Yes, they were 'batsmen' back then, not 'batters' as they are now termed to please the politically correct mob, and the girlies. But to some of us dinosaurs, a batter is, and will always remain, merely a whisked flour and water-based mixture, into which raw fillets of fish are dipped before deep-fat frying. So there!)

But let's just get the Divisional attachments over with, and then wrestle with those exams, but no one was really worried about failing, except perhaps Dogs Dinner over the parade-ground drill, but they'd all see, soon enough.

Over the course of a week, they'd be sent individually or in pairs, dressed in full summer uniform, minus holster, as they were not allowed to draw firearms, out to Divisions for an A or B shift (08.00 to16.00 hours, or 16.00 hours to midnight respectively) to be spent with whomever the relevant Sub Divisional Inspectors directed.

The first unit AV and Yates – seemingly joined at the hip – were sent to was the Traffic/Hong Kong Island Office in Central Police

Station, to be 'mentored' (more like 'neutered') by the Officer in Charge of the Accident Investigation Section, (the OC/AIS/T/HKI) a tall, officious, well up himself, thirty year old ex-Bermudan police officer, whom it turned out knew Norrie Pinkney from the old days. But it was soon apparent they were hardly friends.

They could soon see why, as this Senior Inspector Alex Wynter just sat them in an empty office and gave them a stack of traffic accident and fatal crash investigation files to read through, popping in once or twice to make sure they weren't asleep, and then flitted away, claiming he was really too busy to take care of them.

Come on! Traffic/HKI, as they found out later, was hardly the sharp end of policing in Hong Kong, and surely he could have at least given them a 'ride-around', but, by the state of him, a 'reach-around' would have probably been more in his line.

Perhaps it had been unwise to mention Norrie Pinkney after all, and come 16.00 hours, when the transport came to take them back to PTS, the Bucket and Bob Y were well cheesed off and hungry, as there seemed nowhere to go for lunch, and no one came to see if they needed watering or grazing.

The holidaying Geoff Bottomley had a run-in with Wynter a few years later, which resulted in him being arrested for water wastage during a period when water restrictions had been applied Colony wide, with water only 'on tap' for two three-hour periods daily.

The daft old sod forgot, and left the bathroom tap on, overnight. Bloody tourist! Unfortunately, when the water supply had returned, it flooded out Wynter's flat beneath the one AV had arranged for his parents to stay in through the Police Housing Department. Whoops! Poor Mrs Wynter had awoken to find water flooding-in through her open balcony window, and loose wooden parquet flooring tiles floating around her living room, kitchen and both bedroom floors. Geoff was later merely warned by the ASDI at Happy Valley Police Station, a footballing mate of AVs, to be more careful.

The following day was much better, though, being sent for a B shift at Western Police Station, attached to an Australian fellow named Bradley 'Dunny' McKenzie, who was in charge of the Special Duty Squad there, tasked to combat illegal gambling, dangerous drugs, and sex crimes, such as operating illegal massage parlours, soliciting for immoral purposes, and running 'fish ball stalls' (those wankatoriums, where in describing them as such I have already laid claim to copyright on that word. Hard luck!)

So straight out of uniform and into the plain clothes they'd been told to carry with them. And they didn't come much plainer than the clothes AV and Bob Y wore, both being walking advertisements for China Products.

Bob Y knew Dunny slightly as they had played rugby for the Police First XV together up at Boundary Street, Bob occasionally having won a place on the wing, Bradley a full back who had played semi-pro Down Under.

He was very forthright in telling them that in an area like Western Division, predominantly Chinese, it was extremely hard for expatriates to go out and find their own cases, sticking out like sore thumbs, and it was better to task the Sergeants to sniff around, if not acting on information received, and for the Inspector to execute relevant authorisations (warrants) under the law when something was found to be going on.

That of course was part of their supervisory duty, anyway, but it was nice to get some 'hands on' operational experience too.

He gave them some case files, and they lit up a few buttons from the PTS training received to date, about the gubbins of offences, evidence required to make a case, caution statements and whatnot.

They also had a run out across a series of rooftops, checking for known drug-dealer haunts, and for drug addicts seeking a fix, called '*dough yau*'. But although there were some obvious signs of drug use up there, such as used needles and tin foil for 'chasing the dragon' by heroin fume inhalation, the places were unfortunately quiet.

But not so Western Mess, to where they went for the evening meal, to find Jack Claymore in the chair of honour, as senior resident, with a fine bevvy of expatriates surrounding him, including Luanshya's own Steve Greening, Wolfgang 'Kaiser' Sheitzer and a belligerent Canadian (is there any other kind?) named 'Rocky' Rhodes.

Greening was very offhand, even with fellow Luanyshan Bob Y, obviously wondering why Debbie was sharing her favours with such a palpably, insignificant little nincompoop as AV obviously was, and why Dunny had the temerity to bring them to the Mess amongst real policemen.

In fact, while Debbie was marvellous fun as a 'good-time girl' in Popeye's Bar and as an occasional paid companion, if Greening had any designs on her as a spouse or steady girlfriend, then he certainly had a lucky escape, because after her March 1976 marriage to Inspector J B Farrier, the Headquarters Sub Unit Commander at Wong Tai Sin Sub Division in North Kowloon, she turned into an absolute harridan, making his life hell. She cut off her wonderfully long hair, stayed in their spacious apartment all day, gambling with friends, or watching TV, and ate like a pig until she became a frump, and nagged him incessantly on his whereabouts if he didn't arrive home on the dot of when he said he would.

On one occasion, when he had stayed in the Wong Tai Sin Mess politically drinking with the Divisional Superintendent, amongst others, she burst in with his hot, plated roast dinner and smacked it down on the bar counter, vociferously insisting he consume it there and then and, with arms folded, glared at him until he did so! Hugely embarrassing for both himself and the officers he'd been drinking with. She then smashed him over the head with the half-empty plate, gravy and uneaten mixed veg and mash running down his hair and uniform tunic.

Thank the Lord that AV and Geoff Bottomley (more later) hadn't had any of that from her, although how AV in particular would have liked Greening to have been lumbered, instead of Farrier, who seemed quite a nice chap the one time they had met.

Hell, if poor JB had to put up with that sort of behaviour, he might just as well have married an English girl and have done with it.

On hearing about the incident, which of course had spread like wildfire, it was for many their first ever realisation that domestic abuse and violence isn't gender-based or specific, but a fact that many found hard to believe, even less to understand.

Still, back at Western Mess, Jack Claymore at least made them more than welcome, all 'hail fellow well met,' and was pleased that they were almost done with PTS, informing them that he was due to be posted from South Kowloon Court shortly, and made Assistant Sub Divisional Inspector at Yaumatei Sub Division, where coincidentally AV was due to be sent on the morrow.

Steady Eddie, not wanting to give away the fact his mother was German in case it set off even more fascist sentiments, casually asked about the 'Hitler Party' of a while back, which struck a nerve with Wolfgang (and why was he christened 'Wolf*gang*' when there was only one of him?).

Maybe it had come to attention, somewhere, and he'd been bollocked?

He became defensive and tried to make a link between his views, and those of a certain Irish Superintendent named Drick O'Miscoll (nickname 'Paddy'), who apparently or allegedly burst into pro IRA and Irish Nationalist sentiments when pissed, claiming he'd be on the barricades fighting the murderous British bastards come the next uprising.

His own peculiar take on moral equivalency, obviously.

'Rocky' Rhodes (who according to him, was an ex-lumberjack), merely glared at everyone with contempt at least, and blind hatred at most, a portent of him pistol-whipping a taxi driver some eight months later and being whisked away to Canada as a result, booted out extremely expeditiously.

To paraphrase Nikola Tesla, if Rocky's malevolence and sociopathy could have been turned into electricity, it would have powered half of Kowloon.

Formal Mess life in Divisions had had its day, though, and within eighteen months most single Inspectors had been moved to serviced apartments, both on Hong Kong Island and in Kowloon, and the Mess bars and dining facilities were thereafter usually only used by those working there, not by officers from all over, with very few, if any, then sleeping or residing at the stations where they worked.

Work to do, though, and Dunny's Sergeant had received information that a street newspaper and magazine seller had a stack of obscene dirty magazines for sale, as opposed to acceptable or approved dirty magazines, and they'd go and check it out.

But yes, by jingo, he did have about fifty hardcore publications on offer, hidden behind his *Times* and *Newsweek*s, and the middle centrefold pages left nothing to the imagination, with some white bird becoming extremely 'playful' indeed with her Alsatian dog, although how she probably wished that she'd have had its claws cut first.

And so, the vendor was arrested, the offending magazines seized, and charges laid of Publishing (i.e., offering for sale) Obscene Articles.

Whoop dee la!

AV and Bob Y were on the scoresheet, as it were, and at the end of the shift profusely thanked Dunny for his time and guidance, having thoroughly enjoyed themselves.

Very obviously those magazines would be confiscated and have to be destroyed, but Dunny thought, *What a waste!* and therefore gave copies to some of his many mates at different police formations, and to teammates at the next rugby game, leaving in all about five to show to the Magistrate, which should have sufficed.

Should have, but when the case came to trial, the vendor

pleaded guilty, with AV and Yates on standby to give evidence, which disappointingly then wasn't needed.

But after being duly convicted, he claimed to have not known what was inside the magazines, with the job lot being delivered individually wrapped in plastic, and that the loss of so much stock would cause him financial hardship, a matter which obviously hit at the core of the Magistrate's bleeding heart.

And so – oh hell! – he fined the newspaper seller 500 Hong Kong Dollars but directed that *all* the magazines be returned to him, but with the offensive centrefold pages removed and destroyed!

Poor old Dunny had to make a load of phone calls to his mates to try and retrieve as many as he could, send his team out around other newspaper sellers to try and buy the same magazines, and then make up the shortfall by dipping into his own pocket.

AV and Yates did the honourable thing, obviously, and magnanimously returned their one copy to Dunny. Well, why not? They were officers and gentlemen, after all. And Nev and Tommy Two Dicks *had* finished with it.

But another lesson had been learnt of course. Don't rely on Magistrates!

The next day, as mentioned, AV was on a B shift in Yaumatei, looked after by a one-pipper named Tony Keats, while Bob was in the next Sub Division down, which fortunately for him was Tsimshatsui, yes Chimsy, with none other than 'The Reverend' Bill Robinson mentoring him for the day. Bill had left PTS about three months earlier and was now a Sub Unit Commander in the uniformed branch.

Bill obviously had been informed in advance of who was coming, and thus could plan accordingly, having saved a pile of liquor licence renewal inspections to amuse them both.

Yes, the police were the licencing authority for liquor licences, with conditions to be observed such as cleanliness, no disorderly conduct, no underage staff or customers, and common sensical things like that. But bearing in mind there were so many bars, clubs and pubs in Chimsy, it was a tough job, as Yates would find out, but someone had to do it.

And how strange that Bill's portfolio that day seemed to be exclusively to check the bars that he, the WCH5, and most of the other bar-hopping *'Bon Baans'*, or Inspectors, frequented.

The scenario. Bill and Bob enter a premises. Greetings. There to check licence conditions. Okay, Bill (in most cases). Would you like a cup of tea, gentlemen? No thank you, but your toilets are a bit dirty and don't meet the licencing requirement. Oh, sorry about that, we'll attend to it… would you like a couple of beers? Well, OK then (as if forced) and then into a booth, caps off, Bill's fags out, and a pleasant half hour passes, with second buckshee beers arriving before they even know it.

Bill's approval for re-licencing was then rubber-stamped and annotated on his clipboard, and then on to another licence check in a different watering hole, with the final stop being – where else? – at the Red Lips, where they certainly had no need to worry about underaged staff, nor luckily whether or not oxygen and a defibrillator were in place, just in case one or more of the old dears took a funny turn, nor whether barman Charlie had been trained in cardiopulmonary resuscitation.

But not only were they fulfilling their statutory duty in ensuring those stipulated conditions, of course, but it also had the added bonus of showing a uniformed police presence around the bars to dissuade bad or disruptive elements from encroaching. Proactive policing at its finest. Well according to some, anyway.

When the transport came to pick Bob Y up, having already loaded Bottomley on board, the slip that he had made in having a soda pop with Kiwi during orienteering had been well and truly rectified, and he had to be elbowed a few times to enable him to stay awake.

Yes, licencing checks were hard work but, as mentioned previously, someone had to do it.

Bottomley meanwhile had been in the hands of an absolute nutter, in the form of a very young-looking, and acting, Tony Keats, about nine months out of PTS and another Sub Unit Commander.

He arranged for AV to be driven around the Yaumatei Sub Division in a Land Rover, which provided a fascinating glimpse of locals going about their daily business, street hawkers and markets aplenty.

He then conducted a foot patrol with him, again affording an insight into urban commerce, about twenty times more bustling than the Wong Chuk Hang Market, particularly as the very busy Nathan Road ran through the Sub Division.

Things then however soured a little when, going to buy a McDonald's at the very recently opened first outlet in Kowloon (and only one other in Hong Kong, in Causeway Bay) at the bustling Kansu Street, Tony switched on the Land Rover's lights and sirens to part the crowds and market stalls, like Moses parting the Red Sea.

Of course, the Land Rover pulling up like that meant the crowds immediately reformed, but magnified, to see if there had been a robbery or not. Imagine the embarrassment of then forcing themselves, in full uniform, to the front of the queue and asking for 'A Big Mac with extra fries, please, and a chocolate shake'!

Chocolate shake?? Jesus Christ, Bottomley was close to having one of his own.

After the meal had been eaten back at Yaumatei Police Station, with Bottomley grateful that Tony didn't want to go back for an apple pie, one of Tony's Sergeants came in with information that an illegal gambling house was in operation, just about 500 yards from the station, along the sea front.

He immediately went to the Assistant Divisional Superintendent and obtained the required Gambling Authorisation to enter the premises, then he and AV were straight into plain clothes, and to the armoury where Tony drew a sledgehammer and three shotguns, which he distributed to his Sergeant and two Constables.

Thence into the Sergeant's private car, wherein AV could hardly believe his ears when Tony told them that they could shoot anyone jumping out of the windows, or who otherwise tried to escape. AV caught the Sergeant's eye, with him shaking his head, and an absolute catastrophe was on the cards, make no mistake.

They alighted some little way from the alleged casino, with Sergeant Auyeung telling them to wait a moment or, '*Dang yat jan*,' while he made a phone call from a grocery shop (all local calls were free in Hong Kong) and then after about three minutes he returned and instructed which PC was to guard which entry, window, and rear of the ground-floor premises thought to be used for the gambling.

Tony was really chomping at the bit by then and couldn't wait for the 'off'.

But when they arrived, *what* an anti-climax, with the front door already being open, forty or fifty people lined up against the walls, a wad of neatly folded banknotes amounting to exactly 1,200 HK dollars on a green-baized table, also upon which were cards, and Chinese gambling paraphernalia, and one bloke to the fore who was put forward as the keeper, or organiser or operator, all dead quiet, the silence only interrupted by the telephone ringing.

Mr Keats was highly delighted, his first gambling casino, and on the very day he could show off to a PTS wallah too, with the Duty Officer at Yaumatei Police Station sending two lorries to bring the arrested gamblers and exhibits back to the station for processing and charging.

What with all that excitement, it was soon time to go off duty, with AV not failing to shake Sergeant Auyeung's hand before scrambling into the PTS lorry, only Tony not realising his Sergeant had phoned ahead to the casino saying something to the effect that, 'Crazy Horse is on the way. Pack it in. *Now!*'

And within twenty minutes they'd have been opening and operating a gambling house somewhere else.

So it went, back then.

Tony Keats, incidentally, was sacked some months later for stealing 'information money' which he should have passed to his Sergeant, whilst on the Special Duty Squad in Yaumatei, with AV understudying him at the time and taking over sooner rather than later, having been told by him that they were entitled to half of that cash.

Thank the Lord he didn't listen!

'Information money', as seems obvious, was available to pay 'snouts' or 'touts' for information leading to arrests, or for information about ongoing or forthcoming criminal activity, and as far as the Special Duty Squads were concerned, the Team Sergeant generally forked out the cash first and then, if indeed arrests were made, reclaimed it from the Assistant Divisional Superintendent in his parent Division, who maintained a government-provided fund, or sub-imprest account for such miscellaneous purposes.

The Inspector running the Special Duty Squad prepared and signed the forms to pass to the ADS, who gave cash reimbursements weekly, and thus it could be a fair old whack depending on the type and number of cases involved. The money was then ordinarily and routinely passed to the Team Sergeant through the Inspector who'd signed for it, and everyone was happy. One had to take the word of the Sergeant on trust, however, that there had been an informer in the first place.

There were also registered informants on file at some specialised CID units, incidentally with code names to protect their identities in view of the harm that could befall them in view of some extremely serious crimes on which they'd 'grass' if indeed they were not members of the criminal enterprise themselves.

But before Tony proved to have 'sticky fingers', AV had worried about Tony's maturity, if not sanity, because when having a few beers after a shift, Tony would sit around with a plastic revolver in his holster and a set of toy handcuffs on his belt, not caring who saw them, obviously trying to impress.

It was later learnt that he was by no means the only one who did that either!

So, after attachments and back at PTS, a morning was spent on a debriefing session on their experiences, and in the main the two squads gave positive feedback, apart from several moans about their time at Traffic HKI with Alex Wynter (so it hadn't been only AV and Yates who felt disgruntled then). In addition, one Chinese trainee who said that he hadn't liked going into a number of Chimsy nightclubs and drinking beer in the showgirls' changing rooms, where young ladies in various stages of undress had been milling around, during liquor licence checks, at which he was kicked hard under the table, and then clammed up.

Poor old Nev though hadn't had much excitement at all, having been sent to North Point, Wong Tai Sin and Kwun Tong, all out in the wilds, the biggest thrill being one or two foot patrols.

And so, to all intents and purposes, that was the course completed and all that was left were the exams in five days' time.

It was now officially winter, though, and they had swapped boots and gaiters for the winter PTS uniform of long trousers, shoes that had been tipped and soled with metal bits for marching, rough khaki shirt and a pullover, and they felt and thought they looked much better in that gear too.

The Passing Out Parade, though, would be in official full winter uniform, so time to get those room boys working!

And so to the last Saturday afternoon before the two days of exams the coming week, with the lads having a social beer outside of the Mess, wondering whether it would be advisable to go to the China Fleet Club or not, when Dogs Dinner came across and, completely off his own bat, bought a full round of drinks for what were mainly his fellow 102 squad members, apart from Yates of course.

He even included Two Dicks in the round, the pair still a bit wary of each other after a stupid 'handbags at ten paces' confrontation they'd had a week earlier, over something neither was now quite sure about.

Now while Martin was a generous lad with people that he was close to, he wasn't prone to shell out magnanimously (were any of them?) and so, in Gloucester-speak, summat were up!

And indeed it was. Or soon would be, as Dogs grandly told them that he and Lilly were getting married on Monday and that he was resigning during the coming few days and taking her back to Somerset; the Registry Office was booked and her passport application all sorted!

'*Yat dee dough ho chut kay!*' which means, 'That was one hell of a surprise!'

Yes, resigning before his exams. After all that hard work!

Well, the congratulations were effusive enough, and yes, they'd all attend the wedding if they could get the time off, and certainly would join in the celebratory meal at a private room in the China Fleet Club, but why the rush?

Well apparently, his grandmother was sick, and he wanted to get home during the festive season, but with postings to Divisions scheduled over Christmas, he had presumed it would be impossible to get away.

Leave it to the lads!

They checked at the Administration Office to find their postings had not even been considered yet, and that they were now scheduled to leave PTS seven days later than originally planned, on 3rd January 1976, and not 27th December.

Further, after the Commandant was consulted via Frick Jacobs, and in view of the circumstances, Mr Dinner could take his exams and if successful would be granted leave for his time worked at PTS, and compassionate leave for a period to be determined after that, if required, and could return to Hong Kong as and when, merely letting Perry Sherry (in London) know his plans.

His posting would then be determined.

He would, however, have to pay his airfares back to the UK and return to Hong Kong himself, with no need to reimburse the Hong

Kong government for bringing him out there unless he resigned while on leave. Even better from Dogs' point of view, there was no requirement for him to take part in the squad's Dining Out Night or the Passing Out Parade.

What a deal, and Dogs, with tears in his eyes when it was presented to him, immediately snatched at it.

Not only that, but the lads would have a whip-round amongst all the Recruit Inspector squads at PTS, and his mates at Western Mess, which should more than defray the costs of airfares for him and the missus.

Or he could use it to '*cheng*' (invite and pay for – remember?) a mighty booze-up at his stag party and reception!

(Martin chose to use the cash collected for the air tickets, which was a wise move, though it must be said he didn't skimp on treating his mates to as much booze and grub as they could throw down their gullets.)

Not one person though advised him against marrying Lilly; he'd been with her, on and off, for seven months and obviously knew his mind.

'Just one thing. Please. *Not* a continuously looped playing of Creedence Clearwater Revival (CCR), either at the China Fleet Club or the San Fran Bar, or all deals will be off! We've had enough already!'

Well, there are limits!

And so, ladies and gerbils, we have almost reached the end, and it would be stupid for you to desert the squad now, wouldn't it?

The next piece will have one of them in stitches! And shock the hell out of the others.

See you there.

If you somehow get there before me, please wait, as I will for you. '*Seen dough, seen dang*,' in the local vernacular.

How to recognise me? I'll be the one with a chip on both shoulders; well, I've always been a messy eater.

Chapter Fifteen

End Games!

And so there they were, in the Alan wicker chairs outside the Mess, with good old Martin Dinner getting married, his personal arrangements having been taken care of by his mates via Chief Inspector Frick Jacobs and Paddy Loughlin, the Irish PTS Commandant, most expeditiously indeed, surprisingly so as it was a Saturday afternoon, when the top administrative and senior uniformed staff ordinarily would be on leave, but who had remained on duty to set and print the examination papers for the following week.

And an extra pleasing piece of news was given to them by both instructors who came across and told them that they'd allow Monday as a leave day, no drill, PT or musketry even, for those who wanted to attend the wedding of Dogs and Lilly at the Hong Kong Registry Office in the City Hall, right next door to the Star Ferry Terminal in Central.

They however cautioned them that, with exams scheduled for the following Thursday and Friday, not to get so drunk as to still be hung-over when they started.

As if!

And so they took it easy on Saturday, with Dog's stag party binge taking place on Sunday afternoon at the China Fleet Club, the Godown, Popeye's and finishing at the San Fran, with nothing beyond a Saturday-type booze-up taking place. Nothing outrageous; no fixing Dogs up with May Ling or Ah Cheung, for example, especially with Lilly and a mate or two very likely surreptitiously shadowing the revellers as they progressed.

Very few of 101 squad attended, maybe because Dogs had had a 'set-to' with McMee while playing basketball, and Big Mouth had taken it too far, with elbows and knees flying.

But Billy 'Whizzer' Nairn surprisingly attended, arriving late, escaping from the shackles and clutches of his wife and child (and perhaps having already written his crib notes on empty fag packets), for it seemed the first time in Hong Kong, and he was making a real fool of himself by annoying and lasciviously pestering the girls in each bar they went to. Particularly in the San Fran where he thought or hoped that the women had been laid on, as well as the beer, obviously thinking that he was a real Rudolph Vaselino, although his claims to anyone who cared to listen that his penis was 'like a baby's arm holding an apple' proved to be way off the mark, according to some of the very peeved lady guests, and judging by his next piece of exhibitionism.

If he hadn't been warned to behave by Dogs, backed up by the giant Lats, now back from the UK, it was very likely he would have tried to sexually assault one or more of the girls, there and then, prancing around with his dick out and inviting the ladies to:

'Shake hands with my little friend!'

It was therefore no surprise that he was sacked some two months later, when in CID Wanchai, for several times demanding oral sex from the mother of a young Chinese bloke charged with trafficking in dangerous drugs to reduce the offence to simple possession.

Not only that, but he was using AV and Nev's rooms in the

station Mess in which to conduct such assignations, while they were working across the harbour in Yaumatei, obviously without their knowledge or permission.

No charges laid. Quietly moved on. An Irish Superintendent investigated the incidents and the accountability aspect, but apart from officially and to a very select few, kept the findings extremely close to his chest. Never mind; ask no questions, get no lies; no names, no pack drill.

Still, the wedding ceremony in the City Hall Registry Office was a pleasant enough affair, the best man being Plod, of all people, not because Dogs felt sorry for trying to pee on him so many times, but because he reckoned Plod would be the only one who wouldn't be blind drunk at some stage during the day.

The cheek of it! True though.

The good old China Fleet Club laid on a fine buffet in a private room, and then they all went to the San Fran, which was closed to all but the wedding party, and no, there was no CCR played. Thank you, whomever!

Lilly looked very fetching, with a low-cut white dress, and the strange thing was that not one of their intake squad had ever spoken to her, beyond 'Hello,' as the only times they had seen her was when she was with Martin who, it must be said, was very possessive.

Some wag remarked that it was easier for Dogs to take her to Yeovil than it was for any of his mates to bring her to conviviality, let alone friendship, but no doubt in the two years she'd been working in the San Fran, she'd come across a veritable football stadium's worth of self-important, bumptious *'Bon Baans'* (Inspectors) and loutish, loud-mouthed servicemen, and, in the main, being especially obnoxious when they were in a drunken, laddish group. She probably had had little time or respect for any of them, her Martin being an exception, of course.

Lilly's friends, mainly girls who worked in the bars, and a sister and a cousin or two, were quite standoffish, probably because there were no men there that they were allowed to hustle and hassle, all tit and tassel, for drinks and it seemed they were anxiously waiting for the happy couple to depart, when the bar could perhaps revert to business as usual.

Yes, the reception at the San Fran was actually quite a low-key gathering, only 'Whizzer' misbehaving, once again (freedom unbridled, obviously), and at about 18.00 hours Dogs and Lilly disappeared for a night at the nearby Luk Kwok Hotel, while the lads supped up the remainder of the free beer, the majority of squad 101 attending too, even McMee, who was as subdued as anyone had ever seen him.

Frick Jacobs had put in an appearance, which was jolly decent of him, and 'Fingers' Claymore, after finishing work at South Kowloon Court, poked his head around the curtain and dropped off an electronic bedside alarm clock as a gift, then made for Popeye's, the San Fran obviously outside of his comfort zone with too many people he didn't know in attendance.

The money collected for the newlyweds was indeed sufficient to pay for both air fares, one-way, back to the UK, for which the groom was very grateful, as he should have been, obviously.

The next morning, he was allowed leave to go to the British Consulate to sort out Lilly's passport, which was automatically and immediately granted back then, and book their air tickets back to England, scheduled to depart a week hence, on the Monday.

Well, half-crown and sixpence time again, with a change to the examination schedule; the drill and musketry exams would be held first, but at least they'd have a day to assimilate this.

Firstly, each Recruit Inspector would have to move a squad of senior rank and file around the drill square in an orderly fashion, using all the commands and skills they had so painstakingly supposedly learnt over so many months of toil.

A Drill Sergeant had marched a hand-picked senior squad of thirty Police Constables onto the square, and the three rows of ten abreast stood at ease, awaiting the first contestant, your starter for ten.

AV, Nev and Yates had thought that they'd sit up on the bank overlooking the parade ground with the others while the first couple of lads strutted their stuff and they could judge the standard they had to emulate, or better.

But with half of the two squads being sent for their musketry examination, to be grilled on various types of weapons and their usage, 'Bottomley' was first in alphabetical order of those remaining for the Drill Exercise and thus, unfairly as he thought, he reluctantly became the initial 'Johnny on the Spot'.

But there was nothing else for it – was there? – and so, 'Attention! Dressing! Right dress! Left turn! Quick march! Left wheel!' and all that jazz, and before he even realised it, the squad were back in almost the same position they had started from.

Yes!

The CDMI congratulated him, which was a major boost to his confidence, with Nev next stepping up to the plate and he did just as well, and ditto for Bob Yates and Lats Latimer.

But Two Dicks had to have two goes at it, the squad breaking up at his first attempt, but getting round quite well on the second.

This, as will be seen later, had disastrous consequences for their Dining Out night.

Those who had first completed their weaponry exam snuck back as quickly as they could to see how Dog's Dinner would cope, but despite his own peculiar stiff-limbed marching style, he drove the PCs around quite well, returning them two or three yards from where they'd started, after having admittedly gotten them out of step once, but a pass, and that's all that was required.

The weaponry exam was a doddle, too, with Tony Ho and Franny Fong helping them out tremendously, and who were very forgiving about mistakes made, as long as the candidates could rectify them there and then.

Everyone passed, but there was no hitting the bar. Not quite yet.

It has to be pointed out that all that drill and musketry training, prior to those examinations, was not solely geared to obtain them a pass to satisfy the Police Training School's CDMI as an otherwise pointless activity, but to reach a level where, in a large disciplined and para-military organisation like the RHKP, they'd be competent enough to muster and parade junior police officers later in Divisions. As such, they would take charge in any emergency situation or one that involved a requirement to deploy large numbers of men by using standard commands, and a disciplined set of routines and movements, that should be almost second nature to all of them.

However, on the following day, Friday, talk about nerves!

Three papers to be sat: Evidence and Police Procedure; Criminal Law, and, lastly, Miscellaneous Ordinances and Road Traffic.

None of the papers though presented much of a problem, except that there were some questions about cats and dogs, off-road tractors, repairing vehicles on a road, removal of night soil and unlit road works (no, neither AV nor BY had blabbed – see Chapter 13 – so Brian Wilkins could rest easy) and other minor crap that surely should not have been asked, with the nitty gritty like burglaries and robberies and assaults surely of more import than that wishy-washy kind of stuff.

Still, it was the same for everyone and it was therefore fair enough, but a few wondered if Billy 'Whizzer' Nairn even had the details of the Cats and Dogs Ordinance on his fag packets.

Then finally, at about 13.00 hours, papers please, and away they went to the Mess, or their rooms or to play guitar or bullshit, whatever, having to wait until 17.00 hours for the results to be posted.

Yes, a few post-mortems, and 'What did you put?' and 'Why cats and dogs?' but everyone was quietly confident.

And they had cause to be, for they had all passed, the SM3 and Lats way up on the leader boards in respective courses, and even

Dogs, who originally thought he'd not be sitting the exams, passed comfortably.

The senior squads of rank and file had also been taking their finals, and the routine fortnightly exams for junior and intermediate people had been conducted simultaneously, so it was celebration time all round.

Wednesday was their Dining Out function and Saturday was the Passing Out Parade, and so until the Wednesday they could 'coast', as it were.

Down 'The Wanch', then?

Surprisingly, no, but Saturday night would be party night, that's for sure, but they were still required to front up for the Commandant's Parade the next day, which again went off without a hitch, but the state of the latest new Recruit Inspector squad, tripping over canons and the dais, made them wryly and slyly smile and wince.

How soon they had forgotten!

And so to Saturday night, when the SM3, as they had taken to do, started off the evening with a spaghetti bollock naked, or bolognaise to you, at the La Taverna restaurant in Central, having alternated with the one in Chimsy, Bottomley having observed how Tenspeed ate spaghetti and now no longer spread it all over himself, his mates, or the other diners. Again, progress indeed.

A visit to the Jockey Pub to see if Tony Carpio had learned any new tunes (he hadn't) then the Captain's Bar at the Mandarin Hotel, where beer was served in pewter mugs, then one in the Trader's Bar at the basement of the multi round-windowed Connaught Building, also known as…? Yes, the building of a thousand arseholes, but obviously one thousand and three while the SM3 were there.

And then of course the China Fleet Club, their standby or go-to hostelry, being very surprised that course 101 hadn't made their way there over the past months. Perhaps they had and maybe they were slumming it with the ratings, particularly as it appeared Mungo McMee had been hanging out with schoolkids.

However, AV and Steady Eddie (the latter 'guesting' to bolster the mid field) were playing footie for the Galloping Gwailos the following day, against the full Battalion team at Stanley, rumoured to consist of very fit and talented young squaddies, and far from being a social kick-around, it would likely be a full-on, no-holds-barred affair, and no piss-up after the game either.

Just how had Jerry Benfield dropped them into that?

They'd been asked by Benfield, who did appreciate the cheek bearing in mind it was celebration time, to 'Have an early night,' as they were putting out the best team they could, for once sacrificing the social aspect.

He promised to make it up to them if they won.

And win they did, 5-4, despite a howler by Bottomley, and an own goal by Yates, but t surprisingly *had* meant that down in 'The Wanch' they did indeed 'tap in' and eased back on the reins, as it were.

They met up with other squad members in Popeye's and yes, there was Jack Claymore in his usual seat, along with a few other lads they could recognise as policemen, while Debbie and Tina were chasing around, pushing for drinks as normal.

While many celebrants were 'hitting it', AV took a walk outside to get some air, and watch the world go by, and immediately across the street, and in the fading light, he could just make out the straggly dyed-black hair and grey-coated back of May Ling disappearing up the staircase to where her apartment was located on the first floor, allegedly, hand in hand with some smallish, scruffily dressed, middle-aged Caucasian bloke with long wispy grey hair, and slightly bandy legs.

He just had a fleeting and totally disinterested glance at the punter's back as he disappeared into the darkness, but there was something very familiar about him, very familiar indeed, but he'd met all sorts of people in the bars, and there were a load of eccentric expats they'd encountered in Hong Kong, and that was for sure!

Manfully resisting the beers thrust at him, and rebelling against his own nature, AV sat back down at the bar and chatted to Claymore, with something nagging at him but he couldn't quite think what, until… Hell Fire!

'A surprise in December!' he suddenly thought, remembering mum Gina's letter (Chapter 14). What? Because, if he wasn't very much mistaken, the back of that old git he'd seen disappearing up the staircase belonged to none other than his old man! Geoff!

Hastily grabbing Nev and Yates and without really telling them what was up, he caused them all to leap over the dividing rail to the other side of Lockhart Road, and up the stairs to May Ling's apartment, which many had entered thinking she was pimping and leading them to a young prostitute, and then, after the ugly, sordid truth revealed itself, having to quickly decide, in the later words of The Clash, 'Should I Stay or Should I Go?'

A loud knock on the metal grill and hammering on the wooden door, and it opened, and yes, there, standing in all his trouserless glory, was Geoff, looking terribly sheepish, it must be said.

'Hello son,' he meekly whimpered, 'I've been looking for you!'

'Well, you're not gonna find me in here, are you?' was all AV growled, although inwardly delighted to see his old fella, as he indicated Geoff should dress, and get the hell out of there.

'She must have looked like Titsalina when she was younger,' was all Geoff could pathetically offer as an excuse, but – thank God – he hadn't dipped his wick as he'd been rescued just in time, although he probably didn't see it like that.

The story? He had always intended coming out in December and luckily had been granted a late indulgence flight with the RAF, accompanying a Sergeant Matt Jones from the Royal Electrical and Mechanical Engineers, with whom he worked in Hampshire, hand-delivering some important spares to the Army Base at Shamshuipo, adjacent to the police station.

He'd come out for AV's Passing Out Parade but hadn't wanted

to disturb him because he knew exams were pending, but he would have made contact on Monday as a surprise.

Gina though had to stay in the UK because of her daughter and Henry the Dog.

So where was Sergeant Jones then? In the next apartment, so no, don't tell me… but yes, a frantic rapping on the door was answered by wizened, toothless Ah Cheung, an easy three decades older than Sgt Matt, who obviously *had* done the deed, and was as pleased with himself as anyone ever could be.

They were staying in an Army-leased apartment near the Shamshuipo Army Base, and it was very comfortable, if a bit way out, having been in Hong Kong for two days, this being their first excursion into town.

'Didn't your mother tell you I was coming?'

'No, not in quite so many words!'

So, no pickles then.

Well despite the awful seediness of a whore's boudoir, as it were, Geoff was formally introduced to Nev and Yates, and when Sgt Matt had thrown his clothes back on, after having been firmly told to swill his genitals in the sink, all lolloped across to Popeye's to meet the rest of the crew, with all soon forgiven and forgotten, and something to laugh about in years to come.

Mind you, Gina wouldn't have been amused, that's for sure, and it was fortunate she never got wind of it, or if she had, she was diplomatic enough never to mention it. Or maybe too ashamed to.

Men *can* be such filthy beasts.

Geoff dipped his hand in his pocket and bought a round of drinks, so he was immediately accepted, and then Matt Jones did the same, both congratulating the lads for passing their exams, and a tourist schedule was worked out for Geoff, who wouldn't be leaving until the Monday after the Passing Out Parade, to which he and Matt were immediately invited.

Geoff though didn't want to move into town, quite happy in the

Army flat, which at least gave him some independence, he being the sort of chap who liked poking around back streets and markets, armed with the trusty old camera he'd bought when serving in Germany in the early 1950s, comfortable in his own company, and who several times walked the many miles down Nathan Road into Chimsy and back, stopping to chat to anyone who'd listen.

Yes, my pedigree chums, he was a lot more gregarious and sociable than his son.

After the football on Sunday, Geoff was given a tour round the Peak and many other must-see places, then met up with Dogs and Lilly for a few toots, who left on Monday afternoon, not with a bang but a whimper, back to Blighty, not wanting any final hurrahs or fanfares.

Just handshakes, good luck, and thank you. Would they see Dogs again? Well, some of them would, but not until four years later, when Martin James Dinner, then with a law degree, returned to take up his post as a Junior Assistant Crown Counsel within the Legal Department and, incredibly, some of his former police colleagues would soon be going to *him* for legal advice on *their* cases, and be assisting him in various courts as he prosecuted criminals they had arrested, and even prosecuting the occasional police officer who unfortunately found himself facing charges.

'Never came reformation in such a flood!' And so Lilly had really settled him down, that was for sure. No news for four years and THEN!

Oh well, back to the main story.

To ready him for the Passing Out Parade, AV sprang for a new suit for his old man from – where else? – Bob the Tailor, and didn't he look dapper. Mind you, he picked it up by himself, after the second fitting, and was half pissed through Bob's hospitality by the time he left the shop.

You could rely on Bob!

Nev's parents arrived the following day and were housed at the

Excelsior Hotel, where Tony Carpio played jazz, opposite the Yacht Club and Noon Day Gun, and they saw very little of him outside of normal PTS hours.

However, Bottomley's father and Nev's parents had to fend for themselves on Wednesday evening, their Dining Out night (when two other squads were Dining In, of course).

The Baton of Honour winner in squad 102 was a nice, quiet chap called Jimmy Lam, who had come up through the ranks, and who must have worked his nuts off to achieve what he did, and certainly no one begrudged him his award.

Similarly, in 101 squad, another ex-rank and file officer, a lady named Amy Chan, won the Baton, and no one could dispute that either, and well done to both.

They were due to give short speeches that evening but Jimmy was at a loss how to go about drafting his, and so very unwisely turned to fellow squad members to assist.

Now Dogs Dinner, who by the Wednesday was already back with granny in Yeovil, had been in line to receive what was termed as the 'Wooden Spoon', which was awarded to, or devolved upon, the least coordinated officer at drill, and was a light-hearted jibe usually taken in good fun. But in Martin's absence the dubious honour was passed down the line to – guess who? – none other than Tommy Two Dicks, who for some reason was mightily pissed off with Morgan Effin-Jones, the CDMI, because of it.

So, bearing that in mind, it was unfortunate that the unsuspecting Jimmy Lam had Two Dicks help him with his speech, wherein the CDMI was referred to as a coolie, failed soldier and basically a bloody tosser.

Well, as you'd imagine, it was to be an afternoon and evening of Auld Lang Syne (Times Long Past) with no one in the passing-out squads ever to be as fit, keen and at the very peak of their powers ever again, or be bonded in such friendship and camaraderie. So why *not* have a good old drink on the strength of it?

The function started well enough; the usual penguin suits or Mess Kits, black evening gowns, the band playing, a few (more) pre-dinner drinks, a splendid three-course spread, fine wines, plates cleared, pass the port please, rushing out for a piddle, and then the speeches, Nev chomping at the bit to get down 'The Wanch' and show himself off in his Mess Kit, and AV due to meet his dad in Popeye's.

Neither was to be, however, as Two Dicks had been very quiet all throughout the meal, and indeed during the afternoon, and appeared to be seething over something.

First the Commandant gave a little speech, blah blah blah, then a guest of honour gave one, blah blah blah, then another Nob gave one, blah blah blah, and then it was presentation time, the first awarded Baton of Honour going to Amy Chan who, in a very timid voice, which belied her actual confidence, gave a few words of thanks and sat back down.

And then it was time for Jimmy to receive his, which he accepted with good grace, and then he unfolded his speech which in the main of course had been drafted by Tommy Allcock.

Having no real idea what he was spouting, Jimmy in all good faith read the tirade against Effin-Jones, the steam almost coming out of the terribly slandered ears of the CDMI sitting next to him at the top table.

He folded up the paper, put it back in his pocket and sat down, but even he must have wondered why there was only a slight ripple of applause.

Then it was time to present the 'Wooden Spoon' and on being called forward, Two Dicks damned near ran to the top table, and snatched it from the CDMI and then launched into a vitrio.ic diatribe against him, with calls to sit down and boos all round, and then he tried to break it across his knee, to no avail, so he flung it against the far Mess wall, stomping off, his mission, whatever it was, accomplished.

Talk about a pregnant, awkward silence, only broken when the Commandant declared, 'Let's adjourn to the bar, gentlemen.'

Well it should obviously have been 'Off Ground Galloping Knob Rot' time, but not that night, because as the lads in 102 squad gathered round Two Dicks to find out what the hell had set him off, the CDMI, who was certainly no fool and who had immediately married Jimmy's speech and Tommy's insults together, came roaring across and chinned him with a right hook, immediately causing blood to spurt from Tommy's split jaw.

And once again, where was the Mess Secretary while all this was going on?

I tell you where. Attempting his sycophancy on the Superintendent Bandmaster, a Colin Forest, whom Mungo had called in the presence of others, a 'piccolo-playing poof', stretching situational awareness and good manners to the absolute limit.

It had become quite apparent that McMee was a chocco, melting at the first sign of real confrontation or trouble, shirking his responsibilities in case anything reflected badly on him.

God help anyone working with or under him. Mind you, the lads would soon discover loads like him, hiding behind their warrant cards, talking a good day's work in the Mess, slagging off competitors or anyone seen as a threat, and carping away at anyone else's success, spreading rumours as easily as marmalade jam.

Terry Carpenter took over, trying to pour oil on troubled waters, now back as Deputy Commandant, as David 'Ham Sap' Man had been suspended for allegations of indecent assault against several recruit WPCs who'd finally banded together to report him, a so-called class action.

And good for them!

No criminal or disciplinary charges were laid against him, though, and after an apology to those WPCs, he was moved out to be an Assistant Divisional Superintendent in a busy area where gambling was rife, and where he took personal charge of selecting the WPCs for attachment to the Special Duty Squads, which could be a nice little earner, such was the corruption at that time.

The WPCs hitherto had invariably paid cash for the posting but, under David Man's tenure, a demand for sex was the norm, so it wasn't too long before he was in trouble in that regard yet again. One of the new batch of complainants was AVs later wife (more on her later), although Mr Man had felt 'obliged' to make out-of-court settlements to the ladies, and was then ironically moved to the Police Public Relations Bureau where he bade his time until retirement a year or so later, wisely keeping a very low profile indeed.

But yes, AV *had* finally managed a shag - well, to make love, then - when sober; it was his new girlfriend who'd had to be drunk!

But back on Passing Out night, an ambulance was called and several lads accompanied Tommy to hospital where he had six stitches inserted in his face, and where he ill-advisedly allowed them to take a blood sample on the request of Mr Carpenter.

The Mess on return was close to empty, with names of witnesses taken, all giving statements over the next few days, and Morgan Effin-Jones was defaulted, the police equivalent of a court martial, and was given a severe reprimand, which in fact was all the incident deserved.

Some know-it-alls pressed for formal charges of Wounding or Assault Occasioning Actual Bodily Harm, but the majority bore the view that as it was between two expats, and Morgan had been somewhat provoked, what happened in the Mess, stayed in the Mess, particularly as the blood analysis had revealed Tommy was heavily pissed, although the medical report was couched in more medical and technical terms.

The CDMI later apologised in full view and hearing of the lads, and the matter was ostensibly done and dusted, although it definitely put an end to any ambitions that he may have had in becoming a Sub Divisional Inspector outside of PTS.

The atmosphere in the Mess was obviously tetchy until the

Passing Out Parade, even more so as Bottomley had a small contretemps with a tall, miserable, humpty-backed New Zealander called Dave 'Drongo' Moon, a course below them, and who stood propped at the bar on Thursday night, muttering insults towards AV for some goddam reason, about how he didn't like little men, and why was Bottomley such a stuck-up little shit?

True, many people got that opinion of AV who hadn't been a regular Mess bar visitor, hating small talk and bullshit, only talking to people he trusted or thought something of, with the view that if someone had a problem with him, or he with them, then let's not play the game, and simply just ignore one another.

In fact, as the years went by, AV (who'd turned into a real loner later after being accused of every goddam crime from corruption, to assault, to conspiracy to pervert the course of justice, to being much too gung-ho) made it easier for people by completely blanking them, so they didn't have to go through unfelt pointless greetings and platitudes if they bumped into him, or if they or he hadn't crossed the road on seeing each other approaching.

Because once again, 'It's all Dick!'

Mutism by election, they call it, and for some it's a mental disability.

Ha! As if!

AV, just to 'get on', had never even tried to learn how to say, 'Pleased to meet you', or to converse with people he didn't like, and whom he wasn't at all pleased to meet, when they, in return, just as equally felt the same about him.

In his dotage, though, commencing at thirty five, and with the benefit of hindsight, he did sometimes wish that he *had* learnt the art of *pretending* to be sincere, the same as everyone else, as true sincerity, probity and integrity were very rare commodities indeed amongst most of those he'd encounter in Hong Kong, and it had been very hard indeed, being a loner and outsider, having to butt heads, let alone compete with, a veritable nest of vituperative and venal vipers.

But back in the Mess, 'Drongo' Moon continued with his foul invective and vicious, scathing polemic against Bottomley, being warned several times to pack it in, and to speak to AV when sober, if he was aggrieved about something.

Nothing doing, just carrying on and on…

Now Bottomley of course had backed down early doors on the Piggard arse-stabbing incident, which was a mistake as Piggard later tried it on again in Divisions, with not only AV, but while he had been prepared to also let Moon's verbal attack pass, even from a junior course member, Drongo was trying the patience of a saint, and then, sorry, 'Red Mist Time' and Bam Bang Boom!

A flurry of fists had Moon decked in about twenty seconds, the only witnesses being from AV's own course, with all of them quickly dispersing while Recruit Inspector Moon was left alone, crawling on all fours and crying in his drunkenness, most probably trying to make sense of where he was and what had happened.

Where was the Mess Secretary? Your guess was as good as theirs.

AV wasn't going to apologise, but next day told Frick Jacobs what had happened, who spoke to Moon's instructor, with Moon agreeing he was very much at fault, and would apologise in due course.

AV received what he thought at the time was a mild, tongue-in-cheek verbal warning from Jacobs, but he was to learn that everything was recorded, somewhere. And anything noteworthy or out of the ordinary was bandied around like 'Dunny' McKenzie's obscene magazines, although gossip, speculation, lies and fantasy could not be destroyed so easily as by a Magistrate's order.

Consequently, that incident, significantly enhanced as news of it spread, would damn him for a good while as a punchy trouble-maker, which much later rebounded when he decided to stir up as much trouble as he possibly could, hung for a sheep as a lamb, when the final pieces of straw had broken the camel's back, becoming a very successful and an extremely well paid ICAC informer.

Fuck 'em!

Yes, for some reason he unwittingly had seemed to get up so many people's noses that he had thought of changing his name to Vick Inhaler, but there were a load of people in truth he did want to annoy, and who needed annoying, and whom he was quite content to oblige, his code name at the Independent Commission Against Corruption being – you'll never guess – 'Old Mister Happy.'

But, in fact, it's fine being thought an arsehole as long as you realise what exactly you are, and can live with it, and even profit by it.

('Bam Bang Boom', incidentally, is a very fine modern blues song performed by Dion, and Billy Gibbons, the bearded wonder out of ZZ Top.)

Anyway, Geoff had been hosted by Army Sergeants in Yuen Long over Christmas, having access to every Sergeants' Mess up there in view of his equivalent civilian rank, and had a spiffing time, with AV later being his private tourist guide, and Dee Dee (Debbie) 'looking after' him when AV was busy. She was a far better proposition than May Ling, whom his old man now scampered across Wanchai's Lockhart Road to avoid, not that she would be likely to remember him or the incident at all. All in a night's work and she'd had thousands of nights and a good forty years of infinitely worse memories than of someone running out on her.

Hell, Geoff had even paid her the 200 Hong Kong dollars they'd agreed upon in advance, so in fact he had no reason at all to feel guilty towards her. Towards Gina, yes, but certainly not to May Ling.

But one wonders what Steve Greening would have made of the fact that Debbie was temporarily a Bottomley generational consort, the misguidedly jealous little snob?

As for Sergeant Matt? He had ploughed his own furrow with some army mates, but seemed happy enough with them, meeting Geoff for nightcaps back at his Mess and at their flat.

The Passing Out Parade went off swimmingly, the lads all

dressed in dark-blue full winter uniforms, proudly showing off one pip on either shoulder, with Phillip Yip and Frankie Chan not embarrassing either AV, Yates or the squads they were leading, in full view of the Commandant, invited dignitaries, families and other interested spectators, while Nev as expected was totally professional in marching his unit around the crowded 'dance floor'.

As the squad of WPCs were dismissed for the last time, AV could not help but think that Gobbler Wong was amongst them, and wonder what was she doing the rest of the afternoon?

Oh well, back to the land of dreams.

Geoff and Matt enjoyed the parade immensely and could hardly believe that the standard of drill was better than that at their Borden Army Base back in the UK.

Yes, Dad, it ain't all fun and games.

A few beers in the mess, Geoff kipping it off in AV's room, Nev off with his parents, Yates up at Wong Chuck Hang market after nuts and mangoes, a wash and brush up, then a pint of draft San Miguel beer at the Jockey pub, a quick gin and tonic or two in the China Fleet Club, and then ending up in Popeye's, where the usual suspects were in attendance.

But at about 20.00 hours, who should slink through the curtains but none other than Dave 'Drongo' Moon, sporting a patch over his black eye, and sitting directly opposite Yates and AV. Geoff was sat in a booth with Dee Dee, whilst Nev was in an adjacent one with Tina, having an hour to spare before he was to meet his parents for a '*hoy seen*', or seafood dinner.

AV quietly informed his old man that he'd planted Moon a couple of nights previously, following a series of savage, venomous insults, and his old man laughed until he learnt his son had received a ticking-off because of it, and would no doubt be marked down because of it.

Anyway, the night continued and when Moon slinked off to the toilet, it seemed coincidentally that it was at the very same time that Geoff needed a pee, and who followed behind him in the semi darkness.

Some five minutes later Geoff returned, rudely pushing his way through the throng, and gaspingly saying he'd see his son in the San Fran, then quickly left.

'What's going on?'

The answer became alarmingly apparent when Moon was spotted returning from the toilet, staggering around like Blind Pugh after a heavy night in the Admiral Benbow, holding a bloody nose, his other eye closed, and moaning like hell through a cut lip and a missing front tooth, that some old nutter had attacked him in the gents for no goddang reason, and did anyone know who he was?

'No idea mate, no idea at all!' but Drongo didn't want to bring yet more adverse or official attention to himself following so closely after that incident in the Mess, and so literally took it on the chin as it were and wrote it off as merely part of life's rich tapestry, instead of dialling 999 and requesting Police Emergency assistance, which no doubt would have led to a CID Wanchai investigation.

So, he did have some common sense and a pair of bollocks, after all, then! (Mind you, he'd revenge himself on AV in various sneaky, underhand ways in years to come, which exactly mirrored Moon's dominant character traits.)

The irony however was that he had only been in Popeye's to apologise to AV, getting up Dutch (or New Zealand) courage to do so, but that was now entirely out of the question of course.

Geoff was immediately whisked across to Chimsy, particularly liking the Australian-themed Ned Kelly's Bar, where he was delighted when the band played the traditional blues song, 'St James Infirmary', which he hadn't heard for years, and where he had 'One hell of a night!' with the lads, very chuffed with himself indeed for, as he saw it, upholding the family's honour.

He took his RAF flight back to Brize Norton early on Monday morning, loaded with goodies for Gina and the girls, having enjoyed himself enormously, and had established a friendship with Lats and Yates that would last until he died, decades later.

He would next be in Hong Kong in 1979 for AV's wedding, with Gina accompanying him, Bottomley junior marrying WPC Zoe Cheung Wai-lin, whose stepfather was one of the Station Sergeants who'd escaped with an absolute stash of corruptly obtained loot to Taiwan.

He'd met her as her Sub Unit Commander at Yaumatei Police Station, immediately after leaving PTS, and luckily for him she wasn't a Potential Officer, and thus was not seeking help to get her foot on the ladder, although it would have been helpful if she had, as she could then have helped AV by standing on the bottom rung of *his* ladder when he had a window-cleaning business, many years later.

However, after that wedding, *didn't* Geoff drop him in the shite with his Divisional Detective Inspector in Wanchai, by telling him of his son's temper, and squalid history of drunken incidents before joining the RHKP, and then by upsetting a CID/ Wanchai Sergeant with his over-stimulated, drink-fuelled libido, and obvious attraction towards the Sgt's nightclub hostess girlfriend. All diplomatically, in the end, written-off as good humour though.

Never mind. Family is family after all. There again, so were Caine and Abel.

(And a libido is *not* an inflatable rubber bed or flotation device, in case some of you are dyslexic.)

Back at PTS, the senior rank and file, with their kit and caboodle, were packed off in lorries to the Divisions to which they'd been posted, and because the junior Inspector squads had moved onto the parade square, there was no more drill for the lads, their own postings to various formation due one week later on 3rd January.

The now Probationary Inspectors, as opposed to Recruit Inspectors, had submitted choices on where they wanted to be posted, the so called 'Wish List', with all of the WCH5 placing

Yaumatei Division as their first option, which indeed was to where they were duly assigned. However, they were only informed of this ten minutes before the transport turned up to deliver them to their accommodation at Wanchai Police Station Officers' Mess, the very afternoon they finally left PTS, seemingly for good.

A cock-up on the administration front, so it seemed; there'd be loads of those, they would soon find.

But it had been hard work, filling that final week, with the almost daily social runs to Deep Water Bay with Sgt Bill Wong luckily using up a few hours, as already noted, interrupted by a final fitness test.

Just as Norrie Pinkney had growled, they were expected to have improved on their fitness levels of eight months previously, and how lucky it was that AV had gone from turbo charge to second gear in April, or he could otherwise have had some explaining to do, but nonetheless everyone proved much fitter.

A morning was taken up with a trip to Police Headquarters where they all had photos taken once more, and where their warrant cards were subsequently issued, replacing the blue PTS identity cards so beloved by good old Dave Kensington, who was gone but certainly not forgotten.

'It's all fun and games until someone loses an eye, Lorna,' as my dear old granny used to say – she never *could* remember my name or get my gender right – and just weeks later, poor Norrie unfortunately found himself the subject of an assault charge.

Having been more or less immediately posted to CID Mongkok in view of his former experience as an Aberdonian and Bermudan copper, a report had been made on his shift of an indecent assault on a fourteen year old girl at a Mongkok bus stop, his investigation team handling the case with a steely determination to bring the pervert to book.

While Pinky was in the Officers' Mess, a day or two later, having a few late afternoon snifters, his Sergeant went up and gave him the splendid news that a suspect had been arrested, and was now sitting alone in the 'Daai Fong,' or CID Duty Room.

His ire up, he drained his third glass since lunchtime, and stomped off down to the Duty Room. Seeing a shifty and obviously criminal, middle-aged Chinese chap sat by himself, but strangely with none of his team around to guard him, and who had also neglected to handcuff him, Norrie called him a dirty bastard and a pervert, and then spat on him, with a clip around the ear to finish off with.

Whoops! It turned out the man he had slapped and gobbed on was not the culprit, but the young girl's father who was waiting for his daughter who'd been escorted to the toilet, while the actual suspect was getting a hammering, or perhaps more politically correctly, was being 'interviewed' somewhere more private.

Charges dropped though, once the circumstances had been explained, but Pinky was certainly 'half-crown-and-sixpence' for a little while, that's for sure.

So that aspect was 'NFA'd', which in police parlance was classified as 'No Further Action to be taken,' although in relation to some investigators, in other instances, where they couldn't be arsed to make an effort, or didn't know how to proceed, NFA alternatively, although sometimes jokingly, stood for 'No Fucking Ability'.

Mind you, it wasn't all course 101 people in the mire, as first there was 'Whizzer' from course 102, and then Two Dicks, who after a successful gambling raid in a high-class premises while in charge of a parallel Special Duty Squad in Yaumatei to Alan Bottomley's, he spiked, and thus totally ruined, eight expensive air conditioners as a 'Fuck You!' to the operators, which was actually serious criminal damage, and he was extremely lucky that the person running the illegal casino was a *'Dai Lo'*, or a Big Brother of the Yaumatei Divisional Barrack Sergeant, although the latter was none too pleased.

Now *'Dai Lo'* did not necessarily mean that they were related, being not only a familial term, but also one of respect or deference to someone considered above an individual, either in rank, or on the social or economic scale or even in the Triad hierarchy. It's your guess which, in the above context.

Mind you, Tommy had been very well liked by his Special Duty Squad Sergeant, so much so that Sergeant Tong, on the very first day the new Inspector had arrived on the team, had given Tommy a shiny new Rolex timepiece as a birthday present. But weeks later, the Sergeant was most upset when Tommy, very soon after spiking those air conditioners, was transferred to the Uniformed Branch at Kai Tak Airport, where duties and responsibilities were not quite so taxing, and where he worked under the very same Mr McFyffer who'd proudly paraded before the squads, in all of his glory, on their first arrival in Hong Kong (Chapter Five.)

And so it was that Bob Yates became the Officer in Charge of Yaumatei Special Duty Squad Two, with Bottomley in charge of SDS One, having formerly understudied Inspector Tony Keats, who had, of course, been unceremoniously dismissed over the theft of information money.

But coincidentally, a day after Two Dicks was transferred, Bottomley's own Sergeant tried to present *him* with a splendidly boxed, Rolex Oyster watch, worth more than an Inspector's monthly salary, *his* birthday a full eight months away. And to further complicate matters, Bob Y was approached by the new Sergeant on his squad, who tried to give *him* a very expensive Omega 'Diver's Chronometer' wristwatch, Sergeant Tong having been posted to somewhere in the New Territories over the 'air conditioner incident', and Bob just as surprised and indignant as his mate had been.

Just a goddang minute thar' boy. Surely this can't be right!

Yates and the Bucket conferred, AV with the benefit of 'having the ear' - and other more personal bits - of his girlfriend, WPC Zoe Cheung - now part of his SDS squad - who, after some reluctance it must be said, and in the strictest confidence, informed him the 'gifts' were a tester, to suss out the steadfastness and good character - or otherwise - of the new Inspectors. A bit like Tony Keats previously, who apparently had been very proud indeed to ponce around and show off his Patek Philippe Nautilus watch, along, of course, with his plastic handcuffs and toy revolver.

Both fronted up before their Assistant Sub Divisional Inspector, yes Jack Claymore, of course, who grunted a cynical, 'I told you so', and who summoned the two Sergeants to his office, where Bottomley and Yates made their indignation and displeasure clear, with warnings given and entries made and signed in the police notebooks of all concerned.

Claymore stated to the Inspectors that as markers had been laid down, he wouldn't take the matter further, as to do so might 'embarrass' some officers up the chain of command, who selected the rank and file for those squads, and with whom the lads had to work under, and look-to, in maintaining team harmony and achieving results.

Privately, though, when well outside of the Yaumatei Officers' Mess, Claymore was much less veiled in his thoughts about the affair; they'd had their first experience at how some things stood in 'the real world', and a sharp reminder that they had to watch themselves.

To have 'jumped in with two feet' and overreact, almost fresh out of PTS, without absolute proof and total corroboration of motive, and to have locked horns with long established and very senior NCOs, who had so much to lose, but who might well have been deeply immersed in corruption, could have been dangerous, as an Inspector Mark Foyle at Kowloon City found out. A month after leaving PTS, he had reported his Station Sergeant directly to his Divisional Superintendent for accepting bribes from illegal gambling operators, based on rumour, and then a week later found a packet of heroin secreted inside his own private car's glove compartment. This was after an anonymous tip was received by Narcotics Bureau, and only after his car was searched in his presence by officers from that body.

Goodbye Mr Foyle, whose contract was terminated, despite many being absolutely sure that he had been set up. The Station Sergeant incidentally went on to retire after thirty years of service and relocated to Canada without a blemish on his record.

Tommy Two Dicks' wristwatch was allegedly dropped into Victoria Harbour by 'someone' during a Star Ferry journey between Chimsy and Central. On whose advice? Well, it was none of the rest of the Wong Chuck Hang Five's, that's for sure, with much discussion, despite the possible ramifications bearing in mind what had happened to Mr Foyle, whether the whole matter should have been mentioned to Tony Robling or Linda Bailey at the ICAC. However, it would have been a pointless exercise anyway, as the ICAC already had its investigative claws into Yaumatei Division, and many other Kowloon units as well. This is elaborated upon a few pages hence.

And a course mate of Bill Robinson's, a fine chap, despite bearing the poncey name of Paul Villeneuve, was dropped in the mire through the mis-advice of his Sergeant, when, after Paul and he had arrested someone for possession of a packet of heroin that was below the weight for it to be statutorily presumed to be for trafficking purposes, the Sergeant told him it was normal procedure for them to split the pack into five separate small packets and thus the alternative legal presumption for trafficking would apply.

This would mean a pat on the back, and time off for arresting a drug trafficker, which the arrested bloke obviously was, instead of a person merely having drugs for personal use.

It was the reverse of course of what Billy Whizzer had been doing in CID Wanchai, changing trafficking to simple possession in exchange for sex.

Unfortunately, the Divisional Superintendent walked in on Paul and the Sergeant while they were 'doctoring' the packets, and went apeshit, especially when Paul said he'd thought everyone was in on the act and had assumed he was doing nothing that wasn't standard operating procedure.

Severe bollockings all around – and lucky it was only that – and a lesson learnt very quickly, the denouement spreading like wildfire… don't believe everything you're told, even by senior rank and file with decades of service!

Such cases like that were called '*jo hay*', or manufactured cases, and the joke going around was that the favourite pop group amongst those on anti-drug duties was '*Jo Hay* and the Five Packets!'

Yes, it was an unfortunate fact of life that many officers, both expat and local, of all ranks, were always falling into trouble, in what could often be a high-pressure and sometimes explosive environment, with many pitfalls and temptations that one had to try and cope with and navigate around.

Oh well. So it goes!

Three more activities of note to pad out their final week at PTS:

The Hong Kong Red Cross came again (not all of them) and not for blood this time, but to demonstrate first-aid and instruct on how to stem wounds, apply bandages and conduct CPR, which were essential skills to learn, especially the way that Mess nights seemed to be going.

And then on the shooting range, there was practice on giving a warning before discharging a revolver in anger, such as, 'Police! Stop or I will fire!' in both English and Chinese, but the instructors were not at all happy with someone's 'Stop! I've had a few!'

It was their own fault, really, in scheduling that session so close after the lunchtime piss-up, a lot of that going on as the squads, awaiting postings, were becoming bored with that extra week of doing bugger all, really.

But boredom soon turned to blind panic as the third activity was a run up Brick Hill, which in fact turned out to be more of a scramble, if not an actual crawl, with only half a dozen making it to the top. Bill Wong had gone sick (probably sick of babysitting drunks at Deep Water Bay) with his replacement taking the easy, yet sadistic, option of just pointing to the hillside and turning them loose, while he lounged in the gymnasium. However, there was no direct supervision of the squads during the Brick Hill exercise, so the majority just plonked themselves behind thick bushes about a quarter of the way up, and re-joined those who'd completed the ascent as they were sliding their way back down.

But what a great bloke Callum Colgate was, as being as keen as ever, he had no problems at all in taking Bob Y's 35mm Olympus Trip camera to the top and snapping a series of photos of what proved to be magnificent all-round views that really impressed Bob's family back in Balham.

And true to his word, Jerry Benfield made it up to Bottomley and Yates by having a crate of twelve cold beers delivered to them, which the WCH5 took to the beach and quaffed as aperitifs, although he had included a note saying it would have been two crates if they hadn't collectively been directly responsible for two of the opponents' goals. Charming. They were picked to play again though.

An important final task was to critique the training they had received, mainly a tick-in-the-box affair, with a space at the end for comments, in which everyone noted how impressed they had been with most aspects of their training, although with hindsight, some things had been badly omitted or glossed over.

Corruption in the RHKP had been steadfastly claimed as a thing of the past, but that was definitely *not* the case (as Toby Robling of ICAC and Jack Claymore had intimated) and in fact a very significant number of rank and file from Yaumatei, with whom the lads worked on their first postings, were some six months later lifted by the ICAC. They were charged and duly convicted for corruption offences relating to drug trafficking at the Shek Lung Fruit Market, just along from the police station, and the operation of large-scale illegal gambling houses.

It was alarming, indeed sobering, for some of the WCH5 when they were called to give evidence in that District Court trial of uniformed Station Sergeants, Sergeants and junior rank and file from Yaumatei Division. Not only had they worked with most and socialised with some of them but had also played in the Yaumatei Divisional football team with others who, in the main, seemed straightforward and jolly colleagues, even though that evidence was merely to state that so-and-so had been attached to Yaumatei Division, knowing very little else in truth, apart from some of their nicknames, the ever-churning rumour mill spewing out a story that some of the new officers were ICAC informers.

No! Not then! Most definitely not!

Still, even Jack the Ripper probably had his good points, and was possibly very kind to his dear old mum up there in the Smoke.

Before the trial, several of the accused rank and file approached the lads and begged them not to mention their nicknames when giving evidence, as their accusers generally only knew them by those nomenclatures. These approaches, if reported, could have resulted in further serious problems for the accused policemen, of perhaps attempting to pervert the course of justice, but there was no way in the world anyone could go back on the earlier statements they had given to the ICAC, and especially not under oath in court.

It was up to those charged to prove that the Fatty Cheungs, Tiger Leungs, Big Noses, Teddy Boys, Fat Dogs, Tall Boys, Handsome Lads, Small Heads, Baldies and a whole lot more, as they were known by, but in Cantonese, were such common nicknames that it was not *them* to whom their accusers were referring.

It was not, however, up to the lads to provide them with a defence and, in fact, the way the evidence unfolded over the month of the trial, their actions had been pretty much indefensible, and most had deserved to be sent to prison.

The actual truth of the matter in the case against the 'Yaumatei Syndicate' was that several of the defendants' fellow rank and file, themselves arrested as suspects, had 'turned', and gave statements substantiating corruption allegations made by criminals whose testimony would not have been worth a jot had it not been so corroborated, such were the dubious 'fishing expedition' tactics of the ICAC. This put the fear of God into many who *had* been at it, but who'd do anything to wriggle 'off the hook' at the expense of as many others as it would take.

It was curious that, in all of the mass arrests, very few if any Women Police Constables were charged, it widely being thought that they invariably spilled the beans, mainly being the administrative or personal assistants to the Inspector on the Special Duty Squads, and who, mostly English speakers, often formed the buffer between the Officer and the team Sergeant. They were tasked with making sure that the '*Bon Baan*' (Inspector) didn't find out too much of what the squad were really up to, or how they found enough cases per shift to keep the management happy.

To make matters worse, the Inspectors 'chosen', or rather ordered, to head the Special Duty Squads, never received any worthwhile briefing at all, apart from perhaps an, 'Enjoy yourself, and claim plenty of information money to keep your Sergeant happy! The Inspector you're taking over from will fill you in on your role.'

Yes, Tony Keats had certainly filled AV in, alright, but he most certainly would have been kicked out of the police with Tony, if he had listened!

But where was the accountability, as surely the more senior officers at Yaumatei, with years of service behind them, must have known what was going on, or could reasonably have been expected to know, or else exactly *what* were they in the Police for?

No, not even in Divisions would anyone openly admit the problem, either not thinking it a problem at all, or just glossing it over.

By 1977, though, the ICAC had become too blasé about such

large-scale arrests, and had announced that Kowloon City would be the next Division to fall, at which there were marches to and demonstrations outside of the Commissioner of Police's office block at Police Headquarters by mainly Kowloon City policemen, joined by many others who worked in various different police formations, who feared theirs could well come under ICAC scrutiny in the near future, if they weren't *already* 'of interest' to them.

The vociferous and prolonged shouts from the angry throng of '*CP! Mo lan yung!*' or in English, 'The Commissioner of Police is no fucking use!' were well reported in both the local and English newspapers, as well as on TV, and were severely embarrassing for the Force as a whole, despite how accurate they might well have been. He retired shortly thereafter... with perhaps better memories of being mentioned several times, in the then very popular American television cop series 'Hawaii Five-O', after some episode segments were earlier shot in Hong Kong, to lessen the sting of the vicious barbs thrown at him.

Be that as it may, the unrest, with the authorities dreading it would spread, coupled with a few Sergeants from Yaumatei Division storming the ICAC Offices in Hutchison House in Central, eventually resulted in a partial amnesty, although not for serious individual cases, or for some corrupt cliques of coppers where cases were so advanced that actual charges were imminent, and were held to be in the public interest.

It was a pity there wasn't a requirement, where amnesties were granted, that the individuals be required to come publicly clean about what they had been up to, a sort of Truth and Reconciliation effort, so remedial action could have been taken to stop such general patterns of behaviour forever.

One local Superintendent, Charlie Kwok, who became slightly incautious after several slugs of expensive Hennessy XO brandy mixed with tomato juice (!) told them in the PTS Mess that if he had been corrupt, 'in the old days' of course, he would have put all his money into antiques, the lads not quite sure if he was merely making a statement or dispensing veiled advice, and then he hastily changed the subject.

Quite a while later, when in Divisions, he had been drinking with Yates in Yaumatei Mess, and asked for a lift home, Bob Y obliging as he had bought a motorbike by then, and was grateful to give it a decent spin, with Mr Kwok, half pissed, holding on for grim life the ten miles or so to his apartment in Kwai Chung, in North West Kowloon.

Manners of course dictated that Bob be invited in for a final toot, and as Charlie sorted out the drinks under the furious gaze of his wife, Yates could hardly fail to notice that the living room was decked out like the set of *Going for a Song* and *The Antiques Roadshow* combined, with many beautiful and obviously very valuable vases, screens, pieces of ornately carved rosewood furniture, paintings, and bric-a-brac in display cases, belying the drab exterior of the flat.

No comments made, and none needed really, although Charlie suddenly sobered up, shooting worried glances at Yates, but Bob Y affected a blankness that fooled the Kwoks into thinking he hadn't noticed anything other than the torturous length of time it was taking Chas to get the beer on the table.

Diplomatic, if nothing else, was our Robert, and 'Noble Yeats' was certainly not only the name of the winning horse in the 2022 Grand National at Liverpool's Aintree Racecourse, that's for sure.

Very shortly after leaving PTS and being posted as Sub Unit Commanders or in other responsible positions within the Uniformed Branch, or the Criminal Investigation Department, the new Probationary Inspectors were routinely called upon to complete yearly incremental reports of those under their command, and obviously flicked through the back pages of the Constable or Sergeant's Record of Service (RS), to get a feel for his or her experience, qualifications, commendations and disciplinary record.

It was however quite odd to often see typed entries included in the RS, from the past, such as, 'This officer was part of a seminar conducted by myself and was warned on the perils and pitfalls of corruption,' signed by an Inspector or Chief Inspector who had later, as a Superintendent or indeed a higher rank, been arrested and in some cases imprisoned for the very same corruption they'd apparently warned their subordinates about. Talk about irony. (And perhaps more truthfully at that time, the entry should properly have read, '… warned on the perils and pitfalls of being caught for corruption.') Oh well, all in the past, wasn't it?

As said several times already during this narrative, they had been repeatedly told that there were no Triad Societies in Hong Kong, just small-time thugs using the Triad Society name to commit crime and put victims in fear.

But by 1978, AV was on Anti Triad Duties in CID Wanchai and had been informed by his Detective Station Sergeant that Triad Societies controlled most aspects of life in Hong Kong. From allowing hawkers to operate for 'tea money', to 'protecting' if not actually owning nightclubs, bars and brothels, running both gambling and drug operations, with different Triad Societies in different areas with different spheres of control, with martial arts gyms, clubs and associations very often being fronts where Triad members congregated and recruited new members.

And the RHKP was rife with Triad Society members, with even his large squad mostly being members of different societies so they could quell any disputes between various groups, who were organised into advisors, captains, fighters and soldiers, with secret signs and other ways of identifying each other, a bit more serious than to consider them as merely 'Masons with Attitude' though.

(And so consequently, those *'High bin dough lays?'* at Inter Divisional soccer matches could *indeed* have been as sinister as various young *'Bon Baans'* had been told, or had themselves gleaned, then.)

The Detective Station Sergeant also claimed that some very

senior local officers were also high-ranking Triad officials, with more than a few honorary expat members serving in the police, although AV was very sceptical until he'd been on the squad for a while.

But in 1979 the Hong Kong Security Branch (encompassing Civil Aid Services, the Civil Aviation Authority, Customs, Immigration, and Police Departments, and all Government Medical Services to name a few), after consultation with the HK Legal Department, and recommendation from the top echelon within the RHKP, turned around and said that Triad Societies in Hong Kong *were* in fact extremely active, and powerful, and had been totally underestimated.

(Indeed, they were later called upon to help a smooth transition of Hong Kong to China in 1997.)

The Wong Chuk Hang Five's first Divisional Superintendent, a local officer, was allegedly 'moved on' for being found conducting, in full Triad regalia, a Triad initiation ceremony, this before the 1979 about-face, so it was clear that people *had* known the extent but did nothing about it.

Now surely, if most of the rank and file and the local Inspectorate and above knew this, as obviously many expats must have done, particularly some in CID, why hadn't 'someone' done anything about it, and why was the threat played down?

No mention at all was made of Freemasonry in the Police, or in Hong Kong in general, and how, in certain eyes, favours bestowed by and upon 'Brothers' could perhaps be viewed as corruption at worst and blatant nepotism at best. There was the occasional problem when some bull-nosed, non-Masonic officers refused to drop or amend charges against visiting masons who had committed criminal offences, even though pressurised by Masonic senior officers to do so.

(Some Masonic police allegedly clashed amongst themselves within the police rank structure, when a few junior Inspectors were at a higher level 'On The Square', through their UK Lodges, than their long-serving senior commanders, and indeed some of Hong Kong's high and mighty. Boys will be boys!)

Crown Counsels, with a load being Australian, had been disparaged as merely wanting to do a little time in Hong Kong, get the gratuity, then bugger off to wherever or open up a surf shop, and if they were any good, they'd be in private practice.

It was fortunate that view hadn't been passed to those Crown Counsels taking part in the PTS mock trial exercise, and yes some would just do one tour, but there were many totally professional, dedicated, career-minded people within the Legal Department who were a valuable and vital part of the Judicial System in Hong Kong. Just look at Martin James 'Dogs' Dinner.

And how many expat Recruit Inspectors only lasted one tour or less? Of the initial twenty three expatriate recruits who made up 101 and 102 squads on first arrival in HK, nine did not show up for a second tour for one reason or another, i.e., almost a forty percent wastage. This percentage must surely have been much greater than that of one tour government lawyers.

Why had nothing been mentioned about the homosexual rent-boy rings servicing prominent people, or about how to apply the law which still made homosexual acts, even if consensual, illegal?

(And a 'Cottager' was soon learnt to be not only a supporter of Fulham Football Club, whose team play at Craven Cottage in London, but had anyone in Hong Kong ever arrested a craven cottager for importuning in a public toilet? Just a thought.)

But oh, the stories Mr Claymore told before he left Hong Kong, confirming the rumours of such rent-boy circles, and a Police Special Investigation Unit (the SIU) nicknamed 'The Bum Squad' was formed to look into such activities, to protect young people if any were involved and to investigate government servants who, by their actions, could pose a security risk.

Some of the police officers on that squad were first-class detectives, and kept their cards very close to their chests, but a general 'Poof Mania' seized many in the general police community, and there was much vicious and careless talk on who had funnel-shaped bums, and finger pointing and accusations that 'He's a poof!' and so on and so forth.

The matter came to a head with the suicide of Inspector Mingus Muffet in 1980, as was mentioned in the previous chapter, with Muffet believing he had sensitive information in his possession which should have granted him immunity against committing homosexual acts himself, but when this proved not to be the case, he had some sort of meltdown and shot himself.

He had been in contact with some human rights campaigners before this time, and upon his death, after much publicity, the Muffet Enquiry took place, with many homosexuals coming out and giving evidence before it, which changed many perceptions, one must say. It didn't do Muffet any good, mind you, and yes, after his affair with WPC Stella Lai, he changed tack and began 'to totally bat for the other side', his sexual orientation apparently balancing on a knife edge up to that point. Remember Inspector Fulton Puller, mentioned earlier when being goaded at PTS by Denny 'Mad Dog' Browning (see Chapter 11)? Well, he featured heavily in evidence given, as did a Jim Duffly, a private-sector lawyer, who allegedly tossed some young fellow off his boat while at sea, which may have horrified some casual yachtsmen and the fishing fraternity, but who was given some immunity for his testimony.

And there were also call-girl and female prostitution rings as well, servicing the great and good of the Colony, the client list a veritable 'Who's Who and Shagging What?' of smugness and sordid duplicity.

Most certainly, Claymore wasn't the only police officer or government servant who'd been allegedly, cowering in the closet, along with many in the business community and in the general public at large.

And no mention either had been made of the raging marital infidelity pervading both the highest and the lowest of ranks, it often being thought de rigueur, and perfectly acceptable, to have a wife whilst running a mistress or a veritable hareem at the same time, with very many extra-marital affairs conducted with female police officers within the same station.

In fact, there were so many people shagging like rabbits that there was probably more chance of catching myxomatosis than a sexual transmitted disease!

But was there any moral equivalency between using prostitutes and being a serial adulterer? Was there any morality there at all, in fact?

(With all the various factions and cliques within the expatriate officer cadre, it was jokingly put around that the best way for any of them to succeed, and rise quickly through the ranks, was to be an ex-colonial police, rugby and cricket-playing, alcoholic, backstabbing, gossiping, bullshitting, homosexual, misogynistic Scottish mason, who was married to a rich, university-educated Chinese Woman Inspector, whose prominent family had very well-placed contacts within the police, government, big business, and the Triads.)

More seriously though, why weren't they warned about the terrible back-stabbing, character assassination, gossip, rumour and targeting of certain individuals, even of some people totally unknown to the taunters and their '*ma jai*' (protective clique as explained in Chapter 11), except by notoriety or reputation, which would today count as psychological bullying? This was seemingly encouraged by some senior officers perhaps under pressure themselves from worries about being arrested by the ICAC, or having their own chequered pasts brought into the open.

It drove some people under, with no way to escape it, and no Force Psychologist in those days, and no one caring to spot if anyone was cracking up.

If someone did crack, it was a jolly old laugh for most others, with fingers pointed about LMF, which isn't Little Mo Fo, but Lack of Moral Fibre.

Then there was the drinking culture. Fair enough, rites of passage, and all young men in closed communities, such as the Police, the Oil and Gas explorationists, and the University 'Rag Week and Rugby' fraternity, tend to go at it like men possessed, but there was no control imposed, beyond self-control, but when that got out of hand then surely 'someone' had to advise and see that help was sought, that free-for-alls were not held in the Mess at all hours, encouraging young men to imbibe, or risk being classified as antisocial.

Indeed, many senior officers sought out drinking buddies amongst the lower ranks, probably feeling isolated and fearful for their futures, in a 'lonely is the head that wears the crown' type of thing, particularly when perhaps having the *'ma jai'* system in place, with their favourite ' young horses' obsequiously hanging on their coat tails, and deliciously lapping up every word, rumour and piece of gossip, and ensuring the Boss was always 'topped up' and seldom left wanting for the company of willing lackeys.

It also served to 'head off the Indians at the pass', as it were, as obsequious sycophants or crawlers certainly wouldn't be talked about or stabbed in the back while physically in the company of people whose whole *raison d'être* in some instances was to 'do' as many people down as they could in order to advance themselves or to blow their own trumpets.

And anyone who did go to rehab usually only did so after they'd somehow blown their tops, thus subject to vitriolic polemics and excoriation all around, as 'Dick of the Week' and another bit of gossip and scandal to take pressure off people whose motives, mendacity and dark secrets may not have borne close scrutiny at all.

And woe betide anyone trying to sort themselves out at Alcoholics Anonymous, where they'd meet police officers and others they knew or had heard about, and they'd soon find out there was bugger all anonymous about it, and surely anyone having to resort to AA must of course be lacking in moral fibre, the weak bastards.

AV, on his first visit to an AA meeting in a Central church hall, somewhat later in his so-called career, was shocked, stunned and surprised to find one of his then biggest detractors, a Sub Divisional Inspector in a Sub Division where AV was Officer in Charge of CID, and where the Uniformed Branch and CID sometimes didn't always see eye to eye, as the proud head of the Monday evening meetings, sporting a police-badged, blue blazer and police cravat. The SDI was most aggrieved to have someone there who could possibly rain on his parade or take the wind out of his very blustery sails if it was found out he'd been persecuting and chastising some subordinates he obviously thought had similar alcohol abuse problems as himself, instead of showing empathy and helping them.

Up to that date, no one AV had worked with, or socialised with, had ever twigged that the SDI in question had a drinking problem, although admittedly he had been extremely caustic about those Inspectors and above who frequented the Mess bar after office hours, probably as a defence mechanism or a reinforcer to stop him joining them.

He practically begged AV not to tell anyone about him attending the AA meetings, probably worried about his promotion prospects if word leaked out, and likely scared he'd lose his Monday nights playing the 'Big Man' amongst some very high-powered members of Hong Kong society, all sharing the same disease or, as AV thought of it, a common weakness.

To his indignation and embarrassment, however, AV found that his own visits to AA were the subject of comment in his official Record of Service, or RS, having been shopped and betrayed, obviously, although he couldn't prove by whom, as the daily meetings held at various venues, with a different theme and convenor each night, were attended by, inter alia, a group or gripe of police officers, and some government servants known professionally to him, any of whom may have let the cat out of the bag.

But to this day, AV has still not let on about that SDI, Chief

Inspector Richard Head (yes, a *real* Dick Head! Honest! Would I lie to you?) and he doesn't believe he ever will. And why should he, as the bastard died in 2003 aged sixty three, from cirrhosis of the liver?

Hopefully, in a more understanding and enlightened era, the Hong Kong Police now have teams of psychologists to counsel, treat and address such matters, although AV met the brother of the first RHKP psychologist who had allegedly and dismissively referred to the mainly expats he'd counselled in the nineties as 'a bunch of paranoid drunks'. Whilst there were some very fine senior officers out there, as a general assessment of many people the WCH5 encountered, that was right on the button.

The lack of trust in the integrity and sincerity of some senior officers reached such a state that a few young Inspectors would go into formal interviews with recording devices hidden in their pockets, then discuss what bollocks had been said with colleagues, and use the tape if any promises or agreements made were subsequently broken.

It didn't help matters that there were two records kept in respect of each officer; one was the official record of service, which the officer could inspect, whilst the other contained confidential information, such as attitudes, prejudices, adverse comments, insults given and the like, some items based on the personal, often veiled dislike of the reportee by the senior officer secretly dishing out the poison.

This confidential report was restricted and should never ordinarily be viewed by the individual concerned, but there were ways and means, particularly if one became 'friendly' with senior civilian staff charged with storing those documents, or with the girls who had typed up the notes.

Some officers who thought they were doing well, based on their yearly incremental reports, went near crazy after viewing the confidential snippets written by senior officers whom they had thought themselves 'well in' with.

And racism within the RHKP wasn't broached at all, and while expats were referred to as *gwailos*, as you've learnt before, the Chinese were not always referred to as locals, or Chinese, but increasingly as slopes, slants, chogues or chogeys, which were extremely offensive and derogatory terms.

There were some expats known as 'local killers' who would have no qualms about chastising Chinese officers, but thought twice when an expat came before them, even if having committed the same error, or whatever.

Conversely, there were Chinese officers, despite many being termed as 'plastic *gwailos*', who could be called 'expat killers', especially with the increase in localisation leading up to the 1997 handover to China, by which time the term 'Great British Bastard' was frequently used in the general population instead of *gwailo* when sneeringly referring to their 'Colonial Lords and Masters'.

Obviously an increasingly enfranchised and more politically and socially aware modern generation, as in other former colonies, had taken to questioning some of the duplicity, underhandedness, self-serving interests and cynical machinations of European Imperialism in general and of the British in particular, no matter how much good such colonialisation had left in its wake. Things like Christianity and Hong Kong's legal, administrative and business systems, not to mention cricket and gin and tonic. But fair enough, one can understand how the Opium Wars, syphilis and a continued, overbearing disregard for local sentiment, had exhausted the patience of the anti-colonialists.

Yes, racism was increasing both ways in the lead-up to 1997, with even the then Governor being accused of anti-Chinese sentiments in the suicide note of a top head of a government department in 1980, such letter and investigation being kept very much under wraps.

Obviously, it was a pity that the possibility of rising racial tensions wasn't pointed out to the lads while under training, and it was one hell of a shock and disappointment to find *this* (and many other matters as above) *out*, by rude and bitter experience. However, one wonders quite how modern Hong Kong people now view former British control, bearing in mind the current anti-sedition laws and such, pursuant to and enforced by 'the new management' under its strict political ideology.

All that of course is with the benefit of hindsight, and, notwithstanding, it is very fair to say that the WCH5 had thoroughly enjoyed their eight months at PTS, which brings us to Saturday, 3rd January 1976, the lads all dressed up and packed, but with nowhere to go, sitting in the Mess while the Commandant's Parade was taking place.

Most unfortunately, for some unfathomable reason, their postings had not been arranged, nor accommodation sorted out, but they had time on their side and weren't in a hurry to go anywhere, really, basking in their last hour or two at PTS, and doing nothing important, with sod all required of them.

(But how that would all soon change!)

The administrative staff were apparently frantically working their butts off to rectify both situations.

No hurry. Never mind, or, in one of my final snippets of Cantonese for you all, '*Um gan you.*'

The Wong Chuk Hang Five of Steady Eddie, Nev Tenspeed, Bucket Bottomley, Lats Latimer and Two Dicks Allcock, and presumably most, if not all of the gang who'd lasted the course, did not regret for one moment seizing their 'chances of a lifetime' and, now full of pzazz and panache, were wondering what lay in store for them out in the big wide world. They imagined it would be, basically, all sorts of weird, wild and even wonderfully exotic experiences, tinged with danger, excitement, challenges and even the occasional, very occasional, formal commendation or congratulations for a job well done.

But the 'Dark Side' was out there too (along with some

really nasty bastards hiding amongst a majority, admittedly, of professional and well-intentioned policemen of all ranks), ready to devour any and all, from the greedy, to the stupid, to the naïve, to the lazy, to the promiscuous and all in between, but not even mentioned to fresh recruits except in the most hushed and veiled of tones.

AV, despite his obviously very keen approach, still maintained the general view of the world as being venal and vile, and his growing suspicion that things weren't quite as they seemed in Hong Kong, or in its Police Force, being later starkly confirmed, made him, after his divorce – he was too pissed to poke; she was too proud to push – start to be more of a sociopathic, curmudgeonly cynic than he or anyone else had ever thought possible.

After a ten year stint in the RHKP, he remained in the Far East in the Advertising and Tourism sectors, and then travelled worldwide in the Oil and Gas Industry, but steadfastly and resolutely worked himself down the ladder of success in those roles, where his cavalier, almost reckless disregard for his own interests, and refusing to play 'politics', generally counted against him.

It didn't help that he made some of the most impetuously foolhardy decisions ever made by a drunken arsehole astride a mighty high horse, while in those positions, often after being deliberately wound-up by malicious, or jealous colleagues, who knew that he'd go off the rails, and revert to type, once the blue touch paper had been lit. This resulted in many fights, relocations, much ill-will, and a plethora of psychopathic grudges which he still carries with him, to this very day …

And later in life, him arranging for a highly-educated mail order bride from Eastern Europe proved a total disaster, when the eighteen stone Natasha Sukherov tried to keep him in the same vice-like grip that Debbie (Dee Dee) had on Inspector Farrier, and exhibited the same dogged, resolute, fixed-purpose in obtaining a British passport, through the marriage, as the later Woman

Superintendent, Stella Lai, had so enthusiastically displayed in pursuing her path up through the ranks, Unfortunately for AV, he did not even have the benefit of any of those unbridled sexual favours from Natasha, however temporary, that Stella had seemingly dished out to anyone who was of use to her.

(And with Natasha already being overweight, which increased to twenty stone the way she gorged herself with food the two years before the passport was granted - after which she fled to Lesbos, Greece - he could hardly afford the postage to send his mail order bride back to Eastern Europe, either.)

However, it wasn't all negativity though, as in later life he found a purpose and some happiness in founding and running CARAFA, the Campaign Against Regional and Foreign Accents, which continues to occupy much of his time.

Bob Yates, the original Soda Pop Kid and one of the really good eggs amongst the group, had definitely had his eyes opened about the world and was beginning to question how things had been behind the scenes in Luanshya, and certainly had a load of questions for his father when next they'd meet, even more so after his tour of duty came to an end, bearing in mind how his post-PTS days panned out.

However, The Bucket and Steady Eddie were opposites, perhaps, both in their upbringing and natures, but remain to this day the best of friends nonetheless, and maybe because of it.

'*Semper fi*,' always loyal.

On leaving the Police, after his three year tour, Bob Yates pulled himself together and, away from certain individual and endemically corrupting influences, reverted to being a very moderate drinker, and the fine human being he always had it in him to become. He qualified as a Commercial Airline Pilot after a Hong Kong government gratuity-funded course in California and was last heard of as Chief Pilot and Instructor at Zambia's Horizon Airways, based at Ndola. He has a contract with his father's old company to shuttle mining personnel to and from Johannesburg, which of course suits him ideally, as well as operating other routes within Southern Africa.

And yes he did eventually marry Wilhelmina Mkele, whose marriage to Gordon Banda only lasted a few years, and together they produced two fine boys who are currently studying for doctorates in 'Pre-Spanish Conquest Aztec and Mayan Phallic Art, and its Influence on Staffordshire Pottery and the Horticultural Industry in Pembrokeshire', and 'British Vaudeville and Escapology Acts and their Influence on Politics in America during the Nineteenth and Early Twentieth Century' respectively, at Leeds University in the North of England.

How nice to see that some dreams can and do come true.

And the bigoted 'Yorkie' Bill Towser, (as mentioned in Chapter 5) would surely have been delighted that such bright people had chosen a Yorkshire University at which to study for their higher degrees, especially as both were full-fee paying students, money or 'brass' being oh so important to the famously, and proudly parsimonious locals up in 'Gods Own County.'

Tommy Two Dicks remained in the RHKP for about twenty five years, carrying on much as he had always done, sailing very close to the wind on occasions, but was mainly left alone in view of him not likely or wanting to rise up the ranks, and thus was not a threat to anyone apart from himself, especially if his wife had found out about his few dalliances with the opposite sex.

He married into the Indian community and was content to bumble along as a Senior Inspector, bobbing and weaving, scheming and dreaming, while they ran, and supplemented his police income from their three or four curry houses within Chung King Mansions, and the one they opened, at Tommy's insistence, at the Wong Chuck Hang Estate, which was extremely well patronised by the very many expats at PTS, Ducks' Feet Madras being the specialty of the house.

In the early eighties they added one of Hong Kong's first gay hostelries, the Sniffs and Butts Bar, to their business interests, which is still operating, in the trendy entertainment area of Lan Kwai Fong in Central, a little up from and at the back of the Hong Kong and Shanghai Bank, and which became a popular venue for the young people and trendies who later metastasised and metamorphosised into yuppies.

The 'Sniffs and Butts Bar' was the location where two expat Chief Inspectors, who certainly should have known better, fell afoul of the law by giving false names and addresses to police officers who were on a liquor licence check, but who were recognised by an Inspector with whom they had formerly worked. However, 'their faces fitted', especially as one of their mothers had some association with the Royal Hong Kong Police Commandant General herself, Princess Alexandra.

My oh my, didn't the hierarchy rally-round the flag to save them, as it were!

(Read any good books lately…? That was a 'subject change device' in case you hadn't realised.)

But just mention *this* publication for a twenty percent reduction on your bill at that bar, and AV's name for a twenty percent reduction in the number of teeth in your mouth, and a thick ear, Two Dicks being one of the many he 'shopped' to ICAC, mainly in this instance as revenge for him 'piggy-backing' on Nev and AV's earlier plans to open a curry house outside of PTS themselves.

No, Tommy's 'Sorry lads, it's nothing personal, only business!' didn't quite cut it, and I've news for him which I hope he, and others of his ilk, will possibly bear in mind – 'It's *always* personal to someone.'

Nev, after a spell in Yaumatei Division, and then Traffic Kowloon, and through his high ranking Special Branch cricketing mates, was posted to the VIP Protection Unit, which was considered one of the 'Jewels in the Crown of Postings.' And so it initially seemed, as Nev during training, was part of a team shepherding firstly John Wayne, and then the Miss World contestants of 1977, around the Colony.

Unfortunately for Tenspeed, he was then placed in charge of a small Protection Unit tasked with ensuring the safety and security of minor members of foreign trade delegations, D-list actors, singers and sports personalities, and British backbenchers on publicly funded 'jollies'. And rather than occasional perks like lobster, caviar and champagne while engaged in such duties, he was lucky to be occasionally '*chenged*' (invited) to a free lunch at a hotel, or the YMCA, or to a bowl of noodles from a hawker stall.

In fact, rather than being the Jewel in the Crown, the posting proved to be more of a 'Turd in the Toilet Bowl' when he was assigned to 'look after' Arthur Glossop, that rather self-important, and argumentative British Northern MP (see Chapter 11), and when, rather embarrassingly for Mr Tenspeed, he bumped into Yates and Bottomley down their favourite Chimsy side lane, *again* having a few beers next to where Glossop was seated. Mind you, Nev *was* 'on expenses', and so bought a few bottles of San Mig 'on the company', as their folding table was an ideal place from which to observe his 'client', but then, rather unfortunately, to reluctantly endure Glossop's torrent of drunken, opinionated views, which he more or less 'forced' on the three Inspectors.

Inspector Tenspeed unfortunately and rather mysteriously 'dropped off the radar' after his one and only three year stint with the RHKP, although rumour has it that he was for a while the 'Consiglieri' to 'The Family' back in Jersey, who then moved into the Laos Vegas Entertainment and Casino business in South East Asia, and who apparently made him an offer he couldn't refuse.

(But no, he didn't wake up one morning in St Helier to find Ginty's severed head in bed next to him; things are much more civilised than that in the Channel Islands. On the surface anyway. *Capiche?*)

One would have presumed, though that, as with most people, his 'steaming kettle' would have eventually boiled dry and that he would have settled into a life of conventional conformity and mundanity, with wife, kids and a mortgage and all that brings with it. Let's hope so, because if I have had to put up with it, then why shouldn't he?

Lats Latimer, although never really cutting as loose as the others, became a virtual teetotaller, especially under the loving grip of his later wife Connie, of Chinese descent, a locally joined British Army nursing sister with the rank of Captain at the British Military Hospital in Kowloon. He turned into an avowed family man, doting on his three daughters, and after serving ten years in the RHKP became a 'gentleman farmer' in Suffolk, and very wealthy on the back of getting into organic and free-range livestock farming methods very early, strictly adhering to the adage that, 'Where there's muck, there's money!' And he must have been very mucky indeed to accumulate all he has and so, once again, it's 'Well done that man!'

And so it went for the main characters to date.

But one of these days you must simply remind me to tell you about how the WCH5 fared within the Police, post PTS, but sooner rather than later, as my memory isn't what it used to be, and is getting worse too... all it would take is sponsorship.

And a damned good kick up the arse!

And a final caution to you young policemen, and intended policemen out there, adapted and paraphrased from Ecclesiastes, and as amended by your author:

'Young man, rejoice in thy youth, but watch out for the bastards around you.'

I thank you.

Ecclesiastes, for the unenlightened, has nothing to do with Eccles out of the Goons, or his testicles.

And may I say it's been a pleasure. Yes, it has, though I don't get much chance these days to see whether it still is.

And may I further say that I've been deeply touched while writing this, but my therapist says I'm coming along quite nicely now...

'*High gam dawe*,' or, That's yer lot!
'*Gau deem!*' or 'Job done!'
Victor Blair, c/o the Scrubs. Summer, 2023.

No, not the Wormwood Scrubs prison, but the Scrubs, our local launderette, where I finished off the concluding paragraphs, while keeping a watchful eye on my blue Y-fronts taking a pounding in the tumble dryer, hoping no bastard will steal *this* pair when I pop out to the pub for a quick half pint. Well, two pints then.

Yes, there are some real swine around, as you'll no doubt have gathered from reading my *Made, Laid and Betrayed in Hong Kong*. By the way, Alan Bottomley and Bob Yates are collectively 'Victor Blair'. Oops. The secret's out!

PS. If you are ever in Hong Kong please do not sniff, swallow or otherwise ingest any rhinoceros horn powder or potions, no matter how efficacious people may tell you they are.

AV sniffed some on the advice of an old Police Constable and for weeks thereafter went around chasing and head-butting police Land Rovers and had to be sedated by a vet using a dart gun, which took some doing in the crowded streets of Yaumatei, I can tell you. So it goes.

And I should like to point out that no animals were harmed during the planning, drafting or scripting of this work, and that any similarity to, or mention of, any animal, living or dead herein is on purpose, but was with the fondest memories of Tiger, Henry and Ginty, which should please their descendants, if not their owners.

And now that really is the end. Promise. Thank you and goodbye.

ABOUT THE AUTHOR

Victor Blair is a well-travelled, humorous, rather overly-free spirited 'baby booming' Brit, who is luckily still imbued with an energy belying his years, so hence the slightly provocative gesture above, showing him probably disagreeing with something or someone, yet again… our apologies! He has worn 'many different hats' in UK banking, and in a host of overseas appointments, including ten years in the colonial Hong Kong Police Force, the tourism sector in Asia, and subsequently in worldwide oil and gas exploration and logistics, and finally, engineering consultancy. An as yet unappreciated comedic wit and poet, with a bright, if latent, creative spark, and with early roots in Gloucestershire and Africa, he is now semi-retired in north Thailand, where he busies himself with his sugar cane plantation, scripting away at night time, and as the patriarch of his local wife's ever-increasing extended family.

Intrigued? Have a look at www.victorblairoverthere.com